REPUTATIONS

D1330265

NEVILLE CHAMBERLAIN

David Dutton

Reader in History,
University of Liverpool

A member of the Hodder Headline Group
LONDON
Co-published in the United States of America by
Oxford University Press Inc., New York

First published in Great Britain in 2001 by
Arnold, a member of the Hodder Headline Group,
338 Euston Road, London NW1 3BH

http://www.arnoldpublishers.com

Co-published in the United States of America by
Oxford University Press Inc.,
198 Madison Avenue, New York, NY10016

British Library Cataloguing in Publication Data
A catalogue record for this book is available from the British Library

Library of Congress Cataloging-in-Publication Data
A catalog record for this book is available from the Library of Congress

ISBN 0 340 70626 0 (hb)
ISBN 0 340 70627 9 (pb)

1 2 3 4 5 6 7 8 9 10

Production Editor: Lauren McAllister
Production Controller: Bryan Eccleshall
Cover Design: Terry Griffiths

Typeset in 10 on 12 pt Sabon by Cambrian Typesetters, Frimley, Surrey
Printed and bound in Great Britain by MPG Books Ltd, Bodmin, Cornwall

What do you think about this book? Or any other Arnold title?
Please send your comments to feedback.arnold@hodder.co.uk

Contents

In memory of
Elsie Roderick

General editorial preface

Hero or villain? Charlatan or true prophet? Sinner or saint? The volumes in the Reputations series examine the reputations of some of history's most conspicuous, powerful and influential individuals, considering a range of representations, some of striking incompatibility. The aim is not merely to demonstrate that history is indeed, in Pieter Geyl's phrase, 'argument without end' but that the study even of contradictory conceptions can be fruitful: that the jettisoning of one thesis or presentation leaves behind something of value.

In Iago's self-serving denunciation of it, reputation is 'an idle and most false imposition; oft got without merit, and lost without deserving', but a more generous definition would allow its use as one of the principal currencies of historical understanding. In seeking to analyse the cultivation, creation, and deconstruction of reputation we can understand better the well-springs of action, the workings out of competing claims to power, the different purposes of rival ideologies – in short, see more clearly ways in which the past becomes History.

There is a commitment in each volume to showing how understanding of an individual develops (sometimes in uneven and divergent ways), whether in response to fresh evidence, the emergence or waning of dominant ideologies, changing attitudes and preoccupations of the age in which an author writes, or the creation of new historical paradigms. Will Hitler ever seem *quite* the same after the evidence of a recent study revealing the extent of his Jewish connections during the Vienna years? Reassessment of Lenin and Stalin has been given fresh impetus by the collapse of the Soviet Union and the opening of many of its archives; and the end of the Cold War and of its attendant assumptions must alter our views of Eisenhower and Kennedy.

How will our perceptions of Elizabeth I change in the presence of a new awareness of 'gendered history'?

There is more to the series than illumination of ways in which recent discoveries or trends have refashioned identities or given actions new meaning – though that is an important part. The corresponding aim is to provide readers with a strong sense of the channels and course of debate from the outset: not a Cook's Tour of the historiography, but identification of the key interpretative issues and guidance as to how commentators of different eras and persuasions have tackled them.

Preface

In 1998 Birmingham Museum and Art Gallery mounted a small exhibition on the Chamberlain family to coincide with a meeting in the city of the leaders of the G8 world economic powers. The museum itself is situated in Chamberlain Square, named after Joseph Chamberlain, rightly regarded as one of the founding fathers of the modern city and most of the exhibition was devoted to him. Chancellor Helmut Kohl, attending the summit, expressed an interest in Joseph's elder son, Austen. But the exhibition devoted little space to Neville Chamberlain, even though he had followed his father in serving as Birmingham's Lord Mayor and, unlike his father and brother, had risen to the highest office of government in this country. A brief caption within the exhibition read simply, 'Neville became Prime Minister in 1937 and played an important role in the events which led to the Second World War'.

This seemingly embarrassed reticence tells us much about what has happened to the reputation of a man who, just sixty years earlier, had been hailed as the greatest European statesman 'of this or any other time'. There is, as far as I have been able to ascertain, no public memorial to Chamberlain in his native city. Even scholarships established in his name at Birmingham University by a grateful benefactor at the time of the Munich settlement appear to have vanished without trace. In 1999 English Heritage announced that it was extending the scheme of Blue Plaques, which commemorate distinguished former citizens in their home towns, to Birmingham and invited nominations. I wrote to propose Neville Chamberlain but received no reply or acknowledgement.

Yet Birmingham at least has much for which to thank Neville Chamberlain. Its rightly famous Symphony Orchestra was largely his inspiration. As a young boy of seven, growing up in the city, I, like many of my generation, opened my first bank account with the sum of £4 in the Birmingham Municipal Bank – since swallowed up inside Lloyds TSB – forgivably ignorant that this institution too owed its foundation to the vision of Neville Chamberlain. Yet if the city in which he was born and grew up, and which he represented in parliament for over twenty years, is so reluctant to recognize a man who was, arguably, its most distinguished citizen of the twentieth century, it is hardly surprising that Chamberlain's reputation further afield still stands at such a low ebb.

In writing this study I have incurred many debts, not least to those scholars who have already worked in this area, whose labours and insights are – albeit inadequately – recognized in the notes and bibliography of this book. The staff of the Heslop Room at the University of Birmingham Library where Chamberlain's papers are housed, especially Christine Penney, Philippa Bennett and Martin Killeen, were unfailingly helpful and responsive to my requests. Extracts from manuscript material of which it holds the copyright are reproduced by kind permission of the University of Birmingham. Victoria Emmanuel helped with local information about Chamberlain. Henry Finch aided my understanding of the economic history of inter-war Britain. For their wise comments on an earlier draft of this book I am extremely grateful to Philip Bell, Nick Crowson and Ralph White. As one who still writes books with a pen – and occasionally even a pencil – I am indebted to Alison Bagnall and her now renowned keyboard skills. I must thank my editor, Christopher Wheeler, not only for inviting me to contribute to the *Reputations* series but also for being understanding and supportive, despite my delays in producing a finished typescript. He knows something perhaps of the difficulties which confront those engaged in the bureaucratic paper-chase which is still called 'higher education' in a British provincial university. To all I am indebted, though happy to take full responsibility myself for those errors of fact and interpretation which, despite their endeavours and mine, remain in the finished work.

David Dutton
Liverpool 2000

Acknowledgements

Transcripts of Crown-copyright records in the Public Record Office appear by permission of the Controller of H.M. Stationery Office. Additional copyright material is reproduced by kind permission of Mr Robert Bernays; the Rt Hon. the Earl of Halifax; Mr Robert Harvey; Miss Ishbel Lockhead; Mrs Anne Stacey and the Trustees of the Bridgeman Family Archive; and Dr Tom Shakespeare.

To the best of my knowledge all copyright holders of material reproduced in this book have been traced. Any rights not acknowledged here will be noted in subsequent printings if notice is given to the publisher.

|1|

Introduction

*It is true that he failed and was to a certain extent cast out,
yet all he stood for still goes on, and even as Christ
triumphed in death, so did your father.*[1]

In defining the purpose of this book it is perhaps best to begin
by stating what it is not. It should not be seen as a biography of
Neville Chamberlain. This is not to imply that any entirely satisfactory biography of this vitally important figure of inter-war
British history yet exists. A couple of interim biographies
appeared in Chamberlain's own lifetime. Keith Feiling's official
life probably remains the best single-volume study. But it was
published more than fifty years ago without access to government archives or the benefit of the scholarship of the host of
historians who have investigated the period covered by
Chamberlain's political career in the intervening years.
Subsequent biographies by Iain Macleod and H. Montgomery
Hyde added little to Feiling's analysis. What promised to be the
best – and also the most sympathetic – biographical study, by
Professor David Dilks, remains incomplete. Indeed, the second
volume covering the crucial decade of the 1930s may never now
be written. Even so, the present work makes no attempt to fill
this patent historiographical gap. Rather it seeks to chart a
subtly different course by analysing the evolution of Neville
Chamberlain's historical reputation.

This needs to be considered at a number of levels. A man's reputation lives after him, but the reputation which he acquires during
his own lifetime is also important. Indeed, this reputation can
considerably affect the development of the individual's on-going

career. We shall need, therefore, to consider how Chamberlain
was viewed from the time that he became a well-known figure,
both by those who knew him as a colleague, a friend or a political opponent and by that infinitely more numerous mass of
ordinary people whose perception was altogether more impressionistic. This immediately poses problems of evidence. Though
the political elite tend to leave substantial written records detail-
ing their judgements on their contemporaries, assessing the
views of the broader mass of the population is a much more
difficult exercise. The surviving evidence tends to be fragmentary, random and potentially unrepresentative. Put simply, can
the existence of a packed postbag from the general public
congratulating Chamberlain on his achievements at the Munich
Conference in September 1938 be taken as indicative of opinion in the country as a whole? Is it a valid assumption to
presume that those who make efforts to give expression to their
views on a particular issue are necessarily typical of their more
numerous but silent fellow countrymen?

Politicians in the 1920s and 1930s were very conscious of a
notion of public opinion. Indeed, they often used it as a justification for steps which they were or were not prepared to take.
This was perhaps a necessary reaction to the First World War
and the realization that the ordinary citizen had a right to have
an impact on a decision-making process which might
profoundly affect, or in extreme cases actually deprive him of,
his life. But precisely what they understood by this concept is
unclear. The typical circle of acquaintance of an MP of this era
was probably quite restricted. His idea of the man in the street
may have been based upon those probably atypical members of
his electorate who bothered to write to him or attend his
constituency meetings. At one key moment in the 1930s
Anthony Eden seemed to gauge 'public opinion' on the basis of
what his taxi-driver told him. This may or may not have been a
valid assumption in this particular instance. But applied more
generally it was clearly a risky one. Public opinion polling was
introduced in Britain in 1937, the organisation *Gallup* having
been founded in the United States two years earlier. But as a
means of assessing popular sentiment it lacked the sophistication which is now intrinsic to what has since become a very
important element in the political process. This was true in
terms of the sample selected, the questions asked and the conclusions drawn from the answers given. Contemporary findings,

though interesting, must therefore be treated with considerable caution, even scepticism. The organization *Mass Observation*, set up in 1937, provides the historian with a vast body of recorded public sentiment but it never claimed that its sample was scientifically representative and, because of the methods it employed to collect opinion, its findings must be treated with even greater caution. Yet, however imperfect, such statistical information is certainly a more valuable indication of what people thought than the testimony of journalists and politicians as to what they thought people thought.

In the absence of reliable public opinion polling the historian turns naturally to the evidence of popular feeling provided by general elections. Within the spectrum of reasons prompting the individual citizen to cast his vote in a particular way, his estimation of leading politicians and particularly the Prime Minister of the day probably figures prominently. This is especially the case in the era of increasingly personalized politics since 1918. Yet, uniquely among the British premiers of the twentieth century, Neville Chamberlain never had the opportunity to submit himself to the British electorate either as Prime Minister or as Leader of the Opposition. Failing this form of personal referendum the historian can only fall back upon the fragmentary and sometimes bizarre evidence offered by by-election results. It is a far from satisfactory source but, in the case of Chamberlain's premiership, all we have.

The press is also often taken as offering evidence of a wider opinion on issues and personalities than that of the individual writer of a particular article or leader column, or of the newspaper's proprietor. Yet this source too is fraught with danger. It has long been recognized that the complexion of the British press gives a lop-sided reflection of the opinion of its readers, at least in terms of political affiliation. More generally, there seems no entirely satisfactory answer to the question of whether the press sets out to shape political opinion or merely to reflect it. In all probability there is truth in both propositions. Chamberlain received some harsh press notices at the time of his final retirement from office in October 1940. As he himself complained, 'Not one shows the slightest sign of sympathy for the man, or even any comprehension that there may be a human tragedy in the background'.[2] But it is not easy to assert whether the newspaper columnists were simply articulating widely shared sentiments, or whether with their wide circulations they played their

part in creating that first and most deeply entrenched historical
assessment of Chamberlain's premiership

Once a politician leaves office and more particularly once he
is dead, the custody of his reputation begins to pass into the
hands of the historical profession, aided and abetted for a while
by the writers of political memoirs. (It is perhaps worth adding
that the concept of 'contemporary history', though nothing like
as developed as it has since become, did afford some opportunities for the beginnings of an historical evaluation during
Chamberlain's own lifetime, at least in terms of a number of
interim biographical studies.) In common with most professional
academics, historians in their more fanciful moments like to
suppose that their work exercises a profound impression upon
the nation at large. In some senses it undoubtedly does. There is
a process by which scholarly work percolates down via the
general reading public into the popular consciousness, albeit
often at the cost of over-simplification and even distortion. In
general, however, the historian writes for a fairly limited audience. His work has little relevance for or impact upon the great
mass of his fellow citizens. This raises the interesting possibility
of a clash or dichotomy between the academic assessment of an
individual's career and the popular one. Two distinct and, in their
own way, valid reputations of the same individual can co-exist.
The capacity of the academic writer to change an entrenched
popular perception is often limited. Scholars may have determined that King Richard III was an effective administrator who,
in the course of a brief reign, showed signs of restoring much
needed stability to the realm after a period of turbulence. But the
more common image remains that of Shakespeare's deformed
hunchback who ruthlessly murdered his young nephews in the
Tower of London. Similarly, while there may be no irrefutable
historical evidence that Alexander Borgia ever poisoned anyone,
his popular reputation as the most ingenious and versatile of
murderers is unlikely to be challenged. In the case of Neville
Chamberlain there is an interesting variation of this theme. The
popular perception of a weak and gullible provincial who fell
into the snares carefully laid for him by the evil genius of Adolf
Hitler is certainly at odds with a large corpus of academic literature, particularly that which dates from the 1970s and 1980s. Yet
at the same time the popular image was, at least for a generation,
transmogrified into the academic view, garnished with a suitable
layer of sophistication and scholarly apparatus.

In many instances, of course, it would be naïve to suggest that a popular image of even a prominent British politician persists for very long after his retirement or death. The name of Andrew Bonar Law is unlikely to evoke more than a mere glimmer of recognition from the man in the street; that of Sir Henry Campbell-Bannerman something nearer total ignorance. Yet both like Chamberlain occupied the highest position in British public life within the twentieth century. In the case of Chamberlain, however, something of a popular reputation does subsist to this day. During the 1983 General Election campaign, Roy Jenkins suggested that the re-election of Mrs Thatcher's government would mean the installation of a more right-wing administration than any since that of Neville Chamberlain. Though not a particularly enlightening comment historically speaking, Jenkins presumably hoped to evoke a particular – and obviously unfavourable – image in the minds of at least some of his audience. More recently, in July 1999, the *Sunday Telegraph* published a cartoon by Trog of a smiling and self-satisfied Tony Blair holding aloft a sheet of paper and proclaiming 'It is peace in our time'. The cartoon lacked any caption but was clearly intended to draw an unflattering parallel with Neville Chamberlain returning from Munich. Trog obviously felt confident that he could draw upon a still current image of Chamberlain nearly sixty years after the latter's death.

Chamberlain certainly offers tremendous scope for the study of an evolving reputation. In what Roy Jenkins has called 'the cruel market in political reputations'[3] Chamberlain has experienced the extremes, both in his own lifetime and at the subsequent bar of history. At the time of the Munich settlement the popular journalist Godfrey Winn exclaimed: 'Praise be to God and to Mr. Chamberlain. I find no sacrilege, no bathos, in coupling those two names.'[4] Yet less than two years later many were ready to deem him the most disastrous Prime Minister of the twentieth century or perhaps of all time. It was a transformation which Chamberlain himself called a 'human tragedy':

Only a few months ago I was Prime Minister in the fullest enjoyment of mental and physical health and with what was described by many as an unprecedented hold on the H[ouse] of C[ommons]. Then came the Norwegian withdrawal, the panicky resentful vote which brought down

the majority in such spectacular fashion, my instant reali-
sation that the loss of prestige could only be countered by
a gesture of increased unity here and that that unity could
not be achieved by me in the face of Labour and Liberal
opposition to myself.[5]

Similarly historical and quasi-historical opinions have covered
the full range from outright denigration to near adulation. Even
now no true consensus exists. It was striking that in two studies
published in 1989, and which were based on substantially the
same body of documentation, Chamberlain was presented in
entirely contrasting ways. According to John Charmley, he had
striven manfully to avert the catastrophe of the Second World
War and to preserve the British Empire. His reputation 'stands
better now than it has ever done'.[6] Yet for Sidney Aster the
pendulum of revisionism had swung too far and it was time to
revert to those moral judgements which had so damaged
Chamberlain's standing back in 1940.[7] On balance it is surely
this latter, unflattering image which still prevails. As the mille-
nium came to a close BBC Radio conducted a poll of twenty
academics and politicians to establish a ranking order of the
Prime Ministers of the twentieth century. Out of nineteen candidates considered (Tony Blair was excluded), Chamberlain came
eighteenth, superior only it seemed to Sir Anthony Eden.

Notwithstanding the absence of a fully satisfactory biography, a vast number of books and articles now exist, sixty years
after Chamberlain's death, examining all aspects of his career.
Broadly speaking, this historiography has followed a course
typical of most controversial historical topics, though with
subtle variations peculiar to this particular subject. The normal
pattern allows for the emergence of an early orthodoxy based
upon contemporary or near contemporary accounts. It is
followed in due course by a period of revisionism, as fresh
evidence comes to light and a new generation of writers with
different perspectives and assumptions from their predecessors
takes centre-stage. Almost inevitably, this revisionism eventually
prompts a reaction and a post-revisionist period succeeds it in
which historians tend to take on board some of the conclusions
of their revisionist colleagues, while rejecting their more extreme
assertions and in some cases reasserting arguments used in the
first wave of historical writing. As will be seen, Chamberlain's
reputation has been subjected in full measure to this turbulent

and fluctuating process. Yet in all this vast literature one key element is missing. Unlike many of his contemporaries Chamberlain did not live to write his memoirs. He died only a month after finally leaving office. A politician's ability to get his own version of events, and in particular an account of his own role within those events, into print is an opportunity which many, not least Chamberlain's own successor in Downing Street, have used to the considerable benefit of their longer-term historical reputations. But Chamberlain was denied this advantage and it has been left to others, with varying degrees of skill and success, to make a case on his behalf.

Upon what, however, should Neville Chamberlain's reputation rest? Speaking at a meeting of the Conservative party early in 1957, called to choose a successor as leader to Anthony Eden, Walter Elliot, who coincidentally had served as a minister in Chamberlain's cabinet, suggested that 'a man's life is the whole of his life, and not this or that particular patch of shadow or of sunshine'.[8] This is true enough and an attempt will be made to discuss Chamberlain's reputation in relation to a career in front-line politics which spanned two decades. Yet in one sense Elliot's words were unrealistic if not naïve. He had in mind, of course, the shadow of the Suez Crisis which hung – and continues to hang – over Eden's career to the detriment and partial exclusion of much else that he did and achieved. Chamberlain's career is, in this respect at least, very similar to Eden's own. For 'Suez' we must read 'Munich' or perhaps the enormously loaded word 'appeasement'. Whatever else may be said of Chamberlain's public life his reputation will in the last resort depend upon assessments of this moment and this policy. This was the case when he left office in 1940 and it remains so sixty years later. To expect otherwise is rather like hoping that Pontius Pilate will one day be judged as a successful provincial administrator of the Roman Empire. As Lord Blake has written, 'when national security is at stake one does not judge a statesman by his successes in slum clearance'.[9]

The popular perception of Neville Chamberlain is still that he was the man who pursued a disastrous policy which failed to prevent – and indeed may have contributed to – the outbreak of the Second World War. Because of the magnitude of the issues involved this has also been the aspect of his career which has attracted most scholarly attention. The emotions which Munich and its aftermath evoked, and continue to evoke, help to explain

why Chamberlain does still have a *popular* reputation when the
doings of men such as Bonar Law and Campbell-Bannerman are
largely forgotten. The present writer can recall that his own first
acquaintance with the career of Neville Chamberlain was
derived from a teacher who, combining scholarship with
passion, declared that there had been two occasions in his own
lifetime when he had felt ashamed to be British – at the time of
Munich in 1938 and Suez in 1956.[10] This was perhaps not the
best initiation as far as historical objectivity is concerned but, as
will become apparent, objectivity is not necessarily always
involved in the evolution of a reputation.

As has been said already, this book has no pretensions to
being a biography of Neville Chamberlain. It is, however, written on the assumption that not all of its readers will be familiar
with his career. An outline of Chamberlain's life is therefore
provided below in as factual and dispassionate a way as possible before the detailed discussion of his evolving reputation
begins. The author has scope for putting forward his own views
as to what Chamberlain's reputation and standing *ought* to be
in the final chapter.

*   *   *

Arthur Neville Chamberlain was born in Edgbaston,
Birmingham on 18 March 1869, the second son of the radical
statesman Joseph Chamberlain. During Neville's youth and early
manhood his father was one of the most celebrated men in British
public life. In addition, his half-brother Austen, six years his
senior, was a major political figure in his own right, becoming a
cabinet minister before he was forty years of age. In one sense
then Neville Chamberlain seemed destined for a life in politics.
He was born into an unequivocally political family. But Neville's
father did not intend him for a political career. From an early age
it was Austen whose education and training were shaped with a
view to his eventual succession to the family's political inheritance. It was the elder son who was expected to carry the
Chamberlain name into a second generation of public affairs. So
while Austen went from Rugby school to Trinity College,
Cambridge where he read history and became Vice-President of
the Union, before embarking on a European tour to gain experience of contemporary affairs, Neville's education followed a very
different course. Though he too attended Rugby, which he hated,
thereafter he went to Mason College, the forerunner of

Birmingham University, where he studied metallurgy and science. After two years there Neville began work with a firm of chartered accountants.

Then at the age of twenty-one, Chamberlain was despatched to the island of Andros in the Bahamas to manage an ill-thought-out scheme to grow sisal. The plan was to restore the family's declining financial fortunes, damaged by losses in the Argentinian market where Joseph Chamberlain had invested heavily. Despite difficulties of climate and terrain Neville threw himself with industry and enthusiasm into his task – qualities which would characterize the whole of his adult life. By 1895 6,000 sisal plants had been grown and 800 men were employed under Neville's direction. But the project was doomed from the outset even though it took some time for this reality to be appreciated. The soil on Andros was poor and the crop could not be harvested to commercial advantage. The decision to give up was not easy. Joseph Chamberlain had invested £50,000 in the venture, a huge sum by contemporary values. Finally, after seven frustrating years, Neville returned to Britain, beset it seems with a sense of failure.

He now settled quickly into the life of his native city, prospering in its commerce and industry. He joined Elliot's in Selly Oak, who manufactured copper and brass, and bought up the firm of Hoskins and Son whose main interest lay in the manufacture of cabin berths. In addition, Chamberlain busied himself in the Birmingham Chamber of Commerce, taught at a Sunday school and became Secretary of the city's Liberal Unionist Association. A word about his political affiliation is perhaps appropriate at this stage. During Neville's final year at Rugby in 1886, Joseph Chamberlain had left the ranks of the Liberal party in opposition to Gladstone's policy of Home Rule for Ireland. Thereafter the elder Chamberlain's band of Liberal Unionists had moved ever closer to the Conservatives until he himself entered a Unionist cabinet as Colonial Secretary under the Conservative Lord Salisbury in 1895. The point is not without significance. But for his father's parliamentary gymnastics Neville would probably never have joined the Conservative party. He never felt entirely at home within its ranks, regarded himself as a radical and drew a clear contrast between himself and his naturally conservative half-brother.

By this stage Joseph Chamberlain had become aware of the considerable potential of his younger son. 'You know, of my two boys Neville is really the clever one', he confided to a friend in 1902, 'but he isn't interested in politics – if he was, I would back him to be Prime Minister.'[11] Though Neville campaigned in the Unionist interest during the General Elections of 1906 and 1910, he had no wish or intention to follow Austen into national politics. As he explained,

> [the] fact is, I was intended by nature to get through a lot of money. I should never be satisfied with a cottage, and having chucked away a competence – you know where – I am going to toil and moil till I grub it back again. Of course that doesn't prevent my taking some part in a contest like this [the 1900 General Election] and I am speaking as often as my nervousness and laziness permit me (which is not much) but I haven't begun to think of politics as a career.[12]

It was, however, probably inevitable that he should follow his father and numerous other members of his family by getting himself elected to the City Council in 1911, representing the Liberal Unionists in the All Saints Ward which was part of his father's constituency of West Birmingham. 'Partly the tradition of the family and partly my own incapacity to look on and see other people mismanage things drive me on to take up new and alas! unremunerative occupations.'[13] Early that same year he had married Anne De Vere Cole, the daughter of an army officer. The couple settled in Westbourne, a large house in Edgbaston. Their daughter Dorothy was born at the end of the year followed by a son, Frank, two years later. Meanwhile Neville moved easily up the hierarchy of the City Council and became Lord Mayor in 1915. His father and five of his uncles had also occupied the mayor's chair. Despite the anxieties of European war his mayoralty was characterized by several imaginative measures including the founding of the City of Birmingham Orchestra and the institution of a municipal savings bank. Not surprisingly, he was elected to serve a second term in 1916.

It was, however, the war which suddenly propelled Chamberlain into a prominent position in national politics. On Austen's recommendation he was offered the post of Director-General of National Service by the new Prime Minister, David Lloyd George, though significantly without a seat in parliament. Given no time to consider, Chamberlain accepted this new post though with considerable misgivings. It was a decision which he came to regret. The absence of a parliamentary seat proved a considerable handicap; the scope of his responsibilities was never properly defined; and he found Lloyd George an impossible master. Many considered that no one could have made a success of the appointment in such circumstances. According to the Irish Nationalist MP, John Dillon, 'if Mr. Chamberlain were an archangel, or if he were Hindenburg and Bismarck and all the great men of the world rolled into one, his task would be wholly beyond his powers'.[14] By July 1917 he had decided to resign and he did so the following month. He had been in the post for less than a year.

Once again, Chamberlain was left with a sense of failure. He was 'in a position that reminds me of the Bahamas when the plants didn't grow'.[15] Yet paradoxically this first experience of government office was one of a number of wartime factors which caused him to reconsider his attitude towards national politics. Another was the death in action in Flanders of his cousin Norman, about whom Chamberlain wrote his only book, *Norman Chamberlain: a Memoir* (1923). He had worked closely with Norman on the City Council, come greatly to admire him and was much moved by his death. His book is infused with a sense of enormous loss and of promise unfulfilled, and of the obligation of those who survived to ensure that the world which emerged from the ashes of war was one which justified the sacrifices made on the battlefield. The death of his father in 1914 – though he had not been active in politics since a stroke in the summer of 1906 – probably also increased family pressure to ensure that a new Chamberlain voice should be heard at Westminster. Accordingly, Neville secured adoption as Unionist candidate for the Ladywood division of Birmingham.

He did so without any great expectation of making much of a mark in parliament but with a clear sense of duty:

> My career is broken. How can a man of nearly 50, entering the House with this stigma upon him hope to achieve anything? The fate I foresee is that after messing about for a year or two I shall find myself making no progress. . . . But I can't be satisfied with a purely selfish attention to business for the rest of my life.[16]

Benefitting from the excited atmosphere in which the election was fought only a month after the Armistice, Chamberlain was

returned to parliament with a comfortable majority over his
Labour and Liberal opponents. He made his maiden speech on
12 March 1919 and, unusually, spoke again only a week later.
The topics he chose are indicative of the preoccupations of a
man who had cut his political teeth in an unashamedly provincial setting – the Rent Restriction Bill and the question of canals
and waterways. He gradually warmed to his new environment
but was never at home in the social side of the House where
many new careers have been fostered. 'I am not exactly looking
forward to a Parliamentary life; somehow I seem to have got too
old for much in the way of personal ambition. But I think I can
be of more use this way than any other and so am going to give
it a try.'[17] His relations with Lloyd George had not improved
and he seemed to have renounced any expectation of ministerial
advancement when he turned down the offer of an under-secretaryship in March 1920.

What transformed his prospects, and indeed the whole shape
of inter-war politics, though not necessarily in the way that later
legend would suggest, was the fall of the Lloyd George coalition
government in October 1922. Having departed for a tour of
North America, Neville played no part in the dramatic events at
the Carlton Club when Conservatives and Unionists carried a
motion to withdraw from the coalition and fight the next election as an independent party. But the fact that the majority of
leading Conservatives, including Austen Chamberlain, by that
time the party leader, remained loyal to Lloyd George ensured
that when Andrew Bonar Law formed a new government he was
bound to promote a number of figures from the ranks of obscu-
rity. Neville Chamberlain was one of the beneficiaries, taking the
position of Postmaster-General, outside the cabinet but with
admission to the Privy Council. The appointment caused considerable friction inside the Chamberlain household – indeed the
parliamentary relationship between the two brothers was never
an entirely easy one. Be that as it may, a few months later Neville
was elevated to the cabinet as Minister of Health. It would be
unfair to suggest that, but for the unforeseeable events at the
Carlton Club, Neville Chamberlain would inevitably have
served out his parliamentary career as an obscure backbencher.
His administrative talents and capacity for sheer hard work
might well have forced their way to the attention of
Conservative party managers before too long. But it was
certainly the political upheaval of 1922 which catapulted him

into the front rank with almost unseemly haste for a man who had entered the House of Commons for the first time only months before his fiftieth birthday. The whole batting order of Conservative politics had been transformed in a way that would not be reversed until 1940. It was perhaps inevitable that Law's government should be styled by contemporaries the 'cabinet of the second eleven' and there is a sense in which this slighting description stuck with Chamberlain more than any of his new ministerial colleagues.

A second unpredictable eventuality completed the process of Chamberlain's advance to the front-line of Conservative and national politics. By early 1923 it was clear that Law was seriously ill. In May he was obliged to resign and the succession passed to Stanley Baldwin. The latter's elevation created a vacancy at the Exchequer. When other possible candidates declined to be tempted, Baldwin offered the post to Chamberlain. Thus after little more than four years in the House of Commons and at the age of fifty-four, he had reached the second place in the government, in the process overtaking his brother, who still refused to be reconciled to the events of October 1922, within the Conservative hierarchy. It was an astonishingly rapid advance for such a comparatively late beginner. This seemingly remorseless rise was interrupted by Baldwin's decision to call a general election in December 1923 in order to secure a mandate for tariffs. This meant that Chamberlain as Chancellor did not have the opportunity to introduce a budget during his first spell at the Exchequer. The new Prime Minister had badly miscalculated. Though the parliamentary arithmetic resulting from the 1923 General Election was confusing, it certainly seemed to represent a repudiation of the policy of tariff reform. After a period of manoeuvring the country's first Labour government under Ramsay MacDonald took office. Neville made good use of the period of opposition to heal the breach in the Conservative ranks and Austen returned to the party's front bench, though the old order of seniority was not restored.

Dependent upon Liberal support for its survival in office, the minority Labour government was not likely to last long. It fell over its mishandling of the Campbell Case, the bodged prosecution of an obscure journalist. The resulting General Election of October 1924 was fought against the background of a 'red scare' caused by the publication of the Zinoviev letter which appeared to prove Soviet interference in British politics. The Conservatives now won a resounding victory, though Neville himself came near to defeat in Ladywood at the hands of his charismatic Labour opponent, Oswald Mosley. The Prime Minister was not likely to repeat his mistake of 1923 and the government (and Chamberlain) could look forward to a full parliament in office. Baldwin wanted Chamberlain to return to the Exchequer, but the latter preferred the Ministry of Health which he had shadowed in opposition. It was a wise choice and proved to be the office which gave him his greatest sense of satisfaction. It was also the post in which he secured his most lasting legislative achievements.

After the rapid succession of changing ministries and frequent general elections of the early 1920s, Chamberlain finally had the chance to show his ministerial mettle. He used the opportunity to good advantage, winning the respect and approval of his colleagues in the process. Personally he had no doubts about where the overall emphasis of the new government should lie. 'Unless we leave our mark as Social Reformers', he wrote, 'the country will take it out of us hereafter.'[18] It was typical of his style and approach that, on taking office, he should have drawn up a programme of legislation for the parliament including twenty-five bills to be introduced over the following three years. Strikingly, no less than twenty-one of these proposed measures were enacted within the designated timescale. Chamberlain's health portfolio encompassed responsibility also for housing and it was within this field that he secured some of his most lasting achievements. Developing the schemes of his Labour predecessor, though with greater emphasis on the private sector, he embarked upon an ambitious programme of housebuilding which, by the time of the next general election, had brought about the construction of almost a million new homes. Many of these new dwellings still stand within suburban Britain as ongoing memorials to Neville Chamberlain. At the same time he confirmed fifty-eight programmes for slum clearance.

Chamberlain's was the guiding hand behind the government's Rating and Valuation Bill and also the Widows', Orphans' and Old Age Pensions Bill of 1925. The latter saw Chamberlain emerge as the architect of a system of pensions which would survive until after the end of the Second World War. The National Health Insurance Act of 1928 greatly extended and improved health insurance benefits. In the field of public health there was legislation on food hygiene, clean water and clean air. But his most significant legislative achievement of this period was probably the Local Government Act of 1929. Here his own experience in Birmingham was of considerable importance. This act abolished all the remaining poor law boards of guardians while drawing up new financial relationships between local authorities and central government. The powers of the guardians were vested in the local authorities which were instructed to set up Public Assistance Committees for the relief of destitution. Overall it all represented a significant body of social reform, perhaps the most impressive of the whole period between Asquith's government (1908–16) and that of Clement Attlee (1945–51). Interestingly, much of the legislation involved a constructive working relationship between Chamberlain and the Chancellor of the Exchequer, Winston Churchill. Though Baldwin's government came to an end in 1929 with the feeling that most of its senior ministers were running out of steam, Chamberlain at least had greatly enhanced his stature.

Had the Conservatives won the General Election of 1929, Chamberlain anticipated a spell at the Colonial Office, the ministry where his father had achieved his greatest renown. It was not to be. Labour emerged for the first time as the largest single party in the House of Commons, though still dependent on Liberal support for an overall majority. After his narrow escape at Ladywood in 1924, Chamberlain had transferred to the rock-solid Conservative constituency of Edgbaston which he would represent until his death. Even so, it seemed possible that his own ministerial career had now come to an end. Anticipating that Labour might call another general election in two years time and thereby secure an independent majority in the House of Commons, Chamberlain reflected upon his future prospects:

> In that case we are out for 7 years, and if then we come back I shall be 67 if I am alive, and I daresay politics will have ceased to interest me. On the other hand, the new government may make such blunders that, before two years are up, the country will be glad to be rid of them.[19]

In the event it was the second of his predictions which came closer to the truth.

Baldwin's talents were not well suited to the tasks of opposition and it was in the period after 1929 that Chamberlain emerged as his likely successor. Austen was now felt to be at or near the end of his ministerial career; Churchill ruled himself out of contention by his attitude towards Indian self-government, resigning from the Conservative party's Business Committee on the issue; and Douglas Hogg was effectively excluded once he had accepted the Lord Chancellorship and the peerage which inevitably went with it in 1928. But as discontent with Baldwin's performance mounted, Chamberlain's own position became increasingly difficult. He was glad to leave the country for a time, embarking on a two months' tour of East Africa in late 1929. Austen's main ambition in politics was now to ensure that Neville should not be deprived, as both he and their father had been, of one day succeeding to the premiership. He was therefore greatly concerned when Baldwin succeeded in persuading Neville to take over the party chairmanship from the much criticized J.C.C. Davidson. As this was a personal appointment in the gift of the party leader, Chamberlain's acceptance might well have had the effect of tying his fortunes to those of the apparently sinking Baldwin. The latter was being assailed not only by impatient Conservative backbenchers but also by the press barons, Beaverbrook and Rothermere, keen to commit the party to a policy of 'Empire Free Trade'. In the event Baldwin showed greater resilience than many credited him with and, after the triumph of his supporter Alfred Duff Cooper in the St George's by-election in March 1931, his position was never again seriously threatened. Chamberlain, who had never intrigued against his leader, could only resign himself to waiting for the leadership to be handed over to him, though he probably did not expect that this would take another six years. He now gave up the party chairmanship but continued to have responsibility for the Conservative Research Department.

Chamberlain played an active but probably not decisive role in the negotiations which led to the formation of a National Government in August 1931 following the failure of the Labour cabinet to agree on a package of economy measures to deal with the serious financial crisis which had arisen. In the ensuing cabinet he returned to the Ministry of Health, but after the General Election that October he succeeded Philip Snowden as Chancellor of the Exchequer. Granted the fact that the National Government owed its very existence to the gravity of the economic situation, it was clearly the most important ministerial portfolio. His performance within it was bound to determine his subsequent career. Chamberlain was convinced that the processes of economic recovery would be greatly facilitated by the adoption of preferential tariffs. A cabinet committee on trade, of which he was chairman, recommended a 10 per cent tariff on all imported goods with preferential treatment offered to the Dominions. The details of the latter arrangement were to be worked out at a conference in Ottawa later in 1932. Joseph Chamberlain's last great political crusade had been for tariff reform and it gave Neville enormous personal satisfaction to present these proposals to the House of Commons:

> I believe [Joseph Chamberlain] would have found consolation for the bitterness of his disappointment if he could have foreseen that these proposals, which are the direct and legitimate descendants of his own conception, would be laid before the House of Commons, which he loved, in the presence of one and by the lips of the other of the two immediate successors to his name and blood.[20]

Chamberlain's budgets were cautious and in line with the orthodox thinking of the Bank of England and the City of London. His priorities, like theirs, were to balance the budget and to avoid inflation. By 1934 he was able to report a budget surplus, while restoring most of the cuts in unemployment benefit and in the pay of state employees made at the height of the economic crisis in 1931. 'We have now finished the story of *Bleak House*', he told the House of Commons, 'and are sitting down this afternoon to enjoy the first chapter of *Great Expectations*.'[21] Unemployment, which had peaked in 1932, also fell back though the figure never went below one million for the remainder of the decade.

The Chancellor of the Exchequer is a key figure in any administration but the circumstances of the early 1930s were such that Chamberlain was drawn into areas of policy beyond those with which his office might normally be involved. Many of the most pressing questions confronting British policy makers were inextricably intertwined with economic and commercial considerations. Apart from the issue of imperial preference, there was the long-standing matter of war debts and reparations. More generally, the whole aspect of the international scene had been transformed by the impact of the world economic crisis which had begun in 1929. All this ensured that Chamberlain started involving himself in the realm of foreign policy long before the years of his premiership. It was he, for example, rather than the

Foreign Secretary, who headed the British delegation to the Lausanne Conference in June 1932 called to consider the question of reparations. The Chancellor in fact began a period of close association with international affairs which makes it difficult to sustain the argument that the diplomatic disasters at the end of the decade were largely the errors of an ignorant and untrained first minister with experience only of domestic administration. With the powers of the Prime Minister, Ramsay MacDonald, visibly fading, with Baldwin failing to provide much in the way of leadership and with a Foreign Secretary, John Simon, renowned for his indecision, it was inevitable that Chamberlain became the workhorse of the National Government as a whole. 'It amuses me to find a new policy for each of my colleagues in turn', he told his sister as early as October 1932. By the spring of 1935, however, he seemed less enthusiastic about his position: 'I am more and more carrying this Government on my back. . . . It is certainly time there was a change.'[22]

MacDonald finally stood down from the premiership in May 1935 with Baldwin taking his place. Chamberlain took a leading part in the General Election of November 1935 which saw the National Government returned with a reduced but still impregnable majority in the House of Commons. By this stage he was convinced of the need for rearmament in the face of an increasingly threatening international scene, even though this would jeopardize the financial stability which his whole period at the Treasury had been designed to secure. Indeed, he was the driving force behind the Defence White Papers of 1936 and 1937. In June 1936 he made one of his more celebrated public excursions into the foreign policy arena when, in the course of a speech to the 1900 Club, he declared that the continuation of sanctions against Italy for that country's invasion of Abyssinia represented 'the very midsummer of madness'. Chamberlain remained as Chancellor throughout Baldwin's final premiership, though for much of 1936 he was effectively the day-to-day head of the administration when the Prime Minister suffered what was probably a nervous breakdown. Baldwin recovered sufficiently to show that sureness of touch which tended to characterize his powers of crisis management when the amorous intentions of King Edward VIII towards an American divorcée threatened the stability of the monarchy itself at the end of the year. With a new king safely on the throne Baldwin at last stepped down in a welter of affectionate good wishes in May 1937. By this time the succession of Neville Chamberlain was no longer a matter of debate. No other name than his was seriously considered to take over the premiership at this time. The only blip was the ill-received proposal in Chamberlain's last budget, presented just before he stepped into Baldwin's place, for a National Defence Contribution, a graduated tax on the growth of business profits. It was left to Simon, who took over from him at the Exchequer, to sort this matter out.

By his own admission Chamberlain entered 10 Downing Street at an age when most people are contemplating retirement, if they have not already embarked upon it. At sixty-eight he was the oldest newcomer to the premiership of the twentieth century with the exception of Campbell-Bannerman in 1905. But age seems to have imposed no physical impairment upon him. Apart from periodic attacks of gout Chamberlain enjoyed generally good health until his final collapse after he had ceased to be Prime Minister. Contemporaries were struck by the vigour with which he approached his duties. For many, including the Foreign Secretary Anthony Eden, this was a welcome change after Baldwin's lethargy. But the cabinet which Chamberlain constructed was full of the familiar faces of men who had served for all or most of the years of the National Government. Indeed, the new Prime Minister would periodically bemoan the lack of alternative talent from which to draw on the crowded government benches of the House of Commons.

Almost certainly Chamberlain would have wished his premiership to serve as a fitting climax to the record of domestic administration and reform which had characterized his earlier career. After all, his careful stewardship of the national finances had had behind it the desire to continue to increase the prosperity and happiness of the British people once circumstances allowed. By the spring of 1937, however, it was clear that the government's preoccupations would be dominated by the international rather than the domestic scene. 'What a frightful bill we do owe to Master Hitler, damn him!' Chamberlain complained. 'If it only wasn't for Germany, we should be having such a wonderful time just now.'[23] In fact Hitler's Germany was only the most serious of a number of international threats which had grown up during the lifetime of the National Government and which provided an inescapable backcloth to Chamberlain's premiership. Germany, Italy and Japan were locked together by the Rome–Berlin Axis and the German–Japanese Anti-Comintern Pact. Germany and Japan had already left the League of Nations and would be followed by Italy before the year was out. In such a situation Chamberlain was not alone in believing that the policy of collective security based upon the League was something of a dead letter. In Spain civil war had raged for a year and threatened to boil over into a wider European conflict. While Britain and France adhered to the policy of non-intervention, Germany, Italy and the Soviet Union were busy aiding their respective ideological soul-mates. With British rearmament still in its early stages, it was an altogether unpromising inheritance for the new Prime Minister.

Chamberlain's foreign policy will be discussed in detail elsewhere in this book. At this stage it is merely necessary to note that he seems from the outset to have decided upon a more proactive line than had been adopted by his predecessor. Sceptical of the reliance that could be placed on Britain's potential allies, his overriding concern was to avoid involving the country in another war if this was at all possible and he believed that the best way to achieve this goal was by actively seeking a settlement with those countries which were hoping to revise the existing international settlement. In the first instance he concentrated his attention upon Italy, which he rightly saw as the weaker link in the Rome–Berlin Axis, but he never lost sight of the fact that Germany was ultimately the key to the whole situation. His efforts to reach an accommodation with Mussolini, and in particular his opening of unofficial channels of communication with the Italian dictator, placed increasing strains upon his relationship with Eden. The Foreign Secretary was also disturbed by his apparently dismissive attitude towards suggestions of American mediation in the quest for an international settlement. Chamberlain's personal attention to foreign policy, which Eden had begun by welcoming, became increasingly irksome to the ultra-sensitive Foreign Secretary and Eden finally resigned from the cabinet in February 1938, to be replaced by Lord Halifax. As the new minister was a peer, Chamberlain was obliged to take an increasingly prominent role in presenting the government's foreign policy to the House of Commons. The talks with Italy which had precipitated Eden's resignation now got underway and were brought to an apparently successful conclusion on 16 April, though the agreement itself was not brought into force until the following November. But

Chamberlain's courting of Mussolini never produced the tangible results which he had hoped for.

The new Foreign Secretary had already made contact with the German leadership, including Hitler, in November 1937 when he had accepted an invitation to Germany in his capacity of Master of the Middleton Hunt to attend an international hunting exhibition in Berlin. But the German problem really came to the fore following the Nazi takeover of Austria in March 1938. Though this step was specifically forbidden under the terms of the Treaty of Versailles, there was no willingness in Britain or France to take retaliatory action. The so-called Anschluss served to bring the question of Czechoslovakia to the government's attention. As Austen Chamberlain had warned in 1936, 'If Austria goes, Czechoslovakia is indefensible'.[24] The problem derived from the existence of a substantial number of German-speaking citizens concentrated in the border areas of Czechoslovakia, known as the Sudetenland. To many observers, and certainly in Hitler's propaganda, this seemed to represent a flagrant perversion of the principle of national self-determination. The outlines of British policy were determined in a series of meetings of the cabinet and its Foreign Policy Committee in the spring of 1938, several months before the celebrated meetings at Berchtesgaden, Godesberg and Munich upon which so much historical attention has been focused. In brief, it was agreed that it would not be worth a war to try to keep more than three million Germans inside the Czech state against their will. Czechoslovakia would in any case be merely a pretext for a war with Germany since there was nothing which the British with their existing military capability could do to prevent a German invasion. British policy therefore sought to find out whether the Czech government could be induced to make sufficient concessions to satisfy the aspirations of the Sudeten Germans. The picture was complicated by the fact that Czechoslovakia had a treaty of alliance with France (Britain's only obligations were the virtually moribund ones which arose from Czechoslovakia's membership of the League of Nations) and it was difficult to envisage a situation in which Britain would allow France to go to war with Germany without feeling obliged to join her. Czechoslovakia also had a defensive alliance with the Soviet Union, although the activation of this treaty was dependent on prior French action.

After negotiations through the summer between the Czech

government and its German minority failed to produce agreement, Chamberlain decided upon a dramatic personal initiative. Without consulting the full cabinet he invited himself to Germany for face-to-face discussions with Hitler. In conference at Berchtesgaden a provisional agreement was reached, subject to the approval of the British cabinet, the French government and the Czechs, for the separation of the Sudeten Germans from the rest of Czechoslovakia. The necessary consent was duly secured and Chamberlain returned to Germany on 22 September for what he anticipated would be a relatively routine second meeting with Hitler to finalize the details of the agreement. But at Godesberg on the Rhine Hitler upped the stakes. He now demanded the immediate occupation of the German-speaking area by German troops and promised only not to act before 1 October. Though Chamberlain was inclined to accede to these latest German demands, the cabinet led by Halifax plumped for rejection of the revised terms. War now seemed the probable outcome. On 27 September the Prime Minister broadcast to a nation which was anticipating the worst. 'How horrible', he declared, 'fantastic, incredible, it is that we should be digging trenches and trying on gas-masks here because of a quarrel in a far-away country between people of whom we know nothing.' But Chamberlain clearly regarded it as folly that war should be the outcome of a dispute where the principle, if not the details, of a settlement had already been agreed upon. He declared his readiness to make even a third visit to Hitler if he thought it would do any good.

Chamberlain was actually nearing the end of a long exposition of the whole of the Czechoslovakian saga to the House of Commons when news reached him that, apparently following an intervention by Mussolini, Hitler had agreed to a further meeting in Munich on the following day, to which Mussolini himself and the French Prime Minister Daladier would also be invited. Amidst unprecedented scenes of relief Chamberlain announced his acceptance of the Führer's invitation. These sentiments were widely replicated across the general population which had been brought to the very brink of European war. From the discussions in Munich Chamberlain secured minor concessions from the Godesberg terms, enough to present the new arrangements as a negotiating triumph. He also had little difficulty in persuading Hitler to append his signature to a joint Anglo–German declaration pledging the determination of the two countries never to go to war with one another again. Chamberlain returned to London to an overwhelmingly enthusiastic reception and, in an unguarded moment at the end of a tiring day, declared that 'This is the second time in our history that there has come back from Germany to Downing Street peace with honour. I believe it is peace for our time.' It was a remark which he came to regret and in the Commons debate on the Munich settlement in early October he was altogether more circumspect, reminding his listeners that Britain could not afford to relax the processes of rearmament.

Precisely what Chamberlain believed he had achieved at Munich is a matter of debate and will be considered in a later chapter. But the Prime Minister's public statements became increasingly optimistic. Chamberlain and Halifax visited Paris for conversations with their French opposite numbers in November and in January 1939 the two men went to Rome. The talks with Mussolini achieved little, though Chamberlain seemed well satisfied, hoping perhaps that he could still rely on the Duce to exercise a moderating influence on Hitler. Such expectations were rudely shattered when German troops marched into Prague on the morning of 15 March 1939. This was a significantly different step from any Hitler had yet taken in the foreign arena. He could no longer claim that he was reversing the injustices of Versailles or fighting for the right of German people to enter or rejoin the Reich. Yet Chamberlain seemed at first unwilling to accept that his policy of 'appeasement' had run its course and failed. His speech to the House of Commons that same day was poorly received. Two days later, however, speaking in Birmingham, the Prime Minister struck a very different note. For the first time he seemed ready to contemplate the idea that Hitler's appetite could never be satisfied. 'Is this the last attack upon a small State or is it to be followed by another? Is this in fact a step in the direction of an attempt to dominate the world by force?' If so, Chamberlain insisted, Hitler should know that Britain would 'take part to the uttermost of its power in resisting such a challenge'.

By the end of the month Britain and France had given a guarantee of the independence (though not the territorial integrity) of Poland. On 7 April Mussolini took advantage of the confused situation to launch an attack on Albania. Britain responded by offering guarantees to Romania and Greece and in May issued a declaration of solidarity with Turkey. Though these moves clearly marked a significant departure in British foreign policy, it is probably unwise to stress the extent to which the underlying purposes of Chamberlain's diplomacy had changed. He still hoped to avoid war, but the method of doing so had been modified with the emphasis now placed on deterrence. Chamberlain was probably still willing to envisage further territorial adjustments to Germany's advantage, as his avoidance of a guarantee of Polish integrity appears to suggest.

Britain's batch of guarantees had something in the nature of gesture-politics about it. If Czechoslovakia had been beyond the country's capacity to assist, it was by no means clear how British military support could be brought to Poland or Romania. Increasingly, the government's critics and many of its own members saw that only in alliance with the Soviet Union could Britain's new foreign policy acquire credibility. Chamberlain, however, was reluctant to take this step. He was suspicious of the Soviets on ideological grounds and doubted their military capacity following Stalin's purges of the Red Army. Eventually, however, Chamberlain had to give way, virtually isolated on this issue within his own cabinet. Desultory negotiations began in Moscow but had not made significant progress by the time that the Germans and Soviets shook the world by announcing the signing of a Nazi–Soviet Non-Aggression Pact on 23 August. With his eastern flank thus protected, Hitler was ready to strike again. German forces invaded Poland on 1 September. Largely because of difficulties in synchronizing action with the French, Chamberlain was unable to announce a declaration of war to the House of Commons on 2 September. But under pressure from a sizeable minority of his own cabinet, Chamberlain was forced into action. When Hitler failed to respond to a British ultimatum, Britain declared war at 11am on 3 September.

Chamberlain responded to the war crisis by expanding the basis of his government, bringing in his erstwhile Conservative critics, Churchill and Eden. Significantly, however, the opposition parties with whom the Prime Minister's relations had long been strained, declined his invitation to join the administration. There was criticism of the government's failure to take decisive military action during the period of the so-called Phoney War, irritation at the lack of economic co-ordination of the war effort and some feeling that Chamberlain personally was ill-equipped to take on the role of a war leader. In general, however,

Chamberlain remained firmly in charge until news of the ill-fated Norwegian campaign began to filter back to Britain at the beginning of May 1940. Confidence in the government had been badly shaken by the expedition's failure and a two-day debate on 7 and 8 May turned into a general indictment of Chamberlain's premiership, with stinging attacks delivered not only by Labour and Liberal critics but also by dissident Conservatives such as Leo Amery. The government prevailed with a comfortable majority of eighty-one. But its usual majority was in the region of 240 and over thirty nominal supporters had gone into the opposition lobby and many others had abstained or were absent unpaired. Over the next couple of days Chamberlain reached two conclusions. The first was that the 'national' will was for the creation of a genuinely National Government. That which he headed was still nominally styled 'National' as it had been in 1931, but in practice it was overwhelmingly Conservative. The second conclusion was that such a development would be impossible under his leadership. After momentarily hesitating when the German forces launched their western offensive on 10 May, Chamberlain resigned the premiership later that day and was succeeded by Winston Churchill.

This could easily have been the end of Chamberlain's political career. He was probably already suffering – though he did not yet know it – from the cancer which would kill him before the year was out. But Chamberlain accepted Churchill's offer to take a place in his War Cabinet as Lord President of the Council and, significantly, he retained the leadership of the Conservative party. Only the opposition of Labour prevented him from taking on the Leadership of the House of Commons. In effect he remained for several weeks a key figure in the new government and he continued to chair the War Cabinet whenever Churchill was absent. His task was to co-ordinate domestic policy while the new Prime Minister got on with the task of waging the war. By early September however Chamberlain knew that his days were numbered. 'Any ideas which may have been in my mind about possibilities of further political activity, and even a possibility of another Premiership after the war, have gone.'[25] On 22 September he wrote to Churchill to offer his resignation. Churchill would have been happy to give him time to recover but, recognizing that this was not going to happen, accepted his resignation on 30 September. Chamberlain died on 9 November in his seventy-second year. After cremation his remains were laid to rest in Westminster Abbey with Churchill and members of the War Cabinet acting as pall-bearers.

Notes

1. Chamberlain MSS, BC4/8/9, Hilda Chamberlain to Dorothy Lloyd [Chamberlain's daughter] 21 Dec.1941.
2. Chamberlain MSS, NC2/24A, Neville Chamberlain diary 4 Oct. 1940.
3. R. Jenkins, *The Chancellors* (London, 1998), p.155.
4. C.L. Mowat, *Britain Between the Wars 1918–1940* (London, 1955), p.619.
5. Chamberlain MSS, NC7/6/33, N. Chamberlain to Arthur Chamberlain 12 Oct. 1940.
6. J. Charmley, *Chamberlain and the Lost Peace* (London, 1989), p.212.
7. S. Aster, ' "Guilty Men": The Case of Neville Chamberlain' in R. Boyce and E. M. Robertson (eds), *Paths to War* (London, 1989), pp.233–68.
8. Avon MSS, AP11/11/5, note of party meeting.
9. *Sunday Times* 26 Nov. 1961.
10. It is only just for the present writer to record that his own career as a professional historian of the twentieth century owes much to the interest and enthusiasm engendered by this teacher, Professor R.F. Leslie.
11. J. Amery, *The Life of Joseph Chamberlain*, vol.4 (London, 1951), p.275.
12. Chamberlain MSS, NC7/5/8, N. Chamberlain to A. Greenwood 7 Oct. 1900.
13. *Ibid.*, NC 7/5/17, N. Chamberlain to A. Greenwood 25 April 1909.
14. H.M. Hyde, *Neville Chamberlain* (London, 1976), p.28.
15. Chamberlain MSS, NC18/1/118, N. Chamberlain to H. Chamberlain 1 July 1917.
16. *Ibid.*, NC2/20 , diary 17 Dec. 1917.
17. *Ibid.*, NC7/5/23, N. Chamberlain to A. Greenwood 16 Jan. 1919.
18. *Ibid.*, NC18/1/458, N. Chamberlain to I. Chamberlain 1 Nov. 1924.
19. *Ibid.*, NC2/22, diary 8 June 1929.
20. House of Commons Debates, 5th Series, vol.261, col.296.
21. *Ibid.*, vol.288, cols 905–6.
22. I. Macleod, *Neville Chamberlain* (London, 1961), p.164.
23. Hyde, *Chamberlain*, p.83.
24. *Ibid.*, p.112.
25. Chamberlain MSS, NC2/24A, diary 9 Sept. 1940.

|2|

In his own day

. . . perhaps, when I come to think of it, I don't really care much what they say of me now so long as I am satisfied myself I am doing what is right.[1]

Most of this book is concerned with the judgements of history – what writers and public opinion have made of Neville Chamberlain's career in the sixty years since his retirement and death in 1940. But a prominent figure also develops a reputation during his own lifetime, while his career is still progressing, and the evolution of that reputation can have a significant effect upon the development of the individual's public life. Chamberlain made his first incursion into national politics more than twenty years before he became Prime Minister and it is the purpose of the present chapter to analyse the way in which his reputation emerged from that time. But that reputation was formed largely within the restricted milieu of Westminster politics. To the man in the street Chamberlain remained, even when holding high cabinet office, a largely unknown quantity. Such impressions of him as existed were essentially the creation of occasional comments and assessments in the press. It was striking when he first entered 10 Downing Street in May 1937 how many writers sought to introduce the new Prime Minister to a wider and largely ignorant audience. Perhaps of more significance was the reputation which Chamberlain developed among political insiders, those who worked with and sometimes against him as he made his way steadily up the greasy pole of British political life. Yet even those who moved along the same political corridors as Neville Chamberlain did not find it at all easy to evaluate their colleague. He was not, stressed Duff Cooper, 'a man whom it was easy to know well'.[2] Chamberlain was among the least clubbable of British Prime Ministers. He formed close friendships with very few of his professional colleagues; he unburdened himself to even fewer. Only perhaps within the reassuring confines of his close family circle did he fully relax and remove the mask of his public persona. Nonetheless, by the time that Chamberlain became Prime Minister and indeed for most of his premiership, the reputation which he enjoyed was based upon a perception of positive qualities and achievements in an almost continuously successful political career. Thus what may be thought of as Chamberlain's contemporary reputation sits uneasily alongside the majority verdict of posterity.

It was Chamberlain's competence as Lord Mayor of Birmingham which first brought him to national public notice. The reputation which he gained in that post was the main reason why Lloyd George decided to pluck him from his provincial stronghold and offer him the position of Director-General of National Service in December 1916. Chamberlain was also known as a businessman and his appointment may be regarded as one of several Lloyd George made to bring the enterprise and efficiency of the commercial and industrial worlds into the working of his wartime central government. The *Birmingham Daily Post* did justice to his record at this time:

> One has only to recall the energy with which he has thrown himself into such movements as the establishment of a Municipal Savings Bank, the granting of increased allowances to men broken in the war, the better protection of the Midlands against Zeppelin raids, the preservation of child life, the utilisation of available land for increasing our food supply, civic recreation, and his efforts to elevate the musical life of Birmingham by the formation of a permanent orchestra to realise the scope of his energies and the breadth of his sympathies.[3]

His reputation was that of a constructive radical, 'a strong advocate of town planning and housing and hospital reform'.[4] In marked contrast with the image he would have later in his career, Chamberlain was seen as a man of broad political sympathies, respected and well liked by his political opponents. He would not hesitate to oppose his political friends when their views ran counter to his own; but at the same time he would go 'out of his way to compliment individual members of the Labour group on the [Birmingham] Council'.[5] Trade Union leaders who met him for the first time at a meeting of the TUC in Birmingham in September 1916 were impressed by the broad-minded way in which he regarded the labour problem.

It was inevitable with the name that he bore that contemporaries would be looking for signs in Chamberlain of his famous father. Several observers began to see in Neville rather than his elder and as yet more distinguished brother Austen the true successor to Radical Joe. 'He has more of the piquancy and fire which distinguished his late father', suggested one journalist, 'than any other surviving member of the family, and his gifts of repartee are frequently brought into play.'[6] Despite a somewhat light voice it was his style in debate which prompted most comparisons with his father. Contemporaries described an excellent speaker, lucid, forceful and fluent, with a polished literary style. Early in 1917 the *Birmingham Daily Post* enthused:

> Mr. Neville Chamberlain's voice is light – perhaps a little lacking in robustness and range of tone for him ever to become a great orator. But he has learned how to use it and make the most of it. It was apparent from his first sentence that he was a practised public-speaker . . . The speech was mapped out clearly in his mind. Appropriate language came without a halt, without even a hesitation, without a fault of grammar or emphasis.[7]

Chamberlain thus entered his first national post buttressed by high expectations and considerable confidence. 'What a tribute to the position which N has made for himself!' purred Austen. 'He has had an excellent press and starts with everyone's good will.'[8] Though most historians now consider that Chamberlain's ultimate failure in this position was inevitable granted the brief with which he was entrusted and the limited resources available to him, there can be little doubt that he left office in August 1917 with his reputation badly damaged. A fellow junior minister found it hard to say 'how much NC was to blame, or how much he was hamstrung by the directions imposed by L. George'. Even so,

> nothing in my mind can excuse him for filling his dept. with a huge crowd of officials before there was work for them, many of whom were notoriously incompetent, and

he displayed a good deal of petty departmental animosity which surprised me, after all I had heard of his ability. I cannot believe that he is anything like as good a man as Austen.[9]

But of far greater importance was the opinion of Lloyd George, the man who had elevated Chamberlain to national prominence but who now rejoiced that he 'has resigned and thank God for that'.[10] Lloyd George it was who created the idea that his wartime experience showed that Chamberlain's talents, which appeared formidable when deployed on the restricted canvas of municipal politics, were totally inadequate for the national stage. It was an image from which he would never fully free himself. Though Lloyd George's *War Memoirs* were not published until 1935, it seems likely that he quickly made his views well known within those circles in which he moved. When his memoirs were published, by which time Chamberlain was firmly entrenched as Chancellor of the Exchequer, they assumed a role in the popular historiography of the First World War not unlike that later occupied by Churchill's writings on the conflict of 1939–45. 'Mr. Neville Chamberlain is a man of rigid competency.' Lloyd George's use of the present tense is significant. 'Such men have their uses in conventional times or in conventional positions, and are indispensable for filling subordinate posts at all times. But they are lost in an emergency or in creative tasks at any time.'[11]

Unusually, therefore, when Chamberlain finally decided to enter the House of Commons in 1918, he faced the task of restoring an already tarnished reputation. The legacy of his first experience in national politics would not be easy to shake off. 'I shall always bear the blame for the failure', he had insisted on leaving his post at National Service.[12] Yet, while aspects of his first initiation in government service would return to haunt him, not least in Lloyd George's undying animosity, Chamberlain seemed quickly to put this setback behind him. What is striking about his first years in the House of Commons is the speed with which his reputation recovered. Only in this way is it possible to explain the remarkably rapid advance of a man who had waited until his fiftieth year before entering parliament. To rise to cabinet rank after just over four years and to be appointed Chancellor of the Exchequer only months later was no small achievement and indicated a man who had obviously made a

very positive impression at Westminster. *The Times* passed
judgement upon his elevation:

> By general consent Mr. Chamberlain's ministerial career,
> short as it has been, has proved his capacity for holding
> office; for when he was transferred to the Ministry of
> Health, in order to take charge of the government's hous-
> ing policy, it was at a time when the credit of that
> Department in the House and in the country was low, and
> he has successfully done what he was selected to perform.
> He has been in Parliament only five years, and though his
> elevation to so signal a position as that of Chancellor of
> the Exchequer must partly be explained by the abnormal
> conditions of the present political situation, there will, we
> believe, be a strong disposition to hold that he has attained
> it mainly through his own merits.[13]

In words which clearly ran counter to Lloyd George's sentiments, the *Morning Post* wrote of Chamberlain's statesmanship
and capacity to rise to an emergency, qualities which gave
grounds for the highest expectations as regards his promotion to
the Exchequer. The paper felt confident that he would pursue
sound policies without being tied too rigidly to routine and
precedent. The *Birmingham Daily Post* was equally optimistic.
During his brief period at the Ministry of Health Chamberlain
had shown all the qualities that make for a successful minister.
He had displayed an ability to get to the heart of an intricate
subject, great clarity in putting his views to the House of
Commons, firmness and courage in sticking to those points to
which he was committed and at the same time courtesy and an
open mind in listening to criticism and accepting suggestions for
detailed improvement to his proposed legislation. Above all,
Chamberlain was admired for his efficiency and professional-
ism.

But, as would be the case throughout his career, he attracted
admiration rather than affection. The Chamberlain brothers
always found it far easier to discuss one another's shortcomings
with their sisters than they did to be frank to each other. In a
revealing letter to Ida Chamberlain written in November 1924,
Austen explained Neville's deficiency: 'Boiled down, it all comes
to this. N's manner freezes people. His workers think that he
does not appreciate what they do for him. Everyone respects him
and he makes no friends.'[14] Chamberlain, failing to win many

hearts, had to rely upon the cogency of his argument to win men's minds. Criticisms of this nature were not confined to the family circle and in time they inevitably reached Chamberlain himself, causing him considerable concern. But it was a short-coming in his make-up which he never succeeded in overcoming.

Chamberlain's steady ministerial advancement was inter-rupted by Baldwin's unexpected and ill-advised decision to call a general election on the issue of tariffs in December 1923. Defeat opened the way for the Labour party to take office for the first time. But Chamberlain was back in power following the Conservatives' overwhelming victory in the General Election of October 1924. Offered by Baldwin the choice of resuming his stewardship of the Exchequer or returning to the Ministry of Health, Chamberlain suprisingly opted for the latter. His think-ing at this time reveals much about his attitude to public life:

> I think many of my friends would be disappointed if I didn't return to Downing St. but that would not weigh with me an iota. After all, if one is to look at it from the point of view of personal credit – which I honestly don't – I should eventually get much more if I had been able to make a success of the M[inistry of] H[ealth] than if I had been an ordinary C[hancellor] of [the] E[xchequer]. And if you look back at recent Chancellors you won't find one who stood out sufficiently to be remembered for his work there.[15]

Emerging as a practical social reformer, it was in this office that Chamberlain firmly secured the sort of positive reputation which characterized most of his career before it was forever overshadowed by the impact of his final years. His progressive policies were in fact too advanced for the taste of some of the more right-wing of his parliamentary colleagues. He was seen as one of the most dynamic forces in a government which, as the years went by, seemed increasingly to be plagued by inertia. As a more restricted audience in Birmingham had already learnt a decade earlier, this was a man who could get things done. His talents were of the type which appealed to the senior civil servants with whom he worked. 'Whitehall found in him what it most desires for its normal tasks; industry, order, precision, correctitude, decision.'[16] Indeed, it is perhaps not surprising that the closest associates of his premiership would be drawn from these ranks rather than from among his political colleagues. One who served briefly as his principal private secretary recalled 'a pleasant chief, though shy and reserved, so that those who worked for him could rarely discover the humanity and kindliness that were undoubtedly there'.[17]

It was around this time that Chamberlain overtook his brother in the Conservative hierarchy, notwithstanding the latter's achievement in negotiating the Locarno Treaties of October 1925. Chamberlain was not one to advertise his talents too obviously. For many of his colleagues in the parliamentary party this was their first real opportunity to assess his worth. 'I liked Neville Chamberlain whom I really met for the first time last night', recorded one MP:

> He is immensely superior to Sir Austen – in ability and in general attractiveness. In the House he is wonderfully effective and knows his particular subjects from A to Z. He is a tower of strength to the Government in debate, though his progressive policy in local government may bring the Party into many awkward predicaments before he has done.[18]

After less than a year in office the *Birmingham Daily Post* described the coming man in Conservative politics:

> Mr. Neville Chamberlain undoubtedly has increased his Parliamentary reputation. As Minister of Health he has brought to the House no fewer than ten Bills, and he has now the satisfaction of seeing all of them, if not actually passed, at least well on the way to the Statute-book. The weight of work thrown on the Minister of Health by the special measures called for to enact the proposals of the Budget alone was tremendous. He shouldered it [with] an energy that seemed to defy exhaustion ... Mr. Chamberlain commands the House by his extraordinary grasp of business detail, and he has developed a gift of suavity in dealing with the Opposition which has enabled him to carry through many difficult matters with the greatest economy of time.[19]

For the first time he began to be considered as a potential future party leader and Prime Minister, especially as the decade took a progressive toll of Chamberlain's potential rivals within the Conservative ranks. 'Neville C's answer to L[loyd] G[eorge] was the best thing he has done yet', noted a Conservative elder

statesman in March 1926. 'He is being spoken of as a future
leader of the party.'[20] Viewing the British political scene from
India where he had recently been appointed to the Viceroyalty,
Lord Irwin wrote as one who 'look[ed] forward with some
confidence one of these days to seeing the Party under your leadership'.[21] A little over a decade later Irwin, elevated to the
viscountcy of Halifax, would serve as Chamberlain's Foreign
Secretary. But many accepted Chamberlain's status as Baldwin's
successor-designate in a mood closer to resignation than enthusiasm. He 'certainly improves on acquaintance', conceded
Cuthbert Headlam,

> but it is hard to believe that he is the only possible succes-
> sor if anything happened to Baldwin – and yet many
> people say so. It is not any lack of ability in which he fails;
> it is in the spark of humanity or whatever you like to call
> it. He is more of a machine than a man – at least that is
> how he strikes the ordinary individual who meets him as I
> do.[22]

Notwithstanding these personal shortcomings, it was difficult
for anyone to deny Chamberlain's record of positive achievement as a departmental minister. In a widely reported speech in
Wrexham the Archbishop of Wales declared that the Minister of
Health would go down in history as one of the wisest, most
clear-sighted and resolute benefactors of the physical well-being
of the British working class. A cabinet colleague judged him to
be 'the great success of 1928' as a result of his proposals for
derating.[23] It was clear also that his skills in debate improved
over the course of the parliament. One MP who in 1925 had
found him 'no orator – indeed . . . somewhat of a depressing
speaker', recorded his admiration only two years later:

> Neville Chamberlain made an admirable speech which was
> exactly what was wanted – calm, clear, unanswerable –
> one envies him his power of clear exposition and lucidity –
> one feels that one's own efforts are so hopelessly incoher-
> ent and confused after listening to a man who speaks with
> such directness and logic.[24]

The feather in his legislative cap, both in terms of its intrinsic
importance and of Chamberlain's skill in steering it through the
House of Commons, was the Local Government Act of 1929. It
was, judged *The Times*, one of the outstanding legislative

achievements of the twentieth century for which full credit should be given to the minister himself. The *Morning Post* offered confirmation:

> Mr. Chamberlain, whose praises are on everyone's lips, not only for the boldness of his legislative conception, but for the unfailing resource and skill by which he has piloted his measure through all the rocks and shoals and cross-currents of public agitation. Having in view, not only the antagonisms of opponents, but the misgivings of friends, and the fears of affected interests, it is a remarkable achievement to have carried a scheme of such scope and complexity to third reading without serious resistance, and to have won for it, outside the sphere of party politics, a general, if not always an unqualified, acceptance.[25]

Overall, Baldwin's cabinet had lost much of its momentum by the time of the General Election of May 1929. But Chamberlain was probably unique among the senior ministers of this government as one whose stock stood higher as the administration came to a close than it had at its outset. A period in opposition cannot, by definition, satisfy the ministerial aspirations of an ambitious politician, but it can be critical in reordering the internal dynamics of a political party. So it was in the troubled interlude of Labour government between June 1929 and August 1931. Chamberlain succeeded in enhancing his standing as Baldwin's likely successor, especially once Winston Churchill effectively ruled himself out of contention by his refusal to endorse party policy on the future of India. Indeed, it seemed increasingly clear that Baldwin, whose political talents were ill-suited to the demands of opposition, was dependent for his very survival as party leader upon the continued support of his chief lieutenant. In addition, Chamberlain now emerged as a party manager of some prowess following his period as Party Chairman and his role in establishing the Conservative Research Department. Around this time William Bridgeman, who had served as First Lord of the Admiralty in the out-going Conservative government, penned a perceptive sketch of his leading colleagues. He found Chamberlain

> a very good administrator at the Ministry of Health, perhaps a little too bureaucratic – first-rate at getting a bill through the House on account of his clarity of thought and

speech. A wise counsellor in the Cabinet. He suffers from a rather close habit of reserve which is the one drawback which might prevent him being a good leader. He does not seem to care whether he has friends or not, yet every now and then he seems strangely grateful for any show of friendship from a colleague. He is a little too easily offended and occasionally appears petulant. He has worked very hard to help and support Baldwin, who relies a good deal on his advice, and made a great sacrifice in taking on the temporary control of the Central Office. . . . He is a good organizer and no doubt will do it well. . . .[26]

Yet Austen felt lurking doubts, commenting in November 1930 that Neville still failed to impress a large number of people with his real gifts of leadership. If Baldwin were to stand down at this time, Austen feared that the party would be deeply divided over the succession. For if Chamberlain had his admirers, he had also begun to attract enemies.[27] Indeed, there were those who could admire Chamberlain and dislike him at the same time. Cuthbert Headlam, who had slowly come to appreciate his positive qualities, recorded that he 'dislike[d] him more and more each time I see him'. The reason was clear:

> He never has a pleasant word for one or evinces the slightest interest in the work that one is doing. If you searched the whole world, you could not find a more unsuitable man for his present job [party chairman], or one less qualified to be a leader of men.[28]

One observer doubted whether someone as 'cold and "clammy" as a dead trout' could ever become Prime Minister.[29]

Had Ramsay MacDonald's second Labour government survived for its natural term and overcome the economic crisis which in fact brought about its demise, Chamberlain's political career might well have come to a premature end, leaving him with a very different reputation from that which history has ultimately bestowed upon him. After all, by 1931 he was already sixty-two years of age. As it was, the extraordinary political crisis of that year brought him back to government and, in due course, to 10 Downing Street. The distribution of posts in the National Government formed that August was carefully engineered to emphasize the all-party nature of the new administration. Chamberlain was one of four Conservatives to secure cabinet rank, returning once more to the Ministry of Health. After the General Election in October, however, which served to confirm the overwhelming Conservative preponderance within the government's parliamentary majority, Chamberlain replaced the free-trader Philip Snowden as Chancellor of the Exchequer. Granted that the National Government owed its very existence to the perceived need to save the country from economic disaster, it was clearly the key appointment, even though MacDonald as Prime Minister and Baldwin as Lord President nominally took precedence.

In the history of twentieth-century Britain the Exchequer was not always a launching pad for further political advancement. The country's long-term economic problems offered few openings for easy ministerial achievement. Chamberlain's experience, however, was rather different. His tenure as Chancellor was unusually long (five and a half years); it was also unusually successful. It needs to be stressed that his progress from the Exchequer to the premiership was largely secured on the basis of a contemporary perception that he had presided with competence and authority over the nation's recovery from the worst effects of the world depression. As one newspaper put it at the time he became Prime Minister, Chamberlain 'must have the credit for the financial recovery which has made us the envy of the world, for he would certainly have had the obloquy if there had been failure or distress'.[30] Indeed, it seems reasonable to suggest that, had he become Foreign Secretary rather than Chancellor in 1931, his reputation might have been badly damaged and the chance of becoming Prime Minister lost.

Chamberlain's appointment gave him the opportunity to confirm that his were a safe pair of hands. Contemporary opinion suggested that economic recovery depended above all else upon confidence – and the new Chancellor inspired it. Notwithstanding later criticisms, it was not looking for novel experiments or the sort of high-risk strategy advocated by the minority who had espoused the ideas of John Maynard Keynes. Quite simply, the stakes were too high. It was widely believed that the economy and in particular the pound had teetered on the brink of catastrophe in the summer of 1931, and the important thing was to avoid any repetition. With hindsight Chamberlain may have been condemned for being too orthodox a Chancellor. But at the time this was what was needed. A backbench observer well captured the paradox of Chamberlain's performance at the Exchequer: 'Neville made a good speech, but he was duller than usual I thought and that means very dull: however, the audience seemed to be delighted with him.'[31] 'He does not pretend to see visions or to discover truth by special intuitions peculiar to himself', confirmed the *Sunday Times*. 'He essays no flights, and is content that his processes of thought should be those of the plain man of business . . . the colours that affect his style are those of our native grey skies.'[32]

Chamberlain's standing was greatly enhanced by his handling of the question of tariffs – an issue whose past history was strewn with political corpses. Even a free-trade newspaper such as the *News Chronicle* could voice its approval:

> Mr. Neville Chamberlain has quietly dominated the House. The Prime Minister and Mr. Baldwin have faded into the background. Only Mr. Chamberlain seems sure of what he wants, and he always gets it. He has the quietest manner in the House, and only one gesture – the occasional removal of the glasses from his nose – but no Cabinet Minister has a firmer hold on Parliament.[33]

The fact that most of the country's economic problems in the early 1930s had an international dimension ensured that Chamberlain now became known to a wider audience than hitherto. The final settlement of the long-standing question of German reparations and the need to reassess Britain's commercial relations with the Empire were specific examples. More generally, the state of the national economy was in large measure dependent upon the state of the world economy. Overseas observers now became aware of the same sort of solid qualities which appealed to the domestic audience. As the *New York Times Magazine* put it in the summer of 1933:

> Neville Chamberlain is a man of sterling character all the way through, with a solid but dull exterior, and this combination of character and dullness happens to be exactly the combination that the British like best in their politics . . . He is becoming a warmer and more human speaker than he used to be, but he still belongs to the small band of business men in politics . . . who really know what they are talking about.[34]

Gradually it became clear that, notwithstanding continuing high levels of unemployment, the corner had been turned in

Britain's economic affairs and it was only natural that credit for this achievement should be given to the Chancellor. 'Those who believe in a balanced and honest Budget', observed a Liberal commentator in June 1934, 'will thank the Chancellor for having turned a deaf ear last year to the seductive proposals of Mr. Maynard Keynes and his socialistic disciples.'[35] The economy began to revive from the middle of 1933 and, apart from a temporary check in 1937, the upswing continued throughout the decade. The thirties as a whole witnessed a substantial growth in both national and per capita income. Government accounts were in surplus by the end of 1933, and the following year income tax was reduced by 6d (2.5p) in the pound. The balance of payments was brought into a state of equilibrium in 1933, the wholesale price index was actually lower than in 1930 and the controlled devaluation of sterling after it left the Gold Standard in September 1931 seemed to work well. To what extent the government in general and Chamberlain in particular were responsible for the overall improvement in Britain's economic performance lies outside the scope of this study. The Chancellor's most constructive initiative was probably his successful conversion of a £2,000m War Loan from a 5 to a $3\frac{1}{2}$ per cent stock. In a real sense, though, the question is irrelevant. The important point is that Chamberlain was *seen* to have been successful. 'The Chancellor of the Exchequer has shown much courage and determination and improved our financial position in a marvellous way', recorded a former cabinet colleague in October 1933.[36] When the time came for Chamberlain to move from 11 Downing Street to No. 10, Lord Halifax expressed something more than the dutiful sentiments of a loyal party colleague: 'his five and a half years of administration at the Exchequer will stand out in history, and will be surely recognised to have been the essential condition of all the improvement that these years have seen'.[37] Many thought it the most impressive tenure of the Treasury since Gladstone's day.

Chamberlain's record of competent achievement, especially when set against the failings of his cabinet colleagues, helped strengthen his position inside the National Government. With MacDonald's health in rapid decline and Baldwin finding the experience of non-departmental office too seductive, Chamberlain increasingly emerged as both the creative engine and the workhorse of the administration. The Liberal National, Leslie Hore-Belisha, saw him as a formidable figure in the Tory party, enjoying great support among the rank and file. The Liberal leader, Herbert Samuel, went further. In effect the government was run by Chamberlain. 'What he says goes. When he puts his foot down and says that something must be done, that decision settles it.'[38] This was an exaggeration – but not without its grain of truth.

As throughout his political career Chamberlain remained an essentially private man. But a wider public now at least *believed* that they knew something about him. During the 1930s the medium of film began to play its part in the political battle. Though his efforts may strike a modern audience accustomed to the stage-managed sound-bite as unconvincing, Chamberlain proved in his day to be among the more effective political performers on camera. Despite his somewhat antiquated dress-sense, there was an ordinariness about him which many found attractive. He had at least the ability, which many of his generation lacked, to speak naturally to an audience which was not visible to him. 'At the microphone', judged one observer, 'he does not lecture, he does not hector, he *talks*. Consequently he broadcasts better than he speaks or debates.'[39] Not surprisingly, Chamberlain played a high-profile role in the government's campaign in the General Election of November 1935. In the light of what would be said over the next five years about British preparedness or lack of it for war, it is striking to note the way in which he was now presented by the Labour opposition. The party's deputy leader, Arthur Greenwood, suggested that it was 'the merest scaremongering, disgraceful in a statesman in Mr. Chamberlain's responsible position, to suggest that more millions of money needed to be spent on armaments'. Herbert Morrison concurred. Chamberlain as Chancellor was only too willing to spend millions of pounds on machines of destruction, but had nothing for the unemployed, the social services and the depressed areas. 'He would spend on the means of death, but not on the means of life, and that was the sort of fellow he looked too.'[40] But the electorate as a whole seemed not to agree. The outcome of the election was a comfortable victory for the National Government. A net loss of around ninety seats from the extraordinary result of 1931 was probably inevitable. But it still left the government with a majority of 255 in the new House of Commons.

At one time it had seemed likely that MacDonald and Baldwin would retire together, leaving the road open for

Chamberlain's immediate succession to the premiership. In the event the two nominal leaders of the government exchanged offices in a reshuffle in June 1935, leaving Chamberlain to kick his heels for a further two years. He was not, observed one MP, 'so popular that he cannot be kept waiting'.[41] However, few now doubted that he would reach the ultimate pinnacle of British public life, which had been denied to both his father and half-brother. 'Neville Chamberlain is the most successful Minister in the National Government', opined the *Daily Express* in March 1936. 'He has done more to sustain their position than any other member of the Cabinet.' Austen was now convinced that his brother was the 'dominating mind' of the government and the only possible successor to Baldwin. 'Chips' Channon, Conservative MP for Southend, was of the same mind: 'the Baldwin mantle must certainly fall on Neville Chamberlain, who has earned it, if he wants it'.[42] Only if Baldwin were to hang on too long might Chamberlain's moment pass. As it was, the former spent much of his final premiership contemplating retirement and the attractions of the Worcestershire countryside, except when an issue such as the royal abdication of 1936 served to occupy his particular political skills.

Thus it was that Neville Chamberlain became Prime Minister on 28 May 1937. There was nothing particularly spectacular about his arrival. Indeed, it was one of the smoothest prime ministerial changeovers of the twentieth century. He had reached this political summit on the basis of a proven record of administrative competence and political reliability. An American biographer has well captured the nature of his advance:

> Chamberlain did not rise to political prominence on the basis of surging personal popularity or appeal. He did so by a quiet, steady demonstration of energy and skill. At no point in his career did he blossom forth as a 'man of destiny', as one of those historical figures who appear occasionally in conditions which seem to suggest that Fate had decreed their arrival at that particular point in time.[43]

To a surprisingly large number of people both inside and outside Westminster the new premier remained an unknown quantity. One MP, invited now to join the administration, recorded his experience in a way that revealed that Chamberlain had still not succeeded in overcoming some of the failings noted earlier in his career:

I could not recall that I had ever spoken to Neville and I
did not even know where his room was. I had to ask a
policeman. The interview was awful. It was like a head-
master telling a boy that he had so pleased him for the last
few terms that he had decided to make him a house
prefect. 'You may know', he said, 'that I am forming an
administration, and I have an under-secretaryship to fill.'[44]

Inevitably the press immediately before and after Chamberlain's
succession were full of profiles of the new first minister. Many
writers clearly sought to dispel what they took to be prevailing
misconceptions about the Prime Minister's character and attitudes. The author of one sketch noted that he was often
portrayed as having the mind and disposition of a bureaucrat
and that he was by instinct a Conservative 'Diehard'. But

nothing could be further from the truth. It would indeed be
nearer the truth to suggest that he is inclined more to the
'Left' than to the 'Right' of Conservatism, and no sounder
democrat sits in Parliament.[45]

The idea that he had 'efficiency without feeling' was equally
wide of the mark, though he would certainly have counted for
more in the estimation of his countrymen if he had been able to
'let himself go'.[46]

Perhaps this was the root of the problem. Horace Wilson,
who was the nearest approximation to what a later generation
might have regarded as Chamberlain's spin-doctor, tried to get
the new Prime Minister to go to the Derby and have lunch with
the visiting Australian cricket team. But he never wanted to do
anything 'out of character'. Even visits to the Smoking Room of
the House of Commons were quickly abandoned.[47]
Nonetheless, the verdict of the press upon the new incumbent of
10 Downing Street was overwhelmingly favourable. A piece in
the *Morning Post* may be taken as typical of the mood in which
Chamberlain began his premiership:

As he has passed from office to office his reputation as an
administrator has constantly grown. In the counsels of the
Party and of the Government he has come to be recognised
as the strong man on whom it was safe to lean; and if he
has been chosen now to be the leader of the Party and head
of the Government, it is because he stands in political estimation head and shoulders above any rival. High office it

has been said, makes big men bigger and small men smaller. It will certainly do nothing to diminish the stature of Mr. Neville Chamberlain.[48]

But there was one important sector of political society which did not welcome Chamberlain's elevation. The new Prime Minister could no longer command the respect of his political opponents, particularly on the socialist benches. This would be important in relation to his ultimate downfall and particularly as regards his later reputation. It is impossible to read the diaries and letters of Labour politicians of the late 1930s without realizing that animosity towards Chamberlain reflected something more than the stylized ritual which so often characterizes Britain's adversarial political system. Labour had come to hate him. This development has sometimes been dated too early. Too much has perhaps been made of a conversation with Baldwin in 1927 which Chamberlain himself reported to his sister: 'I always gave him the impression, he said, when I spoke in the H of C that I looked on the Labour Party as dirt. The fact is that intellectually, with a few exceptions, they *are* dirt.'[49] Gradually, however, Chamberlain had come to adopt a style of political debate which increasingly antagonized his opponents. Never one to suffer fools gladly, he became increasingly intolerant of views which did not coincide with his own and found it difficult to conceal the fact. He seemed to delight in opportunities to sneer at those on the Labour benches 'as both fools and humbugs'.[50] In the process he inevitably lost the goodwill of his political opponents. His tactics made it difficult for Labour politicians to support him even when their heads inclined them to do so. 'Fairly good', Hugh Dalton would record of one statement made by the Prime Minister shortly before the outbreak of war. 'If one did not so distrust the man, one would be satisfied with it.'[51] Thus, Chamberlain, however much he had come to dominate his own party, was never likely to emerge as a national leader, as his predecessor might have done and as his successor most certainly did. In times of grave crisis this would be important.

Chamberlain's accession to the premiership inevitably brought him into greater public prominence. The successes and failures of any government are easily attributed to its head, irrespective of the degree of personal responsibility which a Prime Minister may bear for individual policies. In Chamberlain's case this tendency was particularly marked for, in contrast with the increasingly lethargic and detached style of his predecessor, he made it clear that he intended to be the active head of his government. It was a development which many began by applauding; and some continued to do so throughout his premiership. But in time this approach gave rise to complaints that Chamberlain interfered unnecessarily in the departmental affairs of his subordinate ministers, that in defiance of expert professional advice he took decisions in areas of policy for which he had few qualifications and even that he was subverting the accepted norms of cabinet government and thus undermining the constitution. Such perceptions, however, lay in the future. For the time being Eden, who continued as Foreign Secretary, was among those who believed that 'Chamberlain had [the] makings of a really great Prime Minister if only his health held out . . . he had a grip of affairs which Stanley Baldwin had never had'.[52] The press, sensing that the government now had a sense of direction, gave the credit for the change to the new Prime Minister's 'firm grip of affairs'.[53]

The fact that he was now Prime Minister also afforded the general public a greater opportunity to express an opinion upon Chamberlain than, with the exception of the voters of Ladywood and latterly Edgbaston, they had hitherto enjoyed. Though Chamberlain's premiership did not last long enough for him to fight another general election, by-election statistics and the introduction at this time of a relatively unsophisticated form of public opinion polling afford tantalizing insights into the sort of reputation which Chamberlain enjoyed among his fellow countrymen. Specific by-elections in the autumn of 1938 will be examined in due course in the light of the evidence they provide of contemporary reactions to the Munich settlement. More generally, however, while the government experienced a net loss of seats in the contests held between the General Election of 1935 and the end of Chamberlain's premiership, this was not overall on a sufficiently large swing to suggest that the government would have been defeated had the General Election expected in 1939 or 1940 actually taken place. In the last three by-elections which were held before the outbreak of war, the average swing to Labour was just 3.7 per cent. Contemporary evidence, not least the efforts of Labour politicians such as Stafford Cripps to secure a broad popular front to oppose the government, suggests that well-placed contemporaries on both sides of the party political divide expected a government victory, albeit with a somewhat reduced majority, when the election finally took place.

Gallup polls indicate that such expectations reflected a strong personal endorsement of the Prime Minister himself. One writer, clutching at a deceptively seductive yardstick, has suggested that the beleaguered Harold Wilson of the late 1960s was, according to the polls, 'the most unpopular Prime Minister since Neville Chamberlain'.[54] But this unhistorical comparison relates to the sort of standing which the reviled Chamberlain of later years might have been expected to enjoy. It bears no relation to contemporary reality. The monthly Gallup Poll which started in October 1938, whatever its imperfections when compared with modern psephological practice, suggests that Chamberlain regularly commanded the support of a majority of the electorate. Polls taken in February 1939, December 1939 and February 1940 revealed approval ratings of 50, 54 and 51 per cent respectively for his government.[55] These are figures for which many later Prime Ministers would have been exceedingly grateful. And the fact that support for the Prime Minister actually went up when war broke out, even though this event in many ways marked the complete failure of his policies, suggests that this was not just the endorsement of a timorous electorate for Chamberlain's efforts to preserve the peace.

With the agenda of politics and Chamberlain's personal attention increasingly focusing on foreign affairs, one of the guarantees of the new Prime Minister's popularity was the continuing presence of Anthony Eden at the Foreign Office. The latter's youth, charm, good looks and effortless association with popular causes such as the League of Nations and collective security had ensured a popular following unmatched by any other member of the National Government and one which had survived unscathed even when the administration as a whole had fallen out of favour. Not surprisingly, therefore, the breach between Chamberlain and Eden which culminated in the latter's resignation on 20 February 1938 posed the first serious question-marks over the Prime Minister's management of his government and the direction of his policy.

Indeed, some observers doubted whether Chamberlain's government would be able to survive the body-blow of Eden's resignation. According to one Parliamentary Private Secretary the situation in the Commons would be hopeless as more than a hundred of the government's usual supporters were likely to withdraw their backing. Eden himself discussed the government's possible fall with Oliver Harvey, who until his resignation had been his Foreign Office Private Secretary. A week after the event he still believed that the government had been mortally wounded. A Gallup Poll revealed that only 26 per cent of those questioned favoured Chamberlain's foreign policy as against 58 per cent who opposed it and 71 per cent who thought that Eden had been right to resign. (Whether the general public, any more than the majority of backbench MPs, really understood the distinction between the two men's policies and the real reasons for the Foreign Secretary's departure was, however, another matter.) A poll taken in March by the altogether more impressionistic organization, Mass Observation, suggested that 28 per cent were satisfied with the government's foreign policy compared with 32 per cent who were dissatisfied (leaving as many as 40 per cent confused, ignorant or uncertain of their views).

The governmental crisis was discussed extensively in the press. In a piece entitled 'Chamberlain Loses Prestige', *Time and Tide* argued that there had been a 'serious weakening of Mr. Chamberlain's position'. It criticized the Prime Minister in terms which would become the common currency of later historiography:

> His own speech showed the narrow uprightness, the inflexibility, the insensitiveness in dealing with men, of the Birmingham Unitarian. Mr. Chamberlain does not know enough about the world to be an effective Foreign Secretary ... Foreign Affairs began for Mr. Chamberlain when he left his difficult and absorbing work at the Treasury and sniffed the dangerous, intoxicating air of European diplomacy. A man, however gifted, cannot pick up such complicated threads in a few days. Yet Mr. Chamberlain, who had stuck rigidly to his departmental work for years, proceeded to interfere with the Foreign Secretary from the first week he took office as Premier.[56]

But others were less convinced that the Prime Minister's position had been damaged. 'Atticus' in the *Sunday Times* suggested that, while adolescents might hiss Chamberlain's appearance on the cinema newsreels, Westminster was still singing his praises. The veteran editor of the *Observer*, J.L. Garvin, argued that the Prime Minister's hand had been strengthened by Eden's departure. If events were to precipitate a general election, 'he will be upheld by an overwhelming majority of the people in the gravest vote they ever gave'. Chamberlain stood 'like no other man living' between the world and the catastrophe of war.[57]

In the event Chamberlain's position quickly recovered from the events of February 1938. No other cabinet minister followed Eden into the political wilderness. The latter's resignation speech created more confusion than enlightenment and, in the months which followed, he repeatedly disappointed those who now looked to him to lead a broad-based opposition to the government's foreign policy. Within a week of Eden's resignation the Chancellor, John Simon, admittedly a Chamberlainite loyalist, commented on 'an immense swing-over to the PM's side in all quarters where the vaguest idealism does not obscure realities'. 'Chips' Channon, whose regard for Chamberlain was rapidly degenerating into adulation, noted that his stock was soaring: 'I think he is the shrewdest Prime Minister of modern times'. Robert Boothby, MP, traditionally listed among Chamberlain's anti-appeasement opponents, wrote to the Prime Minister as 'a wholehearted supporter of your foreign policy'.[58] A Gallup Poll conducted in March, after Hitler's takeover of Austria, suggested that the earlier poll had represented a personal endorsement of Eden, rather than of his supposed policy of taking a firmer line with the dictator powers. Only 33 per cent now favoured British support for Czechoslovakia in the event of German aggression; 43 per cent opposed such support, while 24 per cent were undecided. Chamberlain himself seemed in no doubt that he enjoyed the overwhelming support of the parliamentary party. Just a month after Eden's departure he recorded:

As for the House of Commons there can be no question that I have got the confidence of our people as S.B. never had it. They show it in lots of ways; by the tremendous reception they give me whenever I speak, by letters and by stopping me in the lobbies to tell me of their wholehearted support.[59]

Many recognized that Chamberlain's determination to negotiate with the dictators represented an enormous gamble, but were prepared to give the Prime Minister the benefit of the doubt. The Edenite MP, Anthony Crossley, told his constituents that it was as yet too early to pass judgement and admitted that if Chamberlain's policy bore fruit he would be hailed as one of the greatest statesmen in English history. Robert Bernays, a

junior government minister, confessed that he would have
resigned had he been absolutely convinced that Eden's line was
correct, but he was not. 'In fact, reluctantly, I am inclined to
think that Chamberlain was right and that his Italian conversations involve a daring act of faith which is . . . in the best traditions of Liberalism.'[60] Anxiously watching the situation from
the other side of the Atlantic, President Roosevelt was fully
aware of the risks Chamberlain was taking:

> If a Chief of Police makes a deal with the leading gangsters
> and the deal results in no more hold-ups, the Chief of
> Police will be called a great man, but if the gangsters do
> not live up to their word, the Chief of Police will go to jail.
> Some people are, I think, taking very long chances.[61]

But he too, still unconvinced that Hitler's ambitions were insatiable, was prepared to go along with the policy of appeasement. A biography of the Prime Minister, written though not
published before the outbreak of war, emphasized this point in
a way that serves as a corrective to later accounts in which the
evidence of hindsight is all too apparent. 'Nothing has occurred
yet', wrote Duncan Keith-Shaw, 'which is conclusive proof that
[the domination of all Europe] is Hitler's intention. It is just
possible that he intends no more than to strive to make sure, in
an aggressive way, that there can never be another Versailles for
Germany.'[62]

In later years no single episode in Chamberlain's career did
more to shape his historical reputation than the Czechoslovakian
crisis of 1938 and its culmination at the Munich Conference that
September. Contemporary reactions to the same episode are
instructive, though the historian must be aware of the limitations
of his evidence. This was an issue upon which strong feelings
were expressed, but there are dangers in automatically equating
vociferous and articulate opinion with the majority view of the
country as a whole. As is usually the case in such situations, we
can speak with greater certainty of the views of the elite at
Westminster and in Fleet Street and of those with pronounced
political opinions. But we know altogether less about the
thoughts of the largely silent masses. Detailed analysis suggests
that much opinion was extremely volatile and even ambiguous,
reflecting both relief that Chamberlain's initiatives had averted
war and also a feeling of guilt about the methods used to do so.

The news of 'Plan Z', that Chamberlain intended to fly to

Germany for face-to-face talks with Hitler over the worsening crisis in Czechoslovakia, took most people by surprise. Inside the Foreign Office Oliver Harvey captured the range of emotions engendered by Chamberlain's initiative:

> British press receives news of PM's visit with marked approval. City is much relieved. Reaction in Germany also one of relief. In America it looks as if it were regarded as a surrender. Winston [Churchill] says it is the stupidest thing that has ever been done.[63]

But it inevitably gave rise to admiration that a man of nearly seventy, with only minimal experience of flying, should make this trip to confront the German Führer on the latter's home ground. Approval of the Prime Minister's initiative cut across party lines. It was, said the Labour *Daily Herald*, an effort to stave off a war which had seemed to be getting dangerously close and, as such, 'it must win the sympathy of opinion everywhere, irrespective of Party'.[64] Predictably, Channon saw it as 'one of the finest, most inspiring acts of all history' and was already confident that Chamberlain by his imagination and practical good sense had saved the world.[65] The Poet Laureate was moved, promptly and appropriately, to verse:

> As Priam to Achilles for his Son,
> So you, into the night divinely led,
> To ask that young men's bodies not yet dead,
> Be given from the battle not begun.[66]

More prosaically President Roosevelt, conscious of the sacrifice that was likely to be demanded of Czechoslovakia as the price of avoiding war, was prepared to go along with the strategy of conceding the Sudetenland to preserve the peace. Only if the exercise revealed that Hitler's appetite remained unsatisfied would he believe that Chamberlain's policy should be reversed. Among the general public Mass Observation reported a 'sensational swing' of opinion in the Prime Minister's favour. One observer, eliciting opinion in a working-class area on the evening of 15 September, got a spontaneous pro-Chamberlain tribute from every second person questioned.[67]

The stakes were clearly high, in terms of world peace and also of Chamberlain's ultimate reputation. As the Chancellor of the Exchequer told the cabinet in an eerie anticipation of Chamberlain's own later phraseology, if he came back 'with the seeds of peace with honour, he will be immediately acclaimed as having carried out the greatest achievement of the last twenty years'.[68] In the event, reactions to the deal hammered out at Chamberlain's first meeting with Hitler at Berchtesgaden on 15 September revealed that combination of an intense desire to avoid war and concern at the price paid to do so which was probably present throughout the Czechoslovakian crisis. A Mass Observation poll conducted on 22 September suggested that only 22 per cent were now in favour of Chamberlain's policy. As many as 40 per cent opposed it. Observers of the first showing of newsreels of the Chamberlain–Hitler encounter recorded that Chamberlain was cheered and Hitler hissed, but a few days later, while the reaction to the Führer remained unchanged, it was noted that Chamberlain was now received in silence. The public mood in the days before the Prime Minister made his second visit to Germany appeared to be hardening against further concessions. The *Daily Herald* reported that ten thousand people massed in Whitehall on 22 September shouting 'Stand by the Czechs!' and 'Chamberlain must go!'[69] When Chamberlain set out for Godesberg he was, as he reported to Hitler, booed by protesters at Heston Airport. Even the Foreign Secretary – though there must be question-marks over how he reached his judgement – warned Chamberlain from London that the great mass of public opinion was now of the view that Britain had gone to the 'limit of concession'.[70]

Having already conceded the basic principle that the status of the Sudetenland would have to be changed, Chamberlain was personally inclined to accept Hitler's new demands as laid out at Bad Godesberg. But he found himself unable to carry the majority of the cabinet with him on this course. Had he done so, it seems likely that opinion would have turned violently against him. The senior Conservative backbencher, Leo Amery, warned that if he were prepared to acquiesce in Hitler's latest demands there would be 'a tremendous revulsion of feeling against' him. Amery admitted that war was an awful thing and that there was much to be said for keeping out of the Czech crisis altogether on the grounds of British weakness. But as the country had been involved since the spring it was impossible now to avoid the consequences.[71] Thus it was that the nation listened to the Prime Minister's broadcast on 27 September in a mood of resigned expectation that war was now imminent. It is not easy for a later generation to recapture the feelings of Chamberlain's audience as he declared that armed conflict between nations was for him a nightmare and that 'we must be very clear, before we embark on it, that it is really the great issues that are at stake'. But one who was soon to be his biographer described emotions which must have been widely shared. He recalled

> the grim memories of another September evening many years ago, clear in my mind. That was the evening of September 27, 1915, the evening of my second day in action in the Battle of Loos, when I had seen my friend, and the best part of my men, die hideously and purpose-lessly, and the good French earth scarred and pitted with shells. These and other such memories of the glories of a 'just' war were in my memory as this tireless worker for peace concluded.[72]

In the event Hitler responded positively to the suggestion of a third meeting in Munich. The dramatic scene in the House of Commons when Chamberlain announced that he would, of course, accept the Führer's invitation has been frequently described. As a piece of theatre it was an occasion for which it is difficult to find a comparison in British parliamentary history:

> Members on both sides stood in their places waving their order papers and cheering frantically for minutes on end. Many were to be seen with tears streaming down their cheeks. It did not accord with Anglo–Saxon tradition or with Dr. Arnold's ideas about the stiff upper lip, it went beyond convention, it was the voice of humanity, the long-ing for life and its abundance. There are no politics and parties when such issues are at stake.[73]

In the galleries above the chamber there was, in defiance of parliamentary convention, a spontaneous outbreak of hand-clapping. Precisely which MPs failed to join in the displays of what Simon described as 'impetuous cheering' and 'unrestrained emotion' will never now be known.[74] That they represented a tiny minority of the House is beyond dispute.

Much was said and written over the next few days which would later, in the light of further broken promises on the part of Adolf Hitler and the outbreak of a second world war, appear foolish, naïve and embarrassingly wrong-headed. 'It was the crowning hour of Mr. Chamberlain's life', wrote one without the benefit of hindsight. 'It was also a decisive moment in the history of the world.'[75] 'I felt sick with enthusiasm [and] longed to clutch him', confessed 'Chips' Channon. 'He seemed the reincarnation of St. George . . . I don't know what this country has done to deserve him.'[76] It is impossible to deny that many of those who later jumped on to an anti-Chamberlain bandwagon wholeheartedly endorsed his latest initiative. If, as some MPs later claimed, it was the contagious atmosphere of the House which exaggerated the Prime Minister's true level of support, then it is only fair to point out that the feelings of relief and approval extended way beyond the corridors of Westminster. Chamberlain was the greatest Englishman that had ever lived, insisted Margot Asquith, widow of Britain's Prime Minister in 1914. The American President reacted with the simple and unambiguous message, 'Good man'. Among the wider public a Mass Observation survey suggested that Chamberlain enjoyed 54 per cent approval, with only 10 per cent in outright opposition.[77]

The scenes which greeted Chamberlain's return from Munich are equally familiar. His reception in Germany immediately following the conclusion of the agreement has received less attention. An American reporter in Munich described the crowds which gathered around his car, the women who wept, the men who became hoarse from cheering and the children who threw flowers. Chamberlain and the French Prime Minister, Edouard Daladier, were taken on a sight-seeing tour of the city to the delight of the crowds. A contemporary writer explained the acclaim of the German people. Quite simply, it reflected the way in which Chamberlain had made himself 'the mouthpiece of the horror with which millions of men and women . . . regard the brutish devilries of modern war'.[78] Back on British soil, it took the Prime Minister an hour and a half to drive the nine miles from Heston to Whitehall, so dense were the crowds. Nothing like it had been seen since the Armistice of 1918. Chamberlain himself described the scene for the benefit of his sisters. The roads were 'lined from one end to the other with people of every class, shouting themselves hoarse, leaping on the running board, banging on the windows, and thrusting their hands into the car to be shaken'.[79] Back in Downing Street the crowds cried deliriously until Chamberlain appeared at the window to wave his ill-fated piece of paper bearing the agreement signed by Hitler and himself, and to utter the fateful words 'Peace for our time', 'unaware that he was handing his critics a nail which they could hammer into the coffin of his historical reputation'.[80]

The Munich settlement provoked strong feelings at the time, just as it has done ever since. Those feelings covered the entire spectrum of opinion from wholehearted congratulation and endorsement to total rejection and denunciation. As will be discussed in a later chapter, there are grounds for suggesting that the national press gave a misleadingly uniform impression of the public mood. There *was* significant opposition to what Chamberlain had done. Large crowds demonstrated against the settlement in Trafalgar Square. Miners in South Wales voiced their disgust at what they took to be Chamberlain's support for fascism. A *Paramount* newsreel showing an anti-appeasement rally being addressed by the Labour MP, Ellen Wilkinson, was withdrawn from circulation following representations by the Foreign Secretary, Lord Halifax. Mass Observation noted that as many as 800 letters of protest were delivered to Downing Street after just one anti-Munich meeting. Despite the 'vast crowds in the streets – hysterical cheers and enthusiasm', recorded Oliver Harvey, 'many feel it to be a great humiliation'.[81] Nonetheless it would seem perverse to deny that, in the immediate aftermath of the Munich Conference at least, the clear balance of public opinion was with Chamberlain who now stood at the pinnacle of popular esteem. Some believed that, whatever else he did in the future, his reputation was now assured:

> He is established today as the greatest of that great triumvirate [of Chamberlains]. Had he achieved nothing else, if he never achieves more, than his restraining of the war-dogs in September 1938, that is enough.[82]

George VI clearly thought he was doing nothing controversial in inviting Chamberlain to join him on the balcony of Buckingham Palace as a token of the 'lasting gratitude of his fellow countrymen throughout the Empire'.[83] Quite suddenly, Chamberlain became what he had never been before – a man of destiny. If his rise to the top had been somewhat staid and prosaic, his presence at this moment of crisis now appeared providential. 'He stood there smiling, the most popular man in the world, more universally acclaimed than any statesman has ever been.'[84] From such heights it was almost inevitable that his reputation would ultimately decline.

The national press (and much of that in the provinces) was overwhelmingly supportive of what Chamberlain had done. Famously, *The Times* proclaimed that 'no conqueror returning from a victory on the battlefield had come adorned with nobler laurels'. The *Daily Express* hailed Munich as an unqualified success, insisting that Britain would not be involved in a European war 'this year or next year either'. Chamberlain had guaranteed 'millions of happy homes and hearts relieved of their burdens'. Accordingly to Beverly Baxter writing in the *Sunday Graphic*, because of what the Prime Minister had done 'the world my son will live in will be a vastly different place. . . . In our time we shall not see again the armed forces of Europe gathering to strike at each other like savage beasts.' In an equally rash prediction the *Western Daily Press* asserted that, whatever the future had in store for him, Chamberlain 'will rest secure in the esteem and affection of us all'. The *News Chronicle* drew attention to the sacrifices made by the Czechs but still rejoiced that peace had been preserved. Even Labour's *Daily Herald*, while admitting that the settlement was open to 'grave criticism', believed that Hitler had been forced to compromise and made to see that there were forces in the world more powerful than the will of a dictator. Only the *Daily Telegraph* of leading publications was unequivocally hostile: 'It was Mr. Disraeli who said that England's two great assets in the world were her fleet and her good name. Today we must console ourselves that we still have our fleet.'[85]

Over the next few weeks Chamberlain received more than 40,000 letters from people of all classes and nations expressing their gratitude and admiration for what he had done at Munich. Among the better known figures who sent messages of congratulation and thanks were General Smuts of South Africa, the Prime Minister of the Netherlands, Cardinal Hinsley on behalf of the Catholic archbishops and bishops of England and Wales, and the King of the Belgians. The last wrote, 'You have done a wonderful piece of work and done it under the guidance and providence of God'.[86] Many members of the general public sent gifts ranging from fishing rods and flies to cases of wine. These were still pouring in at the time of Chamberlain's seventieth birthday the following March. Correspondents to *The Times* demanded a National Fund in Chamberlain's honour. The French went one better with *Paris Soir* offering a corner of French soil with a suitable stream for him to come and indulge his passion for fishing. Old ladies suggested that the Prime Minister's umbrella should be broken up and the pieces sold as sacred relics. The *Daily Sketch* offered readers a photograph of Chamberlain and his wife and received more than 90,000 applications. Lord Lee of Fareham, who had earlier donated Chequers to the nation, now presented a large service of eighteenth-century silver-gilt plate, inscribed 'In grateful homage to Neville Chamberlain' and 'Decori decus addit avito' – 'He adds honour to ancestral honour'.[87] Portugal erected a statue inscribed 'Grateful Mothers' in his honour. The chairman of Blackpool Football Club offered to build twelve houses for the rent-free use of ex-servicemen. Sir Charles Hyde gave £10,000 to Birmingham University to fund a scholarship in the Prime Minister's name. All over France, where the Chamber of Deputies endorsed the Munich settlement with near unanimity, towns renamed a square, a street, a block of flats or a public garden to commemorate Chamberlain's achievement. Many were those who were moved to verse, much of it excruciatingly bad:

> The world looked on, and hopeless, still we prayed
> That war's ignoble die would yet be stayed;
> That this great crime against the human race
> Be stopped in time, by God's eternal grace.
> That prayer was heard, and all the world was shewn
> The power of Faith, in one man's heart alone.[88]

Much of this sentiment was what a later generation would describe as 'froth', the transient expression of an enormous sense of relief that war had, against all the odds, been averted, at least for the time being. 'Men and women reacted . . . with a frenzy of relief that momentarily drove from the minds of most of them any consideration of consequences.'[89] The passage of time afforded the opportunity for second thoughts, especially among those who had not like Chamberlain been charged with the terrible choices posed at the Munich conference table. The volatility of the public mood was ironically captured by one cinema proprietor who advertised a newsreel of Chamberlain's visit to Germany with a poster bearing the headline, 'Chamberlain the Peacemaker: for one week only'. It was certainly evident when the House of Commons debated the settlement in early October. Chamberlain himself was struck by the contrast between his public reception and the 'ceaseless stream of vituperation' to which he was subjected by critical MPs, many of whom had no doubt cheered him to the rafters when he had announced his mission to Munich only days before.[90] Even so, the degree of dissent should not be exaggerated. Few, indeed, were those who were prepared to denounce Chamberlain's actions on the basis that they would have preferred to take Britain into a war on behalf of Czechoslovakia. The Labour front bench was clearer on what it would not have done than in expounding an alternative policy. Many found their feelings articulated by the Conservative Victor Raikes who declared that Chamberlain would go down in history as the greatest European statesman 'of this or any other time'. Support for the Prime Minister was by no means confined to the government benches. The socialist James Maxton insisted that Chamberlain had done 'what the mass of the common people of the world wanted done', while in the House of Lords the Labour peer Lord Ponsonby argued that he had opened the door to the methods of reason to the unspeakable relief of millions. The government won the Commons motion of approval with a majority of more than 200. The majority of Conservative critics abstained rather than vote against their whip. Even Anthony Eden, who in later years thought and wrote of himself as an outright critic, noted that 'we all owe [Chamberlain] a measureless debt of gratitude for the sincerity and pertinacity which he devoted to averting the supreme calamity of war' and was so impressed by the Prime Minister's own speech on the third evening of the debate that he very nearly voted in the government lobby before deciding to abstain.[91]

Though there was much talk of an autumn general election to capitalize on the government's assumed popularity, Chamberlain drew back from an appeal to the country, influenced by doubts at Conservative Central Office as to whether victory was as certain as some imagined.[92] The mood of the country can therefore only be estimated from a series of by-elections held in the weeks after the Munich settlement. Although there was an unusually large number of by-election contests pending when Chamberlain returned from Germany with his piece of paper, with thirteen held between 1 October and 28 February 1939, it seems that only in two – at Oxford and Bridgwater – were issues of foreign policy decisive. Even at this time of international crisis the British electorate revealed its traditional lack of interest in what goes on beyond the English

Channel. Though the Duchess of Atholl, who created the contest by resigning her seat and standing as an Independent in protest at Chamberlain's diplomacy, did her best to place the Munich agreement at the centre of the campaign in Kinross and West Perthshire in December, 64 per cent of those electors who were questioned said that home issues were more important than foreign. At both Oxford and Bridgwater the government candidate was opposed by a single anti-Conservative Independent. Both seats witnessed a swing against the Conservatives compared with the 1935 General Election, but only in Bridgwater was it sufficient to secure the defeat of the government candidate. This somewhat scanty evidence makes it difficult to draw clear conclusions. What is striking is the high turnout at both Oxford and Bridgwater, suggesting that a heightened interest brought out both pro- and anti-Chamberlain voters who might normally have stayed at home.[93]

In the eleven months which followed the Munich Conference whatever hopes Chamberlain may have entertained that he had indeed secured a lasting peace with Germany progressively evaporated. By 3 September 1939 Britain and Germany were at war. While Chamberlain, at least in public, remained optimistic until the spring of 1939, others very quickly turned against what had been done at Munich. Roosevelt was admitting to his shame over his support for appeasement within six weeks of the conclusion of the agreement.[94] The fact that 93 per cent of those questioned in a poll conducted in October 1938 said that they did not believe Hitler when he said that he had no further territorial ambitions in Europe implied a considerable gap between Chamberlain and the man in the street. As the policy with which he had been so closely associated collapsed around him, it was probably inevitable that the Prime Minister's personal standing should also decline. When Chamberlain visited Paris in November plans for a drive in an open car were dropped for fear that he might have things thrown at him. By the end of the year one Foreign Office official judged that Britain's standing in America was 'getting lower and lower owing to the P.M.'s pro-dictator policy, and it is now reacting on sterling'.[95] 'Quite serious people', judged Eden after a visit to the United States in December, thought that Chamberlain was 'a pure fascist' and by the following month returning lecturers of the English Speaking Union were reporting intense feeling against the Prime Minister.[96] Yet it is easy for this process to be exaggerated. If anything, public opinion may have been ahead of the government, but at least the two appeared to be moving in a generally similar direction. The mood of the House of Commons had clearly changed by November 1938. The desire to extol the virtues of the Munich agreement was now altogether less marked. Increasing evidence of Hitler's anti-Semitism culminating with Kristallnacht on 10 November seems to have exercised a profound impact on public opinion. Only 15 per cent of those questioned believed that the Führer's campaign against the Jews should not affect British attempts to reach an understanding with Germany. Over the winter of 1938–9 the press moved progressively away from appeasement. When German forces entered Prague in March 1939 the *Daily Telegraph* was emphatic that Germany had 'perpetrated an affront to the whole civilized world which will not be readily forgotten'. This event clearly threatened the credibility of Chamberlain's foreign policy strategy. As Brendan Bracken explained: 'Chamberlain's political success[es] during the last six months (and they have been very great) were due to the feeling that Munich was a landmark of peace. The crude destruction of what was left of Czechoslovakia must inevitably create doubts in Chamberlain's judgement in the constituencies.'[97]

But Chamberlain at least moved with the changing tide. After a hesitant response in the Commons on 15 March, Harold Nicolson, MP, recorded that the 'feeling in the lobbies is that Chamberlain will either have to go or completely reverse his policy'.[98] But change his policy he did, at least ostensibly so. Speaking in Birmingham on 17 March he appeared to announce the end of appeasement. For the first time he questioned whether any faith could be placed in Hitler's word. Was, in fact, the Prague coup 'the end of an old adventure, or the beginning of a new? . . . is this . . . a step in the direction of an attempt to dominate the world by force?' Gallup in May was still reporting a 55 per cent approval rating for the Prime Minister – though it is worth noting that 56 per cent now expressed a wish to see Winston Churchill invited to join the cabinet. Many of those who had been numbered among Chamberlain's critics as appeasement had reached its crescendo in 1938 now appeared less antagonistic, especially once the Prime Minister had issued a guarantee of Polish independence at the end of March 1939. When the Commons debated Britain's new commitments on 3 April Eden argued that the change of policy had united the nation behind the government and that this would be of enormous importance in future foreign negotiations. What he had in mind was undoubtedly the need for an alliance with the Soviet Union without which the British guarantee to Poland would lack military credibility. Eighty-four per cent of those questioned in March had, unsurprisingly, said that they would like to see Britain and Russia 'being more friendly to each other'. Three months later the same percentage expressed support for a military alliance between the two countries. Once again, Chamberlain moved, however reluctantly and hesitantly, in the same direction, but the startling conclusion of a Nazi–Soviet Non-Aggression Pact on 23 August brought all hopes in this direction crashing to the ground.

With hindsight it is easy, perhaps too easy, to argue that the outbreak of war initiated a process of inevitable decline in Chamberlain's standing to which the events of May 1940 provided a dramatic but inevitable climax. Certainly his statement to parliament on 3 September announcing that the country was now at war contained an unequivocal confession of failure: 'everything that I have worked for, everything that I have hoped for, everything that I have believed in during my public life, has crashed into ruins'. It is also true that, from the point of view of his own reputation, Chamberlain badly mishandled the declaration of war. His delay of 48 hours after the German invasion of Poland before honouring Britain's treaty of guarantee inevitably gave rise to suspicions that he was once again, on the model of Munich, seeking a disreputable way of escape through appeasement and that he had had to be dragged, kicking and screaming, to do his duty. 'In those few minutes', wrote Harold Nicolson of Chamberlain's procrastinating speech to the Commons on 2 September, 'he flung away his reputation. I feel deeply sorry for him.'[99] In fact the delay was almost entirely the result of the Prime Minister's efforts to co-ordinate the declaration of war with Britain's French allies.

Historians have assiduously collected a mass of evidence of growing opposition to Chamberlain over the months of the Phoney War. Mass Observation reported that cinema audiences became increasingly reluctant to applaud the Prime Minister when he appeared on the newsreels. He was not of course a natural war leader. 'How I do hate and loathe this war', he wrote soon after the outbreak of hostilities. 'I was never meant to be a war leader and the thought of all those homes wrecked

. . . makes me want to hand over my responsibilities to someone else.'[100] The presence now of Churchill inside the War Cabinet presented the clear possibility of an alternative Prime Minister with more obvious martial qualities. The *Sunday Pictorial* declared as early as 1 October that Churchill would be the next premier. Thomas Jones compared the speeches of the two men as the first month of war came to a close. While Churchill's were 'arresting', those of the Prime Minister were simply 'costive and dull'.[101] Lady Astor found a speech which Chamberlain delivered to the Junior Carlton Club in November 'so obviously lacking in statesmanship, uplift of any kind, [that] it really got me down for a moment', while Harold Nicolson compared one Chamberlain speech to 'the secretary of a firm of undertakers reading the minutes of the last meeting'.[102] The refusal of the opposition parties to accept Chamberlain's invitation to join the government was regarded by some as evidence of the weakness of Chamberlain's position. A cabinet such as he was able to put together, judged Baffy Dugdale, 'cannot last long'. 'He will soon go', predicted the future Labour minister Patrick Gordon Walker.[103]

The rise during these months of a parliamentary opposition to Chamberlain, extending now way beyond the confines of the Labour and Liberal parties, has been well charted. A variety of groups came into existence convinced that the country was not getting the war leadership it deserved. Central to their critiques was the feeling that Chamberlain had not done enough to co-ordinate the management of the economy. When it became known that the level of unemployment had actually risen during the first few weeks of the war, further ammunition was given to those who argued that Chamberlain's methods had no hope of matching the German war effort. In a letter to *The Times* on 4 December, shortly before he renounced the government whip, the Liberal National MP Clement Davies complained of 'a suspicion that we are not using to the full our manpower, our resources, or our national capacity for initiative and adaptation'.

Yet to an extent this is a classic case of the way in which history is written by the victors, of a process by which relatively minor figures such as Davies, who played a supporting role in bringing about the downfall of the government in May 1940, have been transformed into 'the architects . . . of the government which first saved us from destruction, and then led us to victory'.[104] As has been seen, there were few signs of the country as a whole turning against Chamberlain when war broke out. If anything, the reverse was the case. By November 1939 opinion polls suggested that the Prime Minister was more popular than ever. As late as April 1940 he still enjoyed an approval rating of nearly 60 per cent. Only 30 per cent of those questioned in December 1939 said that they would prefer Churchill as Prime Minister. Much has been made of the somewhat timid cabinet reconstructions which Chamberlain carried out in this period, particularly that which followed the dismissal of Hore-Belisha from the War Ministry in January 1940. But a poll taken in the third week of January showed that 56 per cent of those questioned still approved of the Prime Minister's leadership. The major problems which Chamberlain encountered during the period of the Phoney War derived from the nature of this 'warfare', and would probably have been experienced by any leader in Chamberlain's position. The country was being subjected to innumerable inconveniences ranging from the blackout to the closure of places of entertainment without the compensation of obvious military successes. Hardships would have been easier to bear in the context of mortal danger such as clearly existed in the first months of Churchill's premiership. In a situation in which Britain probably had little to gain from taking the military initiative, many became irritated by the nagging thought that something – precisely what was another matter – ought to be done. As Robert Bruce Lockhart put it in March 1940: 'I cannot help feeling that this present government will never pull us through the war. So far our effort seems, and I think is, only half-hearted. Yet Chamberlain seems quite satisfied, understands nothing about foreign affairs, and gives no lead and no inspiration to the country.'[105] According to a limerick which went the rounds of the Foreign Office,

> An elderly Statesman with gout,
> When asked what this War was about,
> In a Written Reply,
> Said 'My colleagues and I,
> Are doing our best to find out'.[106]

The nature of this period may also have led to a lowering of Chamberlain's standing in the important context of American opinion. The latent conviction that Chamberlain was part of a Wall Street–City of London axis of capital and industry began to resurface among many Democratic New-Dealers. From the Washington Embassy Victor Mallet reported in December 1939 'a quite ridiculous distrust of the Prime Minister'. The relative inactivity of the Phoney War encouraged the erroneous belief that the policy of appeasement was still in place. Roosevelt's 'good man' of September 1938 had, by early May 1940, become 'the evil genius . . . of Western civilization' as far as Secretary of the Interior Harold Ickes was concerned.[107]

For all that, each recorded word of criticism, accorded perhaps excessive teleological significance, can be matched by a complimentary endorsement of Chamberlain's performance as a wartime Prime Minister. The newspapers of the Phoney War period, writes David Dilks, 'contain numerous tributes, some of them rather grudgingly given by political opponents, to the effectiveness of Chamberlain's speeches and to the freedom of gesture, voice and mannerism which he increasingly allowed himself, to the excellent reactions abroad and to the contrast between his own firm but unswaggering declarations of British purpose and the ravings of Hitler and Goebbels. The same impression of vigour and decision is conveyed by film and sound records, as well as by accounts of eye-witnesses.'[108] The *New York Times* judged that Chamberlain's courage had been equal to the cruel test of the war crisis in September 1939. By November the *Observer* concluded that he was showing himself to be as inflexible in war as he had been unremitting in his efforts to preserve peace and that he had strengthened his position in the country. The *News Chronicle* paid tribute that month to a 'forcefully delivered' radio broadcast in which he 'showed a deep understanding of the nation's thoughts and feelings'.[109] Nor was the government as badly run as some contemporary critics and much later legend suggested. Whatever outsiders felt about the War Cabinet its actual members, Churchill included, appear to have believed they worked well together. John Simon described 'an extremely united body, with no internal strain of any kind' and added that the Prime Minister had proved 'absolutely first-class' in promoting team work.[110] Chamberlain in fact proved to be – as throughout his career – an efficient manager of the government's business.

The fall of Chamberlain's government is often loosely attributed to the vote in the House of Commons on the Norwegian campaign on 8 May 1940. Much attention has been paid to dramatic interventions in the debate by figures such as Roger

Keyes, Leo Amery and David Lloyd George, each one helping to ensure the Prime Minister's political demise. In the present context it is important to emphasize that this was not strictly the case. Chamberlain survived the vote with a majority of eighty-one. This was, of course, a significant reduction from the sort of figures which the government had regularly commanded before the outbreak of war. But recent research has shown that the extent of the parliamentary vote against Chamberlain has tended to be exaggerated. Only thirty-eight MPs in receipt of the government whip voted with the opposition. Though these included men such as Keyes, who had written to *The Times* to praise Chamberlain for the Munich agreement, and Quintin Hogg, who had been elected in the Oxford by-election as a committed Chamberlain supporter, the majority of the rebels were long-standing critics. The level of abstentions is difficult to calculate with precision, but was probably less than twenty-five.[111] The parliamentary arithmetic was serious for the Prime Minister but not necessarily fatal. What persuaded him to resign was his inability, in the wake of the vote, to construct a genuinely all-party administration.

Of course, there were those who were delighted to see Chamberlain go. Indeed, it was the Labour party, by refusing again to join an administration still headed by him, which ensured the end of his premiership. 'The fact is our party won't come in under you', insisted Clement Attlee. 'Our party won't have you.'[112] Cecil King of the *Daily Mirror* regarded Chamberlain's resignation as 'the best bit of news since the war was declared'. But others responded very differently. The Queen wrote to express her distress; her daughter Princess Elizabeth was said to have cried. Predictably 'Chips' Channon felt 'sad, angry . . . cheated and out-witted' and drank a toast to the 'King over the water'.[113] More revealing was the reaction of Sir Alexander Cadogan, Permanent Under-Secretary for Foreign Affairs, 'I don't think they'll get a better PM than Neville' – a remark which gives the lie to the idea that Chamberlain had pursued his policies against the united opposition of the Foreign Office.[114] Robert Gower, MP, wrote to Chamberlain on 9 May, in other words after the vote but before his resignation, to assure the Prime Minister that he still enjoyed 'the fullest confidence and the great affection of almost, without exception, the whole of your party colleagues in the House, including the *large major-ity* of those who voted in the Opposition lobby last night. We

would regard it – and I am not exaggerating or being fulsome
when I say so – as a national disaster were you to go.'[115] Once
Chamberlain had resigned, another Tory MP insisted that there
had been no change in the 'confidence which the Party and
Country has always placed in you', while only days after
Churchill's appointment as Prime Minister three-quarters of the
Conservative party were, according to the Chairman of the 1922
Committee, 'ready to put Chamberlain back'.[116]

It seems clear that the decisive change of mood – and the real
damage to Chamberlain's reputation – occurred in the last months
of his life, this despite the fact that he still managed to impress
those who worked closely with him inside Churchill's government, including those new Labour ministers for whom this was
the first experience of having him as a colleague. As Lord
President Chamberlain was 'always very business-like', recalled
Attlee. 'You could work with him.'[117] Perhaps for once there was
something in Channon's assessment that Chamberlain's only
enemies were the people who did not know him. Opinion in the
country seems to have turned decisively against the former Prime
Minister following the return to Britain of the defeated BEF. 'The
men were loud in their cries of resentment against the man who
had let them down through lack of equipment.'[118] Chamberlain
himself received reports from the Party Chairman to the effect
that his position in the country, the party and even his home town
of Birmingham had deteriorated. On 4 June he noted that
Clement Davies and figures in the Labour party were 'whip[ping]
up opinion against me on the ground that I let down the BEF by
under-equipping them'.[119] In July Mass Observation recorded
that 62 per cent of those questioned wanted Chamberlain
removed from the government. A Gallup Poll put the figure at 77
per cent. A campaign got under way inside the trade union movement to secure his dismissal but tended to be discredited by
communist involvement. Bob Boothby and David Lloyd George
were among prominent parliamentarians who tried to convince
Churchill that Chamberlain was now a liability to the country, his
continued presence in the War Cabinet 'a source of mingled bewilderment and irritation to the working classes, with the result that
at perhaps the most dangerous moment in our history it would be
difficult to arouse the unrestrained enthusiasm of the workers,
which was so necessary if we were to win through'.[120] It was
probably only the decisive intervention of the new premier which
saved Chamberlain at this time.

It was, then, a startling reversal of fortunes and one which Chamberlain himself felt acutely. But the key factor in this transformation was not something which he had done or not done. The decisive moment came with the publication in the early summer of 1940 of a slim book of just 125 pages.

Notes

1. Chamberlain MSS, NC18/1/941, N. Chamberlain to Ida Chamberlain 8 Dec. 1935.
2. A. Duff Cooper, *Old Men Forget* (London, 1953), p.188.
3. *Birmingham Daily Post* 20 Dec. 1916.
4. *Picture World* 26 July 1915.
5. *Birmingham Gazette* 26 July 1915.
6. *Picture World* 26 July 1915.
7. *Birmingham Daily Post* 7 Feb. 1917.
8. Chamberlain MSS, AC5/1/4, A. Chamberlain to Hilda Chamberlain 21 Dec. 1916.
9. P. Williamson (ed.), *The Modernisation of Conservative Politics: The Diaries and Letters of William Bridgeman, 1904–1935* (London, 1988), p.125.
10. K. Morgan (ed.), *Lloyd George: Family Letters 1885–1936* (Cardiff, 1973), p.185.
11. D. Lloyd George, *War Memoirs*, vol.3 (London, 1934), p.1368.
12. Chamberlain MSS, NC2/20, diary 17 Dec. 1917.
13. *The Times* 28 Aug. 1923.
14. Chamberlain MSS, AC5/1/339, A. Chamberlain to I. Chamberlain 2 Nov. 1924.
15. *Ibid.*, NC18/1/458, N. Chamberlain to I. Chamberlain 1 Nov. 1924.
16. A. Salter, *Slave of the Lamp: A Public Servant's Notebook* (London, 1967), p.144.
17. P. Grigg, *Prejudice and Judgment* (London, 1948), p.119.
18. S. Ball (ed.), *Parliament and Politics in the Age of Baldwin and MacDonald: The Headlam Diaries 1923–1935* (London, 1992), pp.74–5.
19. *Birmingham Daily Post* 8 Aug. 1925.
20. J. Ramsden (ed.), *Real Old Tory Politics: The Political Diaries of Robert Sanders, Lord Bayford 1910–1935* (London, 1984), p.225.
21. Chamberlain MSS, NC7/11/20/20, Irwin to Chamberlain 4 Oct. 1927.
22. Ball (ed.), *Headlam Diaries*, pp.112–3.
23. Williamson (ed.), *Bridgeman Diaries*, p.217.
24. Ball (ed.), *Headlam Diaries*, pp.63 and 115.
25. *Morning Post* 19 Feb. 1929.
26. Williamson (ed.), *Bridgeman Diaries*, p.232.
27. Chamberlain MSS, AC5/1/520b, A. Chamberlain to I. Chamberlain 16 Nov. 1930. See also *Sunday Times* 18 March

1928: 'Few members of the Cabinet are admired or disliked to such a degree as Mr. Neville Chamberlain.'

28. Ball (ed.), *Headlam Diaries*, p.203.
29. K. Young (ed.), *The Diaries of Sir Robert Bruce Lockhart 1915–1938* (London, 1973), p.179.
30. *Sunday Times* 30 May 1937.
31. Ball (ed.), *Headlam Diaries*, p.298.
32. *Sunday Times* 7 Feb. 1932.
33. *News Chronicle* 23 Dec. 1932.
34. *New York Times Magazine* 23 July 1933.
35. F.W. Hirst in *Contemporary Review*, June 1934.
36. Williamson (ed.), *Bridgeman Diaries*, p.256.
37. *Daily Telegraph* 1 June 1937.
38. A.J.P. Taylor (ed.), *Off the Record: Political Interviews 1933–1943* (London, 1973), pp.48, 50.
39. 'Watchman', *Right Honourable Gentleman: Neville Chamberlain* (London, 1939), p.44. It is worth noting that Chamberlain found his own performance on film 'pompous, insufferably slow in "diction", and unspeakably repellant in "person" '. Chamberlain MSS, NC18/1/1029, N. Chamberlain to H. Chamberlain 21 Nov. 1937.
40. I. Macleod, *Neville Chamberlain* (London, 1961), p.184.
41. S. Ball (ed.), *Parliament and Politics in the Age of Churchill and Attlee: The Headlam Diaries 1935–1951* (London, 1999), p.87.
42. *Daily Express* 16 March 1936; Chambrlain MSS, AC5/1/730, A. Chamberlain to Hilda Chamberlain 28 March 1936; R.R. James (ed.), *Chips: The Diaries of Sir Henry Channon* (London, 1967), p.61.
43. W. Rock, *Neville Chamberlain* (New York, 1969), p.206.
44. N. Smart (ed.), *The Diaries and Letters of Robert Bernays 1932–1939: An Insider's Account of the House of Commons* (Lampeter, 1996), p.310.
45. *Great Britain and the East* 9 July 1936.
46. H. Ashley, 'Neville Chamberlain – the Man and his Methods', *Strand Magazine* June 1937.
47. C. Stuart (ed.), *The Reith Diaries* (London, 1975), p.220.
48. *Morning Post* 31 May 1937.
49. Chamberlain MSS, NC18/1/578, N. Chamberlain to I. Chamberlain 19 June 1927.
50. L. Amery, *My Political Life*, vol. 3 (London, 1955), p.226.
51. B. Pimlott (ed.), *The Political Diary of Hugh Dalton 1918–40, 1945–60* (London, 1986), p.280.
52. J. Harvey (ed.), *The Diplomatic Diaries of Oliver Harvey 1937–1940* (London, 1970), p.34.
53. Chamberlain MSS, NC18/1/1012, N. Chamberlain to H. Chamberlain 18 July 1937.
54. M. Cockerell, *Live from Number 10* (London, 1988), p.143.
55. These and other Gallup figures are taken from G.H. Gallup (ed.), *The Gallup International Public Opinion Polls: Great Britain 1937–1975*, vol. 1 (New York, 1976). Figures for Mass

Observation are taken from C. Madge and T. Harrison, *Britain by Mass Observation* (Harmondsworth, 1939).
56. *Time and Tide* 26 Feb. 1938.
57. *Observer* 27 Feb. 1938.
58. Simon MSS, SP7 fo.70, diary 27 Feb. 1939; James (ed.), *Chips*, p.148; Chamberlain MSS, NC7/11/31/30, Boothby to Chamberlain 12 March 1938.
59. Chamberlain MSS, NC18/1/1043, Chamberlain to H. Chamberlain 27 March 1938.
60. Smart (ed.), *Bernays Diaries*, p.342.
61. C. MacDonald, *The United States, Britain and Appeasement 1936–1939* (London, 1981), pp.73–4.
62. D. Keith-Shaw, *Neville Chamberlain* (London, 1939), p.168.
63. Harvey (ed.), *Diplomatic Diaries*, p.180.
64. *Daily Herald* 15 Sept. 1938.
65. James (ed.), *Chips*, p.166.
66. John Masefield, 'Neville Chamberlain' 15 Sept. 1938.
67. Madge and Harrison, *Britain by Mass Observation*, p.64.
68. Public Record Office, CAB 23/95, cabinet 14 Sept. 1938.
69. R. Douglas, *In the Year of Munich* (London, 1977), p.56.
70. E. Woodward and R. Butler (eds), *Documents on British Foreign Policy 1919–1939*, Third Series, vol.2 (London, 1949), p.490.
71. Chamberlain MSS, NC7/2/81, Amery to Chamberlain 25 Sept. 1938.
72. Keith-Shaw, *Chamberlain*, pp.152–3.
73. D. Walker-Smith, *Neville Chamberlain: Man of Peace* (London, 1939), p.337.
74. Viscount Simon, *Retrospect* (London, 1952), p.247.
75. S. Hodgson, *The Man who Made the Peace: The Story of Neville Chamberlain* (London, 1938), p.103.
76. James (ed.), *Chips*, pp.171–2.
77. N. Nicolson (ed.), *Harold Nicolson: Diaries and Letters 1930–39* (London, 1966), p.371; D.C. Watt, 'Roosevelt and Neville Chamberlain: two appeasers', *International Journal* xxviii, 2 (1973), p.202; Madge and Harrison, *Britain*, p.101.
78. Hodgson, *Man who Made the Peace*, p.144.
79. Macleod, *Chamberlain*, p.268.
80. N. Smart, *The National Government, 1931–40* (London, 1999), p.185.
81. Harvey (ed.), *Diplomatic Diaries*, p.203.
82. Keith-Shaw, *Chamberlain*, p.3.
83. Chamberlain MSS, NC7/3/30, George VI to Chamberlain 30 Sept. 1938.
84. Hodgson, *Man who Made the Peace*, p.1.
85. Useful quotations from the press may be found in W. Hadley, *Munich: Before and After* (London, 1944) and K. Robbins, *Munich 1938* (London, 1968).
86. P. Neville, *Neville Chamberlain: A Study in Failure* (London, 1992), p.100.
87. A. Clark (ed.), *A Good Innings* (London, 1974), p.344.

88. T. James, 'A Man', Oct. 1938.
89. F. Williams, *A Pattern of Rulers* (London, 1965), p.184.
90. Chamberlain MSS, NC18/1/1071, Chamberlain to I. Chamberlain 9 Oct. 1938.
91. D. Dutton, *Anthony Eden: a Life and Reputation* (London, 1997), pp.127–8.
92. R. Parker, *Churchill and Appeasement* (London, 2000), p.208. See also N. J. Crowson (ed.), *Fleet Street, Press Barons and Politics: The Journals of Collin Brooks 1932–1940* (London, 1998), pp.221–2.
93. C. Cook and J. Ramsden (eds), *By-Elections in British Politics* (London, 1973), p.159.
94. J.M. Blum (ed.), *From the Morgenthau Diaries: Years of Urgency 1938–1941* (Boston, 1965), p.49.
95. Harvey (ed.), *Diplomatic Diaries*, p.225.
96. N. Cull, *Selling War: The British Propaganda Campaign against American 'Neutrality' in World War II* (Oxford, 1994), pp.21–2.
97. R. Cockett (ed.), *My Dear Max: The Letters of Brendan Bracken to Lord Beaverbrook 1925–1958* (London, 1990), p.45.
98. Nicolson (ed.), *Diaries and Letters*, p.393.
99. *Ibid.*, p.420.
100. K. Feiling, *The Life of Neville Chamberlain* (London, 1946), p.420.
101. T. Jones, *A Diary with Letters 1931–50* (London, 1954), p.440.
102. W. Rock, *Chamberlain and Roosevelt 1937–40* (Columbus, 1988), p.233; N. Nicolson (ed.), *Harold Nicolson: Diaries and Letters 1939–45* (London, 1967), p.35.
103. N. Rose (ed.), *Baffy: The Diaries of Blanche Dugdale 1936–1947* (London, 1973), p.150; R.Pearce (ed.), *Patrick Gordon Walker: Political Diaries 1932–1971* (London, 1991), p.96.
104. R. Boothby, *My Yesterday, Your Tomorrow* (London, 1962), p.253.
105. K. Young (ed.), *The Diaries of Sir Robert Bruce Lockhart 1939–1965* (London, 1980), p.49.
106. Lord Gladwyn, *Memoirs* (London, 1972), p.96.
107. Rock, *Chamberlain and Roosevelt*, pp.240, 290.
108. Lord Butler (ed.), *The Conservatives: A History from their Origins to 1965* (London, 1977), p.393.
109. *News Chronicle* 27 Nov. 1939.
110. Simon MSS, SP11 fo.35, diary 7 Oct. 1939.
111. N. Smart , 'Four Days in May: The Norway Debate and the Downfall of Neville Chamberlain', *Parliamentary History*, 17, 2 (1998).
112. F. Williams, *A Prime Minister Remembers* (London, 1961), p.33.
113. C. King, *With Malice Toward None: A War Diary* (London, 1970), p.39; James (ed.), *Chips*, p.250.
114. D. Dilks (ed.), *The Diaries of Sir Alexander Cadogan 1938–1945* (London, 1971), p.280.
115. Chamberlain MSS, NC13/17/106, R. Gower to Chamberlain 9 May 1940. Emphasis in original.

116. *Ibid.*, NC13/17/41, P. Buchan-Hepburn to Chamberlain 15 May 1940; A. Roberts, *Eminent Churchillians* (London, 1994), p.142.
117. Williams, *Prime Minister Remembers*, p.37.
118. King, *With Malice*, p.53.
119. Chamberlain MSS, NC2/24A, diary 4 June 1940.
120. R.R. James, *Bob Boothby* (London, 1991), p.262.

|3|

Guilty man

The small men – the mean men – rage but the voice of history is not the voice of the present day and we may confidently await the ultimate judgement.[1]

In October 1940 and suffering from advanced cancer Neville Chamberlain received a letter from his friend and colleague Joseph Ball. The two men had been close since Chamberlain's period as Party Chairman a decade earlier. Ball was concerned about the campaign of denigration to which his former master had been subjected since the end of his premiership the previous May. Unaware of the gravity of the ex-Prime Minister's physical condition, he proposed that Chamberlain should launch a counter-attack:

> The first step in the operations must be a complete and devastating exposure of what is happening, accompanied by an equally pungent and forceful exposure of the vendetta and of the true facts of the situation as it has developed during the past six or seven years, and particularly during the last three years. If you agree that I am right, I will work out a plan of operations for your approval: and I should be prepared if necessary to resign from my present post for the purpose of carrying it out.[2]

It was more than a fortnight before the ailing Chamberlain felt able to dictate a reply, to which he added, conscious it seemed that this was likely to be the last exchange of letters between the two men, a substantial hand-written postscript. Chamberlain's first task was to explain that what Ball proposed was quite impossible. By this stage of his illness he could hardly tolerate any food and was afflicted by 'a most intense depression and general inability to do anything'. But, Chamberlain suggested, a campaign such as Ball wanted was not necessary. So far as his personal reputation was concerned, Chamberlain was 'not in the least disturbed'. The overwhelming balance of his postbag, he insisted, continued to be supportive and 'I do not feel that the opposite view expressed I understand by "guilty men" and elsewhere has a chance of survival. Even if nothing further were to be published giving the true story of the past two years, I should not fear the historians' verdict.'[3] In a career marked by a series of unfortunate statements which have often been interpreted as signs of poor judgement, this represented perhaps Chamberlain's most total miscalculation. Grievous damage had already been done to his long-term historical reputation by the time of this final correspondence with Joseph Ball.

The campaign to which Ball referred and of which Chamberlain was fully aware had its origins in the publication in July 1940 of a short book of just 125 generously spaced pages. *Guilty Men* appeared under the pseudonym of 'Cato', but was in fact the work of three left-wing journalists working at the time for Beaverbrook newspapers, Peter Howard, Frank Owen and Michael Foot. Their identities were not widely known at the time, with Foot even going to the length of reviewing the book himself in the pages of the London *Evening Standard* in order to throw enquirers off the scent of its true authorship. It is difficult to suggest that *Guilty Men* was a work of much intrinsic historical merit. It has few pretensions to scholarship. The three journalists are said to have composed their respective chapters over a weekend before cobbling them together to produce a single text. The seams of conjunction certainly show. The tone of the writing is self-consciously simple, the message it contains unsubtle in the extreme. Its attempts at humour seem, after the passage of sixty years, somewhat laboured. But, as a piece of propaganda, it proved to be a brilliant success. This little book exercised a profound impact not only upon popular perceptions of Neville Chamberlain but also upon the first generation of scholarly writing on the role of Britain and its politicians in the origins of the Second World War. A journalist of a later era, Robin Day, has gone as far as to suggest that *Guilty Men* became the most famous polemic in British political history. Certainly, its impact upon Chamberlain's reputation, both among the general public and within the academic world, was profound indeed. And its central arguments have not yet been laid to rest. We should not perhaps be surprised that Foot, as the only surviving member of the composing trio, should still proclaim the essential truth of what he wrote in his youth. In 1986, eschewing the mass of revisionist literature which had by then appeared, he insisted that 'those who wish to know what actually happened in the 1930s, how the nation was so nearly led to its doom, had better stick to rough-and-ready guides like *Guilty Men*'.[4] Yet it is more surprising that the central argument of this tract, at least as far as it relates to Neville Chamberlain, has, suitably embellished and documented, been resurrected and triumphantly reasserted by at least some historians in the post-revisionist 1990s. *Guilty Men* itself was republished in 1998, as a Penguin 'Twentieth-Century Classic', no less.

To understand this enormous impact the appearance of *Guilty Men* must be placed in its historical context. It was published just a month after the evacuation of the British army from the beaches of Dunkirk and only a fortnight following the fall of France. With hindsight both these landmarks of the Second World War came to assume a positive aura. Dunkirk, a triumph in adversity, epitomized the resourcefulness and dogged determination of the British people. The success of the Royal Navy, supported by a flotilla of small boats, in ferrying the vast majority of the British Expeditionary Force back to safety was certainly a logistical achievement of no small proportions. And there were those who welcomed the fact that Britain could now face her enemy freed from the encumbrance of unreliable allies. King George VI probably spoke for many of his subjects when he told his mother that personally he felt happier since the country had no allies to be polite to or to pamper. In reality, however, the events of the late spring of 1940 represented an overwhelming military defeat and placed Britain in a dire predicament in which her survival as a free nation was gravely imperilled. The British army may have been saved, but most of its equipment had had to be abandoned and it would not be in a position to rejoin the European land war for more than three years. Likewise, though France may not have been the most suitable of allies in many British eyes, the fact remained that Britain had never contemplated taking on the might of Nazi Germany without her military support and her defeat that June left Britain herself apparently vulnerable to imminent invasion.

Contemporaries were no doubt relieved to see the army safely back on British soil, but the mood of deliverance was quickly transformed into one of anger as men began to ask how the country had got into this position in the first place. After all, the Anglo–French forces had withstood everything that the Kaiser's army had thrown at them in the four years and more of the last European conflict. Now allied resistance had collapsed in a period of about six weeks since the launching of the German western offensive on 10 May. Only the fact that the nation's fortunes had been entrusted to men who were criminally negligent could possibly explain the catastrophe that had just occurred. 'Like all successful propaganda, *Guilty Men* caught a public mood, and amplified it into a legend.'[5] 'Cato' succeeded in articulating what the mass of Britons already felt or soon came to feel in 1940. The British army had been defeated not because of tactical mistakes and strategic miscalculations, but because politicians had sent it unprepared and ill-equipped to face the military might of the German Reich. It was 'the story of an army doomed *before* they took the field'.[6] How else could Dunkirk have come about? A generation which had grown up to think of Britain as an invincible world power needed an easy explanation and, more importantly, a convenient scapegoat.

In all probability the central argument of *Guilty Men* was being spread by word of mouth before its authors put pen to paper. The Director of Military Information with the BEF in France told a group of war correspondents that he doubted whether the British army had ever been in a graver position than that 'in which the Government of the past 20 years had now placed it'. One Conservative MP recorded private thoughts which must have been widely shared:

> The losses in material of every description in France have been appalling and apparently there were no supplies in existence at home to replace them – or, at any rate, not nearly enough. This is pretty disgraceful and one feels that there has been no real drive behind our war effort for the last nine months. Chamberlain will have to bear the blame for this. . . .[7]

On the other side of the political spectrum the left-wing Labour MP, Aneurin Bevan, writing in the journal *Tribune*, called for an enquiry into what had happened at Dunkirk and the impeachment of those including Chamberlain who were responsible. His more moderate colleague, Hugh Dalton, had confided to the privacy of his diary secret information about the inadequate equipment of the British forces more than two months before the German blow actually fell.

Guilty Men thus found a ready audience. This was reflected in its astonishing commercial success. By the end of 1940 it had already been reprinted twenty-seven times. Sales, as one of its authors suggested, reached the proportions of a pornographic classic. Despite the refusal of some leading distributors such as W.H. Smith to stock it, more than 200,000 copies were eventually produced and sold. The publishers, Gollancz, even sold it from barrows in Fleet Street. When it is remembered that, in the climate of wartime Britain, it is likely that most copies were circulated among several pairs of hands, the book's impact upon British opinion may be assessed.

As suggested, *Guilty Men* is first and foremost a critique of British defence policy during the 1930s. Indeed the authors asserted that they did not have the scope to give an account of Chamberlain's performance in foreign affairs, restricting themselves to recording only his promises regarding the country's preparations for war should that foreign policy fail. But *Guilty Men* became the essential critique of the years of appeasement. The key elements of its argument, crudely expressed though they are, were to be repeated, developed, embellished and enlarged over the next twenty years or so to become the accepted orthodoxy on the performance of Chamberlain and his contemporaries in the approach to war. Those elements must be isolated and defined.

In the first place this is a uniquely personal indictment. We are dealing with the mistakes of men and there is no place here for the impersonal determinants of historical causation, whether political, economic, social or cultural. The book begins with a cast-list of the guilty men, headed inevitably by Chamberlain himself. Indeed, 'pride of place as Guilty Man number one must surely always be allotted to Neville Chamberlain'.[8] The list of fifteen – fourteen politicians and one civil servant – contains few surprises. Omitted from it are such obvious long-term critics of Chamberlain's policies as Churchill and Vansittart together with those politicians such as Eden and Duff Cooper who, through timely resignations, managed to escape the contaminating embrace of the National Government before it was too late for their own reputations. But the reader is left in no doubt that those who remain are lesser men, not fit for the high offices they held. Cato's duty was 'patiently and clearly [to] trace the origin and monstrous growth of the regime of little men'.[9] Often this involved a process of ridicule. Chamberlain himself was presented as 'umbrella man'; the nomination of his colleague Sir Thomas Inskip as Minister for the Co-ordination of Defence in 1936 represented the most astonishing appointment 'since the Roman Emperor Caligula made his horse a Consul'.[10]

But Cato's charges were no laughing matter. The crimes committed were altogether too serious for that. After all, those who led, or misled, the country through the 1930s 'took over a great empire, supreme in arms and secure in liberty' and succeeded only in 'conduct[ing] it to the edge of national humiliation'.[11] Indeed the concepts of crime, guilt and punishment are important here. A couple of months later another vitriolic little book was published under the title *The Case Against Neville Chamberlain*. Now largely forgotten, but enjoying quite a wide circulation at the time, this work set out to present 'to the great Jury of the British public' the evidence against the man who, as it admitted, had so recently been regarded as a national hero. Some seemed to want to go further than simply considering the evidence. In the early days of the conflict the diplomat Robert Bruce Lockhart recorded a discussion about those politicians, including Chamberlain, who were 'criminally responsible for war and should be hanged on lamp posts of Downing Street'.[12] By introducing such concepts *Guilty Men* ensured that there would be a profoundly moral element in the indictment of Neville Chamberlain. This notion, which often sits uneasily with objective historical analysis, would persist in presentations of him for many years to come. Chamberlain may have been portrayed as a foolish man, totally out of his depth in dealing with the international problems of the 1930s, but he remained someone whose policies needed to be blamed rather than explained.

The Chamberlain portrayed in *Guilty Men* may have been both foolish and short-sighted, but there was at the same time something sinister about the way in which he conducted the nation's affairs. 'What's there behind the Arras?' asked Cato. The answer was Sir Horace Wilson, the government's Chief Industrial Adviser and, according to the account in *Guilty Men*, 'for over two years . . . the second most powerful figure in the public life of the country'.[13] It was he rather than the experts of the Foreign Office whom Chamberlain chose to accompany him on his visits to Germany to meet Hitler. Indeed, he 'enjoyed immense power during the Premiership of Mr. Chamberlain. He was answerable to no one except the Prime Minister'.[14] Thus began a notion that would be expounded and expanded over the years to come – that Chamberlain had acted in wilful defiance of the wiser opinions of abler men, preferring the advice of shadowy figures such as Wilson and a small group of sycophantic ministers.

Guilty Men was self-evidently a critique directed from the Left. Even if its authors remained unknown, the political credentials of its publisher were no secret. This approach enabled Cato to develop the thesis that the mistakes which led to the ignominious defeat at Dunkirk were the responsibility of the National Government which had taken office in 1931. Though nominally a cross-party coalition, this administration had been increasingly dominated by the Conservative party, especially after the General Election of 1935. Cato thus took up a theme evident in the parliamentary debate on the Norwegian campaign which had precipitated the fall of Chamberlain's government. In simple terms the whole of the 1930s could be represented as a unity, a period of gross mismanagement of Britain's external relations. Writing in 1941 the Liberal MP Geoffrey Mander put the point very clearly: 'We now know that the pathway to the beaches of Dunkirk lay through the wastes of Manchuria.'[15] In other words the failure of the National Government, within weeks of its foundation, to take effective action against the Japanese invasion of China had initiated a disastrous pattern of aggression going unchecked and unpunished, which culminated in Hitler's western offensive of 1940. This view became entrenched. Writing in 1959 Winston Churchill's son Randolph suggested that Sir John Simon's appointment to the Foreign Office in November 1931 was 'to commence a disastrous era in which under successive Foreign Secretaries . . . British power and influence steadily declined and Britain was fatuously conducted towards the Second World War'.[16]

In theory this line of analysis could have had the effect of lessening the amount of 'guilt' laid specifically at Chamberlain's door. After all, he did not assume the premiership until May 1937, almost six years after the formation of the National Government. It was possible that Chamberlain's responsibility would be diluted within a more general and wide-ranging indictment. In practice this did not happen. In the first place Chamberlain had been widely recognized as the most forceful element within the administration for some time before he became Prime Minister. But of even more importance, the extension of the critique to the decade as a whole was the first step towards expanding the popular indictment of the 1930s to include not only its foreign policy but its domestic record as well. In short, it was the combination of appeasement *and* the Slump, and not one alone, which turned these years into the 'Devil's Decade'. In this context Chamberlain's key role as Chancellor of the Exchequer for more than five years before he became Prime Minister merely compounded his vulnerability to attack.

Guilty Men was in fact only one, albeit the most significant, in a series of left-wing tracts of the war years, published mostly by Gollancz and Penguin. By 1945 their cumulative effect had been to go a long way towards establishing a broad consensus on the National Government, indeed the whole inter-war period in general and Neville Chamberlain in particular. Much of this writing was at the level of character assassination. Even so, as a barrage of propaganda it proved so successful that it was probably not without its impact on the outcome of the 1945 General Election. The series may be held to have predated *Guilty Men* and indeed the outbreak of war itself, the Left Book Club having been founded in 1936. Of some note was the publication in 1939 of Simon Haxey's *Tory MP* which sought by highly selective quotation to blacken the reputations of all Conservative MPs who had at any time said anything remotely supportive of Hitler or Mussolini. Geoffrey Mander's *We were Not All Wrong* (1941) set out to show that Labour and Liberal MPs, together with just a small number of Conservatives, had in vain warned the government about the threat posed by Nazi Germany. He thus encouraged acceptance of the simple contrast between appeaser and anti-appeaser, the foolish and the wise. For the former, indeed, it was fortunate that 'impeachment has gone out of fashion'.[17] In addition Mander confirmed other key elements in the growing consensus, notably that the war could easily have been averted and that Chamberlain was quite out of his intellectual and imaginative depths in trying to deal with Hitler. His record as a social reformer in Birmingham was 'admirable', but his provincial background and training merely encouraged his belief that, as in the sub-committees of the City Council, international difficulties could always be straightened out by man-to-man negotiations and 'he applied this simple formula with over-weening self-confidence to the problems of Europe'.[18]

With many of these books left-wing authorship was concealed or at least thinly disguised beneath the pseudonyms of public-spirited Roman citizens. *Your MP* (1944) by Gracchus followed the approach of *Tory MP*, listing the votes of MPs in major foreign policy divisions but in a highly tendentious manner. It made the significant point that appeasement had not even ended with the coming of hostilities but had continued through the months of the Phoney War. The primary purpose now was to look forward to the next general election and to ensure a Conservative defeat, for those who had backed Chamberlain in May 1940 could never be trusted again. The responsibilities of such men were grave indeed:

> Because he voted as he did, the dead come into my account of him. In a war that need not have happened – or could have been won and ended quickly and at little cost, if it *had* to happen – men are dead across the beaches, the islands and the hills: beaches of Dunkirk and New Guinea, hills of Norway and of Sicily, islands from Crete to Singapore.[19]

Why Not Trust the Tories, published in 1944 under the name of Celticus but known to be the work of Aneurin Bevan, extended the indictment of the Conservatives' foreign policy as set out in *Guilty Men* to their management of domestic affairs. Drawing strained parallels with what had happened after 1918 Bevan warned that, with the approach of peace, the Tory party would once more 'lie, deceive, cajole and buy time so as . . . to snatch a reprieve for wealth and privilege'.[20] Diplomaticus in *Can the Tories Win the Peace* (1945) offered the same message:

> From [the time of the Russian Revolution] to this the main preoccupation of successive Conservative governments and statesmen has been to preserve the social order and the Empire against the insurgent classes and races rendered militant by the First World War, the Russian Revolution, the great slump and the present war.[21]

The repetition of such extravagant nonsense would serve little purpose were it not for the fact that it seems to have found an attentive audience and that such ideas, suitably refined, would

soon find their place in an academically more respectable historiography on Chamberlain and his foreign policy. One particularly interesting pointer to the future appeared in *Brendan and
Beverley: An Extravaganza* (1944) by Cassius. An imagined
conversation between two archetypal Tories has one saying to
the other, 'In fact, we want your help, not to praise
Chamberlain, but to bury him', a clear anticipation of the way
in which Conservatives themselves would soon seek to disown
their Chamberlainite inheritance.[22] Some Conservatives clearly
recognised what was happening and what its future electoral
implications might be. If the Left was allowed to get away with
the simple contrast between 'the England of the Chamberlains,
the Simons and the Hoares . . . [the] England which condoned
Fascism, consorted with Fascism, connived at imperialist war'
and the 'other England [which] detested Fascism from the day of
its birth . . . the England of the Left, the England of Labour, the
England which inherited . . . the European policy which made
this country the leader of the nations in the nineteenth century',
then the consequences for Conservatism would be grave
indeed.[23] Oliver Stanley warned that the party's pre-war record
had been hung around its neck like a millstone, a millstone
which must be got rid of. Each of the left-wing tracts, charged
Quintin Hogg, 'consists of a deliberate and vicious attack on the
record of the Conservative Party. Each is a variant on the claim
that the only sensible course is to vote for Labour or Liberal
candidates in future.'[24] Labour writers were of course on somewhat shaky ground. Their own party's pre-war record, particularly in terms of opposing rearmament, scarcely offered an
unassailable platform from which to criticize the then government. Yet it is striking how few Tories put their heads above the
literary parapets to challenge the growing orthodoxy espoused
by their political opponents. Quintin Hogg's *The Left was Never
Right* (1945) was probably the most effective riposte from the
political right. But its impact never matched that of *Guilty Men*.
Early attempts to defend Chamberlain's efforts to avert war such
as *Munich: Before and After* (1944) by W.W. Hadley, editor of
the *Sunday Times*, and *The Truth about the Munich Crisis*
(1944) by Viscount Maugham, Chamberlain's Lord Chancellor,
caused only passing notice.

By the end of hostilities in 1945, therefore, a clear picture of
the 1930s had emerged. The reputations of those who had held
office during that decade had been viciously assailed. At times

the quest for a scapegoat seemed to require a living victim and the last years of Stanley Baldwin, Chamberlain's predecessor as Prime Minister, who lived on until 1947, were characterized by abuse and vilification. When the former premier appeared reluctant to sacrifice the metal from the ornamental gates outside his country home for the communal war effort, one MP sarcastically suggested that it was 'very necessary to leave Lord Baldwin his gates in order to protect him from the just indignation of the mob'.[25] At the end of the day, however, Chamberlain towered over all others in the ranks of guilty men. He it was above any other single individual who stood charged with incompetence and deception, diplomatic misjudgements and military miscalculations. Chamberlain it was who had been blind to his duty, failing to prepare the country in the face of an obvious danger and stifling the voices of those who had presumed to speak the truth. In the construction of this new consensus left-wing tracts were joined by articles in the popular press and even by feature films. The role of the Labour-supporting *Daily Mirror* was to be expected; but it was matched by such traditionally Conservative newspapers as the *Daily Express* and *Daily Mail*. The cinema combined entertainment with an important propaganda function. The climax of Michael Powell's film *Contraband* was set in a warehouse packed with plaster busts of Neville Chamberlain which were smashed to smithereens in a final shoot-out. The celebrated *This Happy Breed* was one of several films to contain an unequivocal denunciation of appeasement.

The war had been won by Churchill's defiance rather than Chamberlain's submission. But it also seemed to have been won by the employment of an economic strategy which represented the abandonment of the policies pursued during the 1930s. The historiographical debate over the reality or otherwise of a Keynesian Revolution in Whitehall during the war years lies outside the scope of the present study. What is important, however, is that by 1945 many believed that a new set of ideas had been implemented and had proved successful. The views associated with Chamberlain on the domestic front were thus as discredited as those which he had espoused in defence and foreign policy. Keynes himself had become a key figure after his installation as an adviser to the Chancellor of the Exchequer in 1940. The budget of 1941 is generally taken to be Britain's first structured on Keynesian lines. Keynes's ideas were central to the Coalition government's celebrated White Paper on employment policy of 1944 and had clearly influenced the thinking of *all* the leading political parties by the time of the 1945 General Election. After the budgetary caution of the 1930s, government expenditure had risen rapidly under the pressing necessity of the war. From about £1 billion in 1939 it had climbed to £4 billion in 1943 and £6 billion in 1945, peaking at something like two-thirds of national income. In the process it had had the effect of removing unemployment as a serious problem.

Historians differ about how far and precisely when the post-war Conservative and Labour parties converged in their economic thinking. Broadly speaking, however, by the late 1940s politicians who seriously aspired to power were agreed that there could be no return to the conditions of high unemployment and 'life on the dole' which had characterized Britain before 1939. They also accepted that government now had within its hands the tools of economic management which would ensure the continuing benefits of full employment. Those who protested most loudly against the return of mass unemployment in the 1970s and 1980s, often evoking in the process bitter memories of the 1930s,[26] did so not because they regarded this as an unfortunate phenomenon beyond governmental control but because they saw it as the wilful revival of a suppressed and unnecessary evil. In the Keynesian intervention-ist heyday of the 1940s, 50s and 60s Neville Chamberlain was inevitably seen as an outdated anachronism. Once governments accepted that they could manage the numbers of those without work, it became difficult to defend the policies with which Chamberlain had been associated, with their pre-war insistence that unemployment was an inevitable consequence of the trade cycle. Inter-war Treasury thinking on the capacity of govern-ments to create jobs had been that 'very little additional employ-ment and no real permanent additional employment can in fact, as a general rule, be created by state borrowing and state expen-diture'. It mattered not that these words were uttered by the then Chancellor of the Exchequer, Winston Churchill, in 1929. In the popular mind they summed up the mind-set of Neville Chamberlain.

Chamberlain was thus as 'wrong' in his economic thinking as in his appeasement policy, and as culpable for the suffering of the 1930s unemployed as he was for the outbreak of an unnec-essary war. Apart from his enthusiasm for Imperial Preference he was, asserted A.J.P. Taylor, 'a pure Cobdenite in his reliance on natural forces and individual enterprise'.[27] Presented in 1958 by his Chancellor of the Exchequer with a paper advocating the limitation of public investment, Prime Minister Harold Macmillan declared, 'This is a *very bad paper*. Indeed a disgraceful paper. It might have been written by Mr. Neville Chamberlain's Government.'[28] At the same time post-war governments, whether of Labour or Conservative persuasion, accepted the notion of a welfare state as set out in blue-print during the war by William Beveridge. The notion of the state looking after its citizens at their times of need, from the cradle to the grave, seemed far removed from the cruel austerity of the 1930s means test.

Less than a decade after his popularity had reached its zenith, therefore, Chamberlain's reputation lay in tatters, the victim in part of a grossly over-simplified image of what he had done and stood for in both the domestic and international arenas, and perhaps more particularly of a simplistic certainty as to how governments ought to behave in the future. His foreign policy stood condemned for its craven concessions to aggression and its failure to prepare Britain adequately for a war which could easily have been averted. In the domestic sphere he was inextricably associated with an unbroken period of depression, deprivation and decay, 'a palette made up of dole queues, hunger marches, slum houses, malnutrition and bitter class and industrial relations'.[29] In future, governments would stand up to the aggression of international bullies abroad, while taking active responsibility for the avoidance of social distress at home. In the developing Cold War environment from the late 1940s onwards it was axiomatic that the Soviet threat which had replaced the Nazi one had to be resisted. Few questioned the notion that unchecked aggression only led to a more serious war at a later date and the conviction that there could be no more Munichs was engrained as an article of faith. 'Containment' and the nuclear deterrent owed much to a reaction against the policies of Neville Chamberlain. Just as assuredly all British governments now understood that they could never revert to the socioeconomic policies of the 1930s if they wanted to retain their hold on power. Such assessments were not offered as statements of opinion subject to possible contradiction but as the veritable certainties of the post-war era.

The picture might not have been so absolute had the Conservative party tried to launch a concerted counter-offensive, designed to rehabilitate its own performance in government during the 1930s. But the post-1945 party was dominated in succession by Churchill, Eden and Macmillan, men who, with varying degrees of credibility, had established their reputations as critics of government policy, and particularly its foreign policy, before the war. Others who failed to reach the absolute top of the Tory hierarchy – most noticeably R.A. Butler – repeatedly found themselves being reminded of their appeasement-orientated pasts. Many, including the author himself, considered that Iain Macleod damaged his own career prospects within the Conservative party by the mere act of publishing a sympathetic biography of Chamberlain in 1961. The personnel of the Conservative high command had in fact undergone a considerable transformation during the war and the 1945 General Election served to sweep away many long-serving MPs. Sir Kingsley Wood, who died in 1943, was the last Chamberlainite loyalist to sit in Churchill's War Cabinet. After a period of caution in 1940 itself Churchill, his own position now unassailable, had begun to reshape the party and preferred to promote maverick figures such as Beaverbrook or new men like Oliver Lyttelton rather than drawing from the ranks of the Chamberlainite party. As minds turned to the next election the desire for a new beginning was apparent. 'I understand', noted Leo Amery, 'that they are now very keen on young Service candidates who, after the war, can disclaim any responsibility for the failures of pre-war years.'[30] Any lingering inclination to defend the past was surely destroyed by the outcome of the election with its resulting massive majority for the Labour party. 'This has been a vote against the Tory party and their records from 1920 to 1939', declared Colin Coote, deputy editor of the *Daily Telegraph*.[31] Harold Macmillan confirmed this interpretation: 'It was clear to an unbiased observer that it was not Churchill who had brought the Conservative party so low. On the contrary it was the recent history of the Party, with its pre-war record of unemployment and its failure to preserve peace.'[32] Central Office noted that the election had witnessed

calculated misrepresentation of Conservative policy between the wars. The general socialist line was to paint a picture of Britain in grinding poverty, misery and unemployment before the War ... British governments before the War were accused of deliberately 'sabotaging' the

League of Nations, of nourishing Hitler and encouraging
the growth of fascism. Every effort to maintain peace was
misconstrued or distorted.[33]

This may have been unfair but it was the reality with which the
Conservative party had to live after 1945.

Everything therefore pointed to drawing a line under the
party's pre-war record and starting again. So strong was this
tendency that there was even serious discussion of a change in
the party's name. Condemned by the electorate for being out of
touch with the popular mood in 1945, it made little sense for
Conservatives to focus on the essential continuities of their
party's history. Attempts to defend the pre-war record were
therefore limited to domestic policy and even these were of short
duration. A party pamphlet of 1947 spoke of the 'lie about Tory
misrule' before 1939, but the launching that year of such policy
documents as the *Industrial Charter* encouraged a contrary
approach of stressing, indeed exaggerating, the extent to which
the party *had* changed under Chamberlain's successor. This
involved playing down the very creditable pedigree derived from
the social and industrial policies of the 1930s, but it made good
political sense to do so. With Labour still conducting its elec-
toral strategy in part around the idea of the dangers of a return
to pre-war conditions if the Conservatives were again victorious,
the Tories were well advised to emphasize that this possibility
did not enter their own calculations. Speaking to the 1947 Party
Conference as President of the National Union, Harold
Macmillan dismissed the 1930s as a barren period across the
board as far as Conservative policy was concerned.

Rather like a disgraced Bolshevik, therefore, Chamberlain
found himself largely air-brushed from the Conservative party's
history book. The most damaging charge against his biographer
Iain Macleod, suggested *Time* magazine, was that 'instead of
rehabilitating a hero, he has merely disinterred a ghost whose
miasmal presence still haunts the Conservative Party'.[34] But the
policy with which Chamberlain had been most closely associated
could not be forgotten. Instead it stood as an awful warning to
later generations. Understandings of what appeasement had been
about were now distorted almost beyond recognition. The word
itself lost its original sense of the attempt to defuse conflict
through the pacific settlement of disputes and took on the more
sinister connotation of granting unwarranted concessions and

sacrificing the interests of the weak in order to purchase peace at the expense of a third party. Notions of idealism, magnanimity and righting wrongs went out of the linguistic window. Like 'Munich', 'appeasement' became a symbol of shame which prompted strong emotion rather than rational discussion. A term that had been part of the common political parlance of the 1920s and 1930s became almost a dirty word. The process began surprisingly early. In June 1939 Lord Chatfield, then Minister for the Co-ordination of Defence, was told that Chamberlain himself wished the word to be employed as little as possible because it was already subject to considerable misconstruction. The following year Lord Halifax decreed that it should no longer be used in Foreign Office papers. During the war 'appeasement' became a taboo. 'It must never be mentioned.'[35] By 1945 the negative symbolism was all pervasive. Even dictionary definitions came to be modified to embrace the new concept of surrendering to threats. 'The word appeasement is shunned', wrote one anonymous journalist in 1961, 'for it lost all its Victorian virtues twenty-three years ago and is useful now only in the vocabulary of political abuse.'[36] Those who had used the term without condemnation before 1939 were anxious to explain their intentions. The word, insisted Anthony Eden when he came to write his memoirs, could have two meanings. He had employed it solely to imply the bringing of peace and the settlement of strife. To this day no serious politician would allow his policies to be labelled as 'appeasement', even though many actions and manoeuvres in the diplomatic arena clearly merit such a description.

With hindsight everyone seemed to have been against appeasement as practised by Neville Chamberlain. For many this involved a process of self-induced amnesia and a distortion of the historical record. Eden's attitude in the 1930s had at best been equivocal, reflecting the contemporary complexities of Chamberlain's appeasement policy rather than later condemnatory over-simplifications. After 1945, however, he emerged among the doughtiest opponents of appeasement, someone who had learnt the costly lessons of the 1930s and intended to apply them to later events. In his conduct of the Suez Crisis of 1956 he had before him the mistakes made twenty years before, the failure to resist Hitler when he reoccupied the Rhineland and curiously drawn parallels between Mussolini and the Egyptian dictator, Colonel Nasser. Even when the Suez episode went tragically wrong, Eden remained unrepentant. 'With every day that passes', he insisted, 'more people in all free countries understand that the consequences of appeasing dictators who break international agreements are the same in 1957 as they were in 1938.'[37] In his retirement Eden was always ready to assail anyone who dared to challenge the simplistic condemnation of Chamberlain as a 'guilty man'. Revisionism as regards the 1930s was not only bad history but dangerous for the future of international relations. It was, he believed, unfortunate that Iain Macleod's biography of Chamberlain should have been published in 1961 at the height of the Cold War. In the existing international situation, he told a reporter for the *Sunday Times*, appeasement was certainly not a policy the West could afford to pursue if it intended to survive.

But it was not just survivors of the political generation of the 1930s such as Eden who espoused the new orthodoxy. Throughout the post-war era and through to the present day there has been no shortage of political leaders, throughout the western world but particularly in Britain and the United States, ready to trundle out platitudes about the dangers of replicating the mistakes of the Chamberlain era. Incidentally, it is perhaps reasonable to suggest that the consequences of misapplying the suggested lessons of Munich to later situations have probably outweighed the original mistake of 1938. Be that as it may, a few examples of those post-war evocations will help to illustrate the continuing impact upon Neville Chamberlain's reputation. As has already been suggested, the Cold War was very much played out against the background of the 1930s. Many of those who supported United Nations action in Korea in 1950 had the earlier decade clearly in mind, arguing that action at that stage might mean not having to fight a bigger war later on. President Truman 'remembered how each time that the democracies failed to act, it had encouraged the aggressors to keep going ahead'.[38] When the Soviet leader Bulganin commended unnamed public figures in America for their support of a nuclear test ban, Vice-President Richard Nixon was quick to compare the liberal Adlai Stevenson to Chamberlain. At the height of the Cuban Missile Crisis in 1962 so-called Young Americans for Freedom picketed the White House with placards calling upon the United States to invade Cuba and insisting that 'appeasement is for cowards', even though the logical consequence of their advice might well have been all-out nuclear war. The spectre of Munich was never far from the minds of American policy makers as their country became embroiled in Vietnam in the mid-1960s. President Johnson explained the commitment of ground troops to Indo-China with the argument that 'from Munich until today, we have learned that to yield to aggression brings only greater threats and brings even more destructive wars'.[39] Soon afterwards Henry Cabot Lodge sought to justify the American approach before the students of the Oxford Union in terms of the need to resist aggression, the inevitable price that would be paid for appeasement and the inexorable progression from Munich to Dunkirk. When the Cold War showed signs of thawing, the hard-line Senator Henry Jackson reacted to news of the SALT-2 agreement on arms limitation with references to appeasement, Munich and Neville Chamberlain. Nearer our own day British Foreign Secretary Douglas Hurd insisted, following the Iraqi invasion of Kuwait in 1990, that the appeasement of aggression would only lead on to further violations of international law. And even the present Prime Minister, Tony Blair, referring to the menace of Slobodan Milosevic, stated in a 1999 interview that 'we have learnt by bitter experience not to appease dictators. We tried it sixty years ago. It didn't work then and it shouldn't be tried now.'[40]

While Chamberlain's pre-war policies continued in this way to be an issue of current politics in the post-war world, it was inevitable that the academic profession would begin the process of historical evaluation. As has been seen, by the end of hostilities in 1945 a large and persuasive body of popular literature was already in the public domain. What is surprising, however, is that when professional historians began to get their teeth into the subject they did not sweep away these wartime polemics and start afresh. Rather they built upon existing assumptions and prejudices, giving them in the process a considerable degree of academic respectability. The first generation of historians of the inter-war years may, very broadly, be divided into two groups – anti-appeasement Conservatives and left-of-centre internationalists. Of the two, the former were probably the more important precisely because they came from a very different starting point from the authors of *Guilty Men* and yet still reached essentially the same conclusion. The most significant figures in this group were Sir Lewis Namier and Sir John Wheeler-Bennett, ably supported as the next chapter will show by none other than Winston Churchill. It should be stressed that both of these writers, especially the first, were distinguished exponents of their craft.

Namier's meticulous research into the political structure of the mid-eighteenth century is widely regarded as an historical work of the highest order. But both men sought to play a dual role in analysing the history of the 1930s for they wrote not only as historians but also as contemporaries and participants. Each one had come to hold strong views about British policy in the 1930s – though Wheeler-Bennett took some time to reach his final position, claiming after a visit to Berlin in 1933 that Hitler was a man of good sense who did not want war and that *Mein Kampf* was a book to which no particular significance need be attached. Their task now was to justify their existing convictions through the processes of historical enquiry. But reconciling the motives of the scholar with those of the participant is one of the most demanding tasks to face the professional historian and it is doubtful whether either Namier or Wheeler-Bennett met the challenge successfully. Their analyses were deeply coloured by a sense of personal involvement. An editorial in *The Listener* of October 1948 well captured the problem:

> Historians of the events, moved by shame or regret or pride, employ an adjective here, a verb there to colour their narrative so that their readers find difficulty in disentangling themselves from the emotions of the chronicler. Truth, it was once said, always arrives in time for history; but Munich has not passed into history yet.[41]

At much the same time Chamberlain's surviving sister Hilda wrote to the BBC to protest that the Corporation had presented Wheeler-Bennett's 'story' as impartial history, whose purpose was to 'inform youth so that they should not repeat the errors of the past'.[42]

Both writers adopted a moralizing tone and style which perpetuated the impressions of crime and condemnation set out in *Guilty Men*. D.C. Watt, one of the first historians to speak out against the ever strengthening orthodoxy, suggested that Namier sought to combine in himself the functions of detective, prosecuting counsel, judge and jury – 'the entire process from the discovery of the criminal's finger-print to the donning of the black cap'.[43] In like vein Wheeler-Bennett appeared more interested in blaming Chamberlain for what had been done than in trying to understand his motives:

> Surrender to blackmail is always damnable because it sets a higher value upon mere self-protection than upon principles,

which, in fact, we know to be sacred and inviolable. Such appeasement is justly condemned because it is felt to be an act of treason against all we stand for – the purchase of life at the expense of those ultimate ends of which the pursuit alone makes life worth living.[44]

Both authors presented Chamberlain as a man of limited imagination whose experience in no way fitted him for the duties he had to discharge as Prime Minister. According to Namier,

His experience was that of a middle-class business man, and he infused into politics the atmosphere of the 'pleasant Sunday afternoon', dull and sober. He was shrewd, ignorant, and self-opinionated, and had the capacity to deceive himself as much as was required by his deeper instincts and his purposes, and also to deceive those who chose to be deceived.[45]

Wheeler-Bennett concurred. His Chamberlain was a man guilty of 'political myopia':

Himself essentially a business man, he could not conceive how any problem could possibly be settled by a recourse to arms, nor could his mentality envisage that any other national leader in Europe, whether democratic or totalitarian, could think otherwise.[46]

It was perhaps true that Chamberlain could not have been expected to understand the depths of Hitler's infamy, the ghastly proportions of which were only fully exposed during and at the conclusion of the war. Even so, the Nazis' very public catalogue of broken pledges still left the British Prime Minister *'culpably credulous'* in his dealings with Hitler.[47]

Neither Wheeler-Bennett nor Namier showed much understanding of the narrow constraints within which British politicians of the 1930s, and in particular Chamberlain, had been forced to operate. Perhaps neither wished to have such an understanding. Their writing was instead suffused with a sense of injured national pride and an unwillingness to recognize that British power to influence the course of events was in decline. For them something had gone radically wrong in British politics in the years between the wars. There was nothing for pride or congratulation in the story of this whole period, claimed Wheeler-Bennett. 'British statesmanship has never been so humbled by a foreign Power since the Dutch burned the British fleet in the Medway.'[48] Namier, who had served in the Foreign Office during the First World War and was a great admirer of Churchill, seemed to suppose that Britain could have intervened single-handedly to preserve the European balance of power. The focus of both men is almost exclusively upon the German threat with practically no appreciation of the strategic constraints posed by the simultaneous challenges of Italy in the Mediterranean and Japan in the Far East. The German bid for world domination could on several occasions have been halted 'without excessive effort or sacrifice'.[49] But, as a result of the sins of omission between 1933 and 1937, Britain under Chamberlain was forced into sins of commission in 1938, condoning 'chicanery, aggression and injustice and [becoming] an accessory to these outrages'.[50]

This assault upon Chamberlain's reputation from the right was matched by an equally uncompromising offensive from the internationalist left. Among the more important representatives of this school were A.L. Rowse, Elizabeth Wiskemann and Margaret George. Their approach may have been different from that of Namier and Wheeler-Bennett, but their fundamental message was the same. Miss Wiskemann, who twenty years after the end of the Second World War still had to confess that she could 'make no claim to detachment about the history of Europe between 1919 and 1945', found Chamberlain 'stubborn, vain, naif and ignorant'. Nothing could have been more futile than the elderly Prime Minister's pilgrimage to Germany to ask Hitler what would satisfy him. 'Hitler was insatiable, and he asked for everything in the name of preserving the peace which he despised.'[51] Rowse and George at least sought explanations for what Chamberlain did. The former indeed seemed to have a mission to explain the apparently inexplicable:

> What could have possessed [the appeasers]? How to explain their blindness? That is the problem. There can be no question now that these men were wrong; but how they could be *so* wrong, in face of everything, and *why* they were so wrong – there is a problem. It is a formidable one. . . .[52]

But they found their explanations not in a sympathetic examination of the underlying determinants of British foreign policy, but in dark tales of self-interested conspiracy and deceit.

Rowse's interests were wide-ranging. He was as at home speculating upon the possible authorship of the plays attributed to Shakespeare as he was discussing the history and topography of his native Cornwall. But his analysis of inter-war politics and diplomacy lacked nothing in confidence. Indeed, it is a feature of this early literature as a whole that it was not put forward with the diffidence which might rightly characterize a near contemporary account written without access to public and private archives and lacking the benefit of historical perspective. Instead, what is presented is an unfolding and unchallengeable truth, given greater authority in most cases by the very fact that the writers lived through and felt passionately about the events they describe. Rowse's confidence in his own judgement is matched only by his contempt for Chamberlain and his belief that he could do business with a man like Hitler: 'Vain old fool – his *impression* against all the evidence of perjury, torture, murder, thuggery that had accumulated since 1933, and was there before!'[53] For Rowse and George the key lies in the corrupting influence of a decadent ruling class. All the historian needs to observe, opined Rowse, is that Britain in 1914 under a Liberal government entered the First World War with France and Russia at her side. Twenty or so years later, however, after two decades of Tory domination, 'this country was on the verge of war with both Germany and Italy, alone save for a France that *we* had broken, only half at our side'.[54] What Rowse had observed was 'a class in decadence' which had nearly ruined the country and reduced it to the status of a second-rate power.[55] In this he confirmed the assessment of none other than Benito Mussolini. For the Italian dictator, Chamberlain and his colleagues were 'not made of the same stuff as the Francis Drakes . . . who created the empire. These . . . are the tired sons of a long line of rich men.'[56] Again we come back to the image of Chamberlain as 'a rather simple-minded businessman', the representative of a political generation which had 'none of the old eighteenth-century aristocracy's guts'. They were 'middle-class men with pacifist backgrounds and no knowledge of Europe, its history or its languages, or of diplomacy, let alone of strategy or war'.[57] Chamberlain and the appeasers were in opposition to the men of the Foreign Office who had a far better knowledge of Europe in general and Germany in particular. In their smug ignorance the former had not even bothered to read *Mein Kampf* in which Hitler 'practically told them beforehand what he intended to do'.[58]

Margaret George developed the same themes. The political leadership of the 1930s was the best that was left after the slaughter of the First World War which 'had decimated the sons of the upper class, the suitable candidates for political places'. After the fall of the Lloyd George government in 1922 power had passed into the hands of 'a kind of league of the mediocre', men who would never have risen above 'under-secretarial level' in more talented administrations. The Chamberlain era was thus conveniently sandwiched between the premierships of the two giants of twentieth-century British history, David Lloyd George and Winston Churchill. But the thirties were a decade 'in desperate need of men of acumen, unusual sensitivity and perception'. Instead Britain was left in the hands of a group of 'businessmen-politicians', nothing in whose experience had prepared them for the European problems they had to face. Appeasement was pre-eminently a policy of the Conservative party, conducted by men more determined to protect their own social positions than to defend the country. Their sympathy for the fascist Right was explicable simply in terms of their fear of the Left and the threat it posed to their own class. Inter-war Tories like Chamberlain were 'conducting a last-ditch defence of property and privilege and, consequently, willing to risk nothing, dare nothing, and deviate only with painful caution from a preferred policy of absolute inaction'. Not even the coming of war had changed the situation. Chamberlain's speech to parliament on 3 September 1939 was 'a wail of personal tragedy' in shockingly bad taste of which he was completely unaware. As a war leader he was still fearful of offending the Germans. This attitude crippled the war effort and poisoned the national spirit.[59] As must be apparent, Mrs George pulled no punches. But, insisted Rowse, 'her book is history . . . she has got it essentially right'.[60]

Many writers of this period straddled an uneasy line between history and personal memoir. Their purported aim was to write the former, but their inability to break free from their contemporary prejudices left them perilously close to the latter. At the same time their writings were joined by a steady trickle of works which had no pretension to be other than personal recollections. The political memoir is a source of which the professional historian is rightly wary. Human nature determines that its primary purpose must be less to aspire towards objective truth than to place the individual's role within any given historical situation in the most favourable possible light. But the memoirs of the political generation who had shared power with Chamberlain, actively opposed him or merely observed him at close quarters played a not insignificant role in shaping his evolving reputation, not least because such works tended to be more widely read than were volumes of conventional history. Those individuals who could now claim to have been 'right' about the 1930s enjoyed a particular authority. Their accounts were eagerly awaited.

Sir Robert Vansittart, Permanent Under-Secretary at the Foreign Office from 1930 to 1938 was well placed to pass judgement. He stood, perhaps second only to Churchill, as a consistent opponent of Nazi Germany, a man who had repeatedly warned of the looming menace of Adolf Hitler. He epitomized the fact that Chamberlain had wilfully pursued his appeasement strategy in defiance of the expert professional advice of the Foreign Office. Indeed, his removal to the high-sounding but largely powerless post of Chief Diplomatic Adviser to the Government in January 1938 reflected the Prime Minister's determination to prosecute his ultimately fateful policy without hindrance or obstruction. Vansittart's memoirs, *The Mist Procession*, were published posthumously in 1958. Indeed, he never completed his account which ends rather abruptly in 1936, some months before Chamberlain reached 10 Downing Street. This was probably to the latter's advantage. Even so, Vansittart had managed to write enough to let his views be known. Memorably, Chamberlain was described as 'an earnest and opinionated provincial [who] was bound to err if he plunged into diplomacy'.[61] A fellow diplomat, but one with less obvious grounds to crow, echoed this point. Chamberlain was not well versed in foreign affairs, suggested William Strang. He had no touch for a diplomatic situation, did not fully realize what he was doing and showed a naïve and misplaced confidence in his own judgement and powers of persuasion.[62]

Alfred Duff Cooper, as the one cabinet minister who had resigned from Chamberlain's government over the agreement reached at Munich, was another with impeccable credentials to pronounce on his old chief. Chamberlain, he stressed, had many admirable qualities, but he 'lacked experience of the world, and he lacked also the imagination which can fill the gaps of inexperience'. He had been a good Lord Mayor of Birmingham but for him

The Dictators of Germany and of Italy were like the Lord
Mayors of Liverpool and Manchester, who might belong
to different political parties and have different interests,
but who must desire the welfare of humanity and be
fundamentally reasonable, decent men like himself. This
profound misconception lay at the root of his policy and
explains his mistakes.[63]

Former ministers whose own roles in the 1930s were not beyond
criticism also weighed in. The Earl of Swinton, dismissed by
Chamberlain in May 1938, took up Cooper's point. It was
Chamberlain's domestic expertise which had proved his undoing:

He brought to the home field the experience and knowledge of a successful Lord Mayor of Birmingham, and here
he knew and understood the vocabulary and alphabet
from A to Z. When he attempted to translate this know-
how to world affairs his range was limited from A to B.[64]

Chamberlain, judged Lord Winterton, was fundamentally a
'sober, intelligent, very able businessman turned administrator
and Prime Minister in his later years . . . The world of Europe
was a *terra ignota* to him' – scarcely a ringing endorsement from
one who had served quite happily in his cabinet for more than
two years.[65]

The maverick Conservative MP Robert Boothby described
the 1930s in predictably colourful terms. The government of
those years was no truly 'national' administration, but simply a
'get together on the part of the Boys of the Old Brigade'. Having
climbed on the bandwagon, they sat there rain or shine until
they had conducted the British Empire to the very brink of
destruction.[66] Those who did not read Boothby's memoirs might
have seen his frequent contributions to the press. Here he baldly
stated that Chamberlain in his public life was 'aloof, arrogant,
obstinate and limited. He was also a failure.'[67] Boothby did his
bit to present appeasement as some sort of establishment
conspiracy:

The verdict of the Deity and of posterity will, I fear, be
hard on the pre-war Establishment; on Baldwin, Halifax,
Simon, Chamberlain and Hoare, who constituted its political core; on Geoffrey Dawson [editor of *The Times*], its
Secretary-General; on Montagu Norman [governor of the

Bank of England], its Treasurer; and on Cliveden, which constituted, with All Souls, its G.H.Q. Between them they conducted us to disaster.[68]

Echoing *Guilty Men's* reference to Sir Horace Wilson, it seemed necessary to Boothby that Chamberlain should have had behind him some sinister mafia or *eminence grise* to have come up with such a damnable policy. The reference to Cliveden, the country home near Maidenhead of the Astor family, picked up an idea first presented back in November 1937 by the Communist journalist, Claud Cockburn, that British foreign policy was being composed behind the scenes and in defiance of the nation's democracy at country house weekends. It was a variation too of the Rowse-George theme of a corrupt governing class consorting with fascism in order to protect itself against the revolutionary left. Such ideas came to be widely accepted in the United States and also in Soviet historiography.[69]

It would be wrong to suggest that any of these memoirs had by itself a decisive impact in shaping Chamberlain's historical reputation in the generation after his death. Each, however, contributed to the steady drip effect which cumulatively made it very difficult for an alternative interpretation to make much headway. This was part of a wider phenomenon. Academic study of the whole question of the origins of the Second World War had not at this stage taken on the intensely controversial tone which in the 1920s and 1930s had so quickly characterized the analysis of the coming of the first great world conflict. For many the war of 1939 was Hitler's war and little more needed to be said. Such an assessment had received judicial sanction with the verdict of the post-war Nuremberg trials. Indeed, the more evidence that was uncovered of Hitler's unlimited capacity for evil, the more misguided – stupid even – appeared those like Chamberlain who had believed that they could deal with him through the methods of conventional diplomatic negotiation. This was a conveniently simple historical scenario which did not readily invite revisionist interpretations.

The twenty-year period following the publication of *Guilty Men* thus witnessed the setting in of something approaching historiographical paralysis, with the vast bulk of the literature displaying a perspective which had been frozen in the summer of 1940. The popular view and the academic tended to reinforce one another in a stultifying embrace. Popular works such as

Collin Brooks's *The Devil's Decade* (1948), William McElwee's *Britain's Locust Years* (1962) and Ronald Blythe's *The Age of Illusion* (1963) – these titles are in themselves revealing – ensured that the image of Chamberlain which had been conjured up in the last months of his life did not fade from the public mind. McElwee's description of Chamberlain as a politician out of his depth could have been written by just about any of the authors discussed in this chapter:

> The clarity of intellect which enabled him to move with skill and certainty through the intricacies of rating adjustments and pension schemes and budgetary calculations wholly deserted him when he came to consider foreign affairs.[70]

From this historiographical consensus it was inevitable that the same picture would find its way into undergraduate textbooks, ensuring the survival of this unflattering picture of Neville Chamberlain into a second generation of minds not directly influenced by personal experience of the 1930s. C.L. Mowat's admirable *Britain Between the Wars 1918–1940* (the terminal date is worthy of note) may be taken as a touchstone of this process. While generally readier than many previous writers to take a charitable view of the performance of the National Government in the social and economic field, Mowat's overall interpretation was still firmly fixed in the framework suggested by Cato a decade and a half before:

> The history of the National government was one long diminuendo. From its triumph in 1931 it shambled its unimaginative way to its fall in 1940, when the failure of the campaign in Norway and the Nazi invasion of the Low Countries brought Great Britain to the crisis of the new world war.[71]

Mowat's Chamberlain, like so many other assessments of this era, was a man of tunnel vision who mistrusted the officials of the Foreign Office and relied instead on the baleful advice of Sir Horace Wilson. His fatal mistake was to believe that there was a human side to the dictators which could be successfully appealed to, especially in tête-à-tête conversations.

What the average reader found on the printed page was reinforced by what he heard and later saw. As early as 1948 Hilda Chamberlain complained about the way in which her brother was represented in the BBC radio programme *The Story of*

Munich. Though the listening public was informed that no attempt had been made to reproduce the actual voices of the speakers from whom quotations were read, there were 'variations of speech to denote the psychology of the speaker at the moment'. But, as Miss Chamberlain protested,

> The selection of a voice to read quotations from my brother's speeches . . . completely destroys their significance. An unpleasantly high key, a mincing accent, the intonation of a smug, self-satisfied and superficial man, is such a travesty of my brother as could only have been made deliberately to indicate to the audience that he was the villain of the piece.[72]

More than thirty years later BBC television showed Chamberlain represented by the actor Eric Porter in a production of *The Wilderness Years*. The character portrayed was weak, defensive and unattractive, relying heavily for support on his equally unsympathetic minister Samuel Hoare.

It would be difficult to say that there was a particular moment when Chamberlain's reputation finally broke free from the chains of Cato's 'Guilty Man'. In one sense, indeed, it has never done so. Certainly, while the first generation of writers remained active they were unlikely to be impressed by alternative analyses, even if these were supported by compelling new evidence. Writing in 1992, and apparently oblivious of the great mass of revisionist literature by then available, Michael Foot insisted that, had he and his two co-authors of 1940 had in their possession all the historical evidence that had come into the public domain in the intervening half-century, they would have presented their indictment against Chamberlain with even greater assurance and ferocity.[73] But the *Guilty Men* thesis did enjoy one last great triumph with the publication in 1963 of *The Appeasers* by Martin Gilbert and Richard Gott. Significantly, the authors were men of a younger generation, able presumably to take a more dispassionate view of the pre-war era than their seniors. Yet here was another swingeing indictment of the political leaders of the 1930s in general and of Chamberlain in particular. The book's commercial success, not only in Britain but in Europe and the United States as well, suggested a still ready appetite for its well-rehearsed message. The vivid passage with which the authors chose to close their narrative encapsulates a whole era of historical writing:

The fate of one other man illuminates the end of a policy and of an era. In 1937 Chamberlain had installed Sir Horace Wilson in a room adjoining the Cabinet Room at No. 10, looking out over the Horse Guards parade. On May 11 1940, Wilson arrived as usual. As he opened the door, he saw, on the sofa confronting him, Brendan Bracken and Randolph Churchill: 'They stared at Sir Horace, but no one spoke or smiled. Then he withdrew, never to return to that seat most proximate to power.'[74]

But the less than ecstatic reception of Gilbert and Gott's book by professional historians suggested that, in the academic world at least, the mood was beginning to change. Other new writers *were* prepared to look again at the record of the pre-war years, free from the prejudices of contemporary authors and suspicious of the neat simplicity of their judgements. *The Appeasers* may not have been the swansong of the orthodox view, but reactions to it showed that this view was at last open to challenge. We must therefore turn to the growth of a revisionist historiography. Before doing so, however, one further key element in the blackening of Chamberlain's name must be considered, one which straddles the realms of history and historiography – the man who succeeded him as Prime Minister, Winston Churchill.

Notes

1. Chamberlain MSS, NC1/15/4/7, Hilda Chamberlain to Annie Chamberlain 14 June 1940.
2. *Ibid.*, NC13/18/788, Ball to Chamberlain 12 Oct. 1940.
3. *Ibid.*, NC L.Add.131, Chamberlain to Ball 28 Oct. 1940.
4. M. Foot, *Loyalists and Loners* (London, 1986), p.181.
5. S. Hoggart and D. Leigh, *Michael Foot: a portrait* (London, 1981), p.80.
6. 'Cato', *Guilty Men* (London, 1940), p.16.
7. P. Addison, *The Road to 1945: British Politics and the Second World War* (London, 1975), pp.107, 112.
8. Foot, *Loyalists and Loners*, p.180.
9. *Guilty Men*, p.21.
10. *Ibid.*, p.76.
11. *Ibid.*, pp.16,19.
12. K. Young (ed.), *The Diaries of Sir Robert Bruce Lockhart*, vol.2 (London, 1980), p.42.
13. *Guilty Men*, p.87.
14. *Ibid.*
15. G. Mander, *We Were Not All Wrong* (London, 1941), p.27.

16. R.S. Churchill, *The Rise and Fall of Sir Anthony Eden* (London, 1959), p.65.
17. Mander, *Not All Wrong*, p.78.
18. *Ibid.*, pp.16–17.
19. 'Gracchus', *Your MP* (London, 1944), p.7.
20. 'Celticus', *Why Not Trust the Tories* (London, 1944), p.13.
21. 'Diplomaticus', *Can the Tories Win the Peace* (London, 1945), p.11.
22. 'Cassius', *Brendan and Beverley: An Extravaganza* (London, 1944), p.47.
23. 'Cassius', *The Trial of Mussolini* (London, 1943), pp.80–1.
24. Q. Hogg, *The Left was Never Right* (London, 1945), p.81.
25. K. Middlemas and J. Barnes, *Baldwin* (London, 1969), p.1060.
26. At one point the TUC adopted the slogan, 'Forward to the 80s not back to the 30s'.
27. A.J.P. Taylor, *English History 1914–1945* (Oxford, 1965), p.375.
28. H. Jones and M. Kandiah (eds), *The Myth of Consensus* (London, 1996), p.104.
29. S. Constantine, *Social Conditions in Britain 1918–1939* (London, 1983), p.1.
30. J. Barnes and D. Nicholson (eds), *The Empire at Bay* (London, 1988), p.845.
31. J. Ramsden, *The Age of Churchill and Eden 1940–1957* (London, 1995), p.88.
32. H. Macmillan, *Tides of Fortune, 1945–1955* (London, 1969), p.287.
33. Ramsden, *Churchill and Eden*, pp.61–2.
34. *Time* 8 Dec. 1961.
35. Young (ed.), *Lockhart Diaries*, vol.2, p.236.
36. *Times Literary Supplement* 1 Dec.1961.
37. Avon MSS, AP23/60/7, Eden to Salisbury 28 Aug. 1957. See also P. Beck, 'Politicians versus Historians: Lord Avon's "Appeasement Battle" against "Lamentably Appeasement-Minded" Historians', *Twentieth Century British History*, 9, 3 (1998).
38. H.S. Truman, *Years of Trial and Hope 1946–1953* (London, 1956), p.351.
39. J. Ramsden, *"That will Depend on Who Writes the History": Winston Churchill as his own Historian* (London, 1997), p.17.
40. *Newsweek* 19 April 1999.
41. *The Listener* 14 Oct. 1948.
42. Chamberlain MSS, BC4/8/90, H. Chamberlain to D. Lloyd 16 Oct. 1948.
43. D.C. Watt, 'Sir Lewis Namier and contemporary European history', *Cambridge Journal*, June 1954, p.597.
44. J. Wheeler-Bennett, *Munich: Prologue to Tragedy* (London, 1948), pp.3–4.
45. L. Namier, *Diplomatic Prelude, 1938–9* (London, 1948), p.41.
46. Wheeler-Bennett, *Munich*, p.268.
47. *Ibid.*, p.16, emphasis added.
48. *Ibid.*, p.434.

49. Namier, *Prelude*, p.ix.
50. Wheeler-Bennett, *Munich*, p.434.
51. E. Wiskemann, *Europe of the Dictators 1919–1945* (London, 1966), pp.5 and 145.
52. A.L. Rowse, *All Souls and Appeasement* (London, 1961), p.13.
53. *Ibid.*, p.83.
54. *Ibid.*, p.84.
55. *Ibid.*, p.117.
56. M. Muggeridge (ed.), *Ciano's Diary 1939–1943* (London, 1947), p.10.
57. Rowse, *All Souls*, p.19.
58. *Ibid.*, pp.8–9.
59. M. George, *The Hollow Men: An Examination of British Foreign Policy between the years 1933–1939* (London, 1965), pp.41, 39, 61, 57–8, 36, 228.
60. *Ibid.*, p.7 (preface by Rowse).
61. R. Vansittart, *The Mist Procession* (London, 1958), p.430.
62. W. Strang, *Britain in World Affairs* (London, 1961), p.321.
63. A. Duff Cooper, *Old Men Forget* (London, 1953), p.200.
64. Earl of Swinton, *Sixty Years of Power* (London, 1966), p.110.
65. Lord Winterton, *Orders of the Day* (London, 1953), p.260.
66. R.Boothby, *I Fight to Live* (London, 1947), p.93.
67. R.Boothby, *My Yesterday, Your Tomorrow* (London, 1962), p.124.
68. *Ibid.*, pp.130–1.
69. See article by James Driscoll in *New York Herald Tribune*, 15 May 1938. For a recent corrective, see N. Rose, *The Cliveden Set* (London, 2000)
70. W. McElwee, *Britain's Locust Years 1918–1940* (London, 1962), p.257.
71. C.L. Mowat, *Britain Between the Wars 1918–1940* (London, 1955), p.413.
72. Chamberlain MSS, NC1/15/5/6–7, H. Chamberlain to W. Clark and to Secretary to the BBC 13 Oct. 1948.
73. *Evening Standard* 14 May 1992.
74. M. Gilbert and R. Gott, *The Appeasers* (London, 1963), p.352.

|4|

The Churchill factor

No man alive has more right to tell the world 'I told you so'
. . . than Winston Churchill.[1]

It was to the infinite disadvantage of Neville Chamberlain's
long-term reputation that his successor as Prime Minister was
Winston Churchill. To this day Churchill retains a unique place
in the popular pantheon of British statesmen. In a radio poll held
in 1999 to determine the Briton of the millennium, Churchill
emerged as a creditable second to William Shakespeare, trailing
the bard by a mere 760 votes. It has become usual to see the
hand-over of May 1940 from one first minister of the crown to
another in very different terms from those associated with most
other changes of British government. This was not part of a
continuum in the on-going evolution of British politics. Rather
the arrival of Churchill in 10 Downing Street represented an
abrupt break with the past, a new beginning, indeed a rebirth of
the British national will for survival. It was a prime ministerial
changeover which confirmed the unsubtle, black and white
historical analysis of this period pioneered by the authors of
Guilty Men. The fall of Chamberlain's government in May 1940
came to mark the end of a sorry period in British history and the
mighty figure of Winston Churchill was there to symbolize a
new and altogether happier beginning. The contrast between the
two men could not, it seems, be more stark. On the one hand we
have the dull and opinionated provincial, the man who, as Lloyd
George once suggested, would have made a reasonable Lord
Mayor of Birmingham in a lean year but who, confronted with
problems way beyond his own capacity and competence,

brought the country to the very brink of disaster. On the other stands the great statesman of truly global stature, quite simply, as A.J.P. Taylor once put it, 'the saviour of his country'.[2] The historian C.L. Mowat, whose study of inter-war Britain published in 1955 was for many years the best general account of this period, well captured this point:

> The end of Chamberlain's government was the end of an era. The National government, with its nine years of Conservative rule, prolonging the dominance of the Conservatives during the twenties, had reached its term; the indecision, the weaknesses of leadership – Baldwin's indolent optimism, Chamberlain's misdirected zeal – the disunity within the nation, all had run their course to this fatal moment.[3]

Churchill is a key factor, in several different ways, for our understanding of the destruction of Neville Chamberlain's historical reputation.

In the first place Churchill, as the great outsider of the 1930s, bore no responsibility for the mistakes and misdeeds of the National Government. When that administration was formed in August 1931, no place was found for him within it. Though his recall was frequently mooted in the years which followed, Churchill did not in fact rejoin the government until invited to do so by Chamberlain at the outbreak of war in his old post of First Lord of the Admiralty, in itself an apparent admission that he had been right and Chamberlain wrong in their respective diagnoses of the international situation over the preceding period. Churchill's exclusion from office for most of the decade was to be explained, as Lloyd George once argued, as the consequence of the 'distrust and trepidation with which mediocrity views genius at close quarters'.[4] The historian, A.L. Rowse, confirmed that 'among the personal motives of this coming together in 1931 was the determination, among these second-rate men, to keep out the two men of genius, Lloyd George and Churchill'.[5] Be that as it may, the very fact that Churchill held no office in these years worked to his great advantage and, by extension, to Chamberlain's detriment. This was something which the great man appreciated full well. When in his memoirs he came to describe his continued exclusion from the cabinet after the General Election of 1935 he admitted that the then Prime Minister, Stanley Baldwin, 'knew no more than I, how great was the service he was doing me in preventing me from being involved in all the Cabinet compromises and shortcomings of the next three years'.[6] In this way the picture developed of Churchill as the voice in the wilderness, the almost isolated prophet who had consistently warned the government, without obvious impact, of the dangers posed by Hitler's Germany and of the calamity towards which the Guilty Men were remorselessly leading the country. It was an analysis which well-placed contemporaries later came to endorse. 'The truth is', wrote Lord Halifax in June 1940, by which time Churchill's lonely critique seemed to have been vindicated, 'that Winston is about the only person who has an absolutely clean sheet.'[7]

An uneasy member of Chamberlain's wartime government from September 1939, Churchill was at hand in the crisis of 1940 to emerge as the National Saviour. It was surely more than mere coincidence that the end of the period of the Phoney War coincided with Churchill's assumption of the premiership. In the weeks and months which followed, the new Prime Minister forged a symbiotic relationship with the British people. 1940 was the 'finest hour' for both Churchill and the British people. As the latter awaited the Battle of Britain, they 'found themselves again, after twenty years of indecision. They turned away from past regrets and faced the future unafraid.'[8] Whatever else Churchill did in his long career, 1940 represented a peak of achievement which he could not hope to repeat. Asked during the 1950s to name the year he would most like to relive, Churchill could only give one answer, '1940, every time, every time'.[9] It was at this point that the British people embarked upon a national epic which would take them from Dunkirk to Hitler's defeat and death five years later, via the Battle of Britain and Churchill's incomparable speeches of resolution and defiance. Isaiah Berlin put the relationship between leader and led in these terms:

> After he had spoken to them in the summer of 1940 as no one has ever before or since, [the British people] conceived a new idea of themselves which their own prowess and the admiration of the world has since established as a heroic image in the history of mankind. . . .[10]

Churchill was the one man who could put a definitive end to one era and embark upon another. As he himself recorded: 'At last I had the authority to give directions over the whole scene.

I felt as if I were walking with destiny, and that all my past life had been but a preparation for this hour and for this trial.'[11] His motives belonged to a different plane from those of ordinary mortals. According to J.H. Plumb, 'the long policy of appeasement, the weakening of Britain's world role, the acceptance of oppression . . . were to Churchill a denial of England's historical destiny and because a denial, bound to end in disaster'.[12] But the transition from Chamberlain to Churchill, from the era of the Guilty Men to that of the few who had been right all along about the menace of Nazi Germany, but who had not been listened to, could not have been secured by man alone. Providence itself was surely involved. Dining with Churchill during the war, Lady Halifax confessed that she 'got slightly confused as to his meaning when he said with some emotion: "That old man up there intended me to be where I am at this time" until [she] realized that he was talking about the Almighty and His Divine Providence and Purposes.'[13] More than four decades later Lord Hailsham, who as Quintin Hogg had entered national politics in 1938 as a supporter of Chamberlain before withdrawing his support in the critical Commons division of May 1940, was of the same mind. 'The one case, in which I think I can see the finger of God in contemporary history, is Churchill's arrival at the premiership at that precise moment in 1940.'[14]

Placed in the supreme office by the hand of God, Churchill in 1940 himself began to experience that process of deification by the British people which, to this day, renders a rational and scholarly reappraisal of his actual contribution to the British war effort a somewhat hazardous endeavour. This is not the place to embark upon such an enquiry though there is more than a grain of truth in Clement Attlee's suggestion that his chief contribution to winning the war lay in talking about it.[15] With his magnificent oratory Churchill came to epitomize the determination of the British people, at whatever cost, to resist and overcome the Nazi aggressor, becoming in the process the very incarnation of John Bull. And certainly this meant playing a role which Chamberlain would have been constitutionally incapable of fulfilling. As one contemporary put it, 'Remembering the Man of 1940, one is inclined to think of him as the *one* ringing voice, speaking determination and fury in contrast with Neville Chamberlain's pathos and perturbation'.[16] Contemporaries had long recognized that war was Churchill's natural milieu. 'War is the only thing that interests him in politics', Lord Robert Cecil declared as long ago as 1927.[17] The MP A.P. Herbert suggested that Churchill 'rather enjoyed a war'.[18] No one would ever have written this of Neville Chamberlain. But in the face of national peril it was Churchill's approach which the nation needed and the people showed their approval. In July 1940 a public opinion poll revealed Churchill enjoying an approval rating of 88 per cent, a figure which did not fall below 78 per cent before Germany's final defeat.

By 1945 history itself seemed ready to confirm that Churchill was indeed the saviour of his nation. As the man who had won the war – in itself a rather curious accolade in the light of Britain's contribution to the allied cause relative to that of the United States and the Soviet Union – his prestige had never been higher. But, as John Ramsden has persuasively shown, the glory of Churchill's achievement did not, notwithstanding his electoral rejection by the British people in July 1945, fade with the passage of time. Far from it. It was in the post-war era that the process really began which transformed him into the 'greatest living Englishman'.[19] Churchill still had political ambitions at the end of the Second World War. The fact that he remained leader of the Conservative party until 1955, by which time he was in his eighty-first year, is testimony to this fact. But he also now had a second objective, to justify himself before the bar of history. And, though he often proclaimed his readiness to accept the verdict of history, he was also determined to be one of the historians. Churchill 'acted as his own Boswell to his own Dr. Johnson – and no more zealous Boswell ever scribbled about a grander Johnson'.[20]

Churchill's six volume history of the Second World War was published between 1948 and 1954. It was widely accepted that the author was uniquely placed to give a definitive account of the great events he described, an impression of authority which was confirmed by the great weight of documentation which his writing contained. The first volume, entitled *The Gathering Storm*, focused largely on the period before the outbreak of hostilities and sold more copies than any of the succeeding tomes. Like all political memoirs Churchill's books aimed first and foremost to justify his own role and to glorify his own achievements. Yet, thought one distinguished historian, 'with his huge resources he was able to cast his work into an almost official mould and often it rises to a degree of objectivity rare in the memoirs of a great statesman'.[21] In private Churchill was open about his intentions. 'Winston's attitude to the war memoirs was "this is not history, this is my case".'[22] 'Give me the facts', he is reputed to have told one of his young researchers, 'and I will twist them the way I want to suit my argument.'[23] But the combination of Churchill's enormous prestige, the fact that he was the first significant writer in the field of Second World War historiography and his magnificent command of the English language – recognized in 1953 by the award of the Nobel Prize for Literature – ensured that the War Memoirs set the tone for writing on the period 1931–45 for at least a generation. For most people what happened in this period evolved into what Churchill said had happened. 'Churchill the historian', wrote Jack Plumb in 1969, 'lies at the very heart of all historiography of the Second World War *and will always remain there.*'[24] Later writers adopted Churchill's ideas and even sometimes his vocabulary as their own. His notion of the 'locust years' found itself evolving into the title of a popular American study of the inter-war era. Writers could give added credibility to their own interpretations by stressing coincidence with what Churchill had written. 'This is not merely my judgement', asserted A.L. Rowse of the view that the Second World War need never have happened, 'it is also Churchill's.'[25] Few in the years following the publication of Churchill's account dared to challenge his intellectual command. Churchill had spoken and for many that was enough. 'For the bulk of the historical profession in America', suggested D.C. Watt in 1976, 'Sir Winston Churchill's view of British policy before 1939 has hardly required a moment's critical examination.'[26] Those who did venture to question the new Churchillian orthodoxy could be sure of a hostile reception. One reviewer of Iain Macleod's sympathetic biography of Neville Chamberlain suggested that 'this book is astonishing. . . . So far as this generation is concerned, Churchill has spoken, and nothing will make anything out of Chamberlain except the fact that he accepted Munich in 1938 and that, a year later, Churchill was proved right.'[27]

Chamberlain was not in fact the chief target of *The Gathering Storm.* Churchill's most withering indictment was reserved for Stanley Baldwin, Chamberlain's predecessor as Prime Minister. He it was whom Churchill's celebrated index entry described as confessing to 'putting party before country', a gloss on Baldwin's 'appalling frankness' speech of November 1936 which it is impossible for the objective historian to sustain. In his *History of the English Speaking Peoples*, only published in 1954 but largely written before the outbreak of war, Churchill wrote of the 'squalid conduct' of the Conservative party in the period 1932–7, the years *before* Chamberlain became Prime Minister. But there was also plenty in *The Gathering Storm* to damage Chamberlain's reputation. Conscious, over-conscious indeed, of his historical destiny, Churchill was captivated by an epic view of history and the way in which great men could divert the course of events. This was very apparent in his life of his ancestor, the Duke of Marlborough, perhaps his most distinguished piece of historical writing, published in four volumes between 1934 and 1938. The developments of the 1930s are also painted in simple terms as a battle between good and evil and, if Hitler provided, obviously enough, the epitome of evil, Churchill left his reader with few doubts that those like Chamberlain who had failed to appreciate Hitler's evil were themselves guilty of grievous crimes. The protagonists of appeasement are presented as weak men whose cowardice was matched only by their lack of insight. Indeed, there was much here about 'what ought to have been done', an approach which should in itself have thrown into serious question Churchill's credentials for historical objectivity. No appreciation was shown of the determinants of the government's policy particularly in the domestic arena. Appeasement was a policy which was not only wrong but also wilfully wrong. The idea that Chamberlain and Churchill were separated by irreconcilable differences owed much to this book.

Chamberlain's supporters were understandably annoyed by Churchill's account, but mostly felt disinclined to contradict him. Churchill's main purpose, judged Lord Halifax, was not only to write history but also to 'make a record for himself'.[28] Chamberlain's widow was 'naturally very much strained by Churchill's remarks', especially as 'these are not real misstatements which could be corrected, but wholesale omissions and assumptions that certain things are now recognised as facts which actually have no such position'.[29] But outright rebuttal would have served little purpose other than to arouse renewed contempt for Chamberlain's memory. In a cautious review of *The Gathering Storm*, Chamberlain's long-time cabinet colleague Samuel Hoare praised Churchill's record, but suggested that the jury on appeasement would remain out until more documentary evidence was available. As it was, Churchill's 'master hand makes the picture look very simple. Appeasement and blindness versus courage and foresight, disarmament versus defence, butter versus guns. The issues seem so clear that no one should be in any doubt about them.'[30]

To understand the full impact of Churchill's writings upon Chamberlain's reputation, the main elements of the former's argument must be outlined. He had given a clear indication of his likely approach in a speech in Brussels in November 1945, arguing that a strong allied stand against Hitler at an early stage in his career would have encouraged his German opponents to remove him. Central to Churchill's analysis indeed is the contention that the Second World War could have been avoided, that it was the 'unnecessary war'. In fact, 'there can hardly ever have been a war more easy to prevent than this second Armageddon'.[31] This implied that those charged with the conduct of Britain's affairs had much to answer for. Indeed, Churchill declared it to be his aim to show how the 'malice of the wicked was reinforced by the weakness of the victims'.[32] However warlike Hitler's intentions, steps could and should have been taken to stop him in his tracks. The Churchillian argument suggested that faster British rearmament could have deterred the German dictator, that a readiness to take a stand at crucial moments could have halted his rake's progress before it was too late and that a Grand Coalition was not only a realistic proposition in the 1930s but something which might even have led to Hitler's overthrow without armed conflict. In each case Chamberlain as Chancellor of the Exchequer or Prime Minister was vulnerable to Churchill's charges. Chamberlain personally was presented as 'alert and businesslike' but 'opinionated and self-confident in a very high degree'. Sadly 'he ran into tides the force of which he could not measure, and met hurricanes from which he did not flinch, but with which he could not cope'.[33] In many ways, therefore, Churchill added respectability to the charge sheet already drawn up by Cato's *Guilty Men*.

Over specific events where Chamberlain had been intimately involved, Churchill's offensive was aimed at an open goal. The former's rejection of Roosevelt's peace initiative in January 1938 represented 'the last frail chance to save the world from tyranny otherwise than by war'.[34] When it came to the Munich agreement Churchill needed to do little more than cite his speeches of the time:

And do not suppose that this is the end. This is only the beginning of the reckoning. This is only the first sip, the first foretaste of a bitter cup which will be proffered to us year by year unless, by a supreme recovery of moral health and martial vigour, we arise again and take our stand for freedom as in the olden time.[35]

Churchill argued that the year's breathing space, which some said had been 'won' by the Munich settlement, in fact left Britain and France in a worse position relative to Hitler's Germany than was the case in September 1938. He dealt with the more difficult period after September 1939, when he had shared cabinet office with Chamberlain, by subtly distancing himself from the Prime Minister. 'The sedate, sincere but routine character of the Administration did not evoke that intense effort, either in the governing circles or in the munition factories, which was vital.'[36] Even the disastrous Norwegian campaign which served as the prelude to Chamberlain's overthrow and Churchill's assumption of the premiership, was presented in the most favourable light from the latter's point of view. 'Had I been allowed to act with freedom and design when I first demanded permission, a far more agreeable conclusion might have been reached in this key theatre, with favourable consequences in every direction.'[37] The reader is thus prepared for the moment of Chamberlain's replacement by Churchill, with the latter ready to lead the British people into a new and more glorious era. 'I was conscious of a profound sense of relief. . . . My warnings over the last six years had been so numerous, so detailed, and were now so terribly vindicated, that no one could gainsay me.'[38]

So persuasive is the Churchillian version of events that Churchill's own position must be subjected to closer analysis. Many were those who were ready to accept Churchill at his own estimation. Even a sympathetic biographer of Chamberlain's loyal Foreign Secretary, Lord Halifax, could suggest that Churchill was 'the one man whose record was entirely clean, who had predicted this moment [Munich] with the prescience of genius, and for years seen his warnings disregarded'.[39] Yet it is now clear that acceptance of Churchill's interpretation of the 1930s involves a sleight of hand to conceal clear inconsistencies on the part of the Great Man. In the first place we must dispel the idea that his exclusion from office in this decade was part of a conspiracy by lesser men to control one of far greater ability. His departure from the Conservative shadow cabinet may have been 'the most unfortunate event that occurred between the two wars', but it was his own fault.[40] It was not so much a case of a man of decision being cast outside as it was the very quality of Churchill's decisions which tended to put him beyond the political pale. Having resigned from the Conservative front bench in January 1931 as a result of the bipartisan policy on India to which Baldwin had committed the party, he had no real claim to office at the formation of the National Government a few months later. In any case his career to date had been strewn with errors and misjudgements which took much of the shine from his positive achievements. Chamberlain's assessment of his then governmental colleague, written in August 1925, was not the shortsighted assessment of one myopic observer, but one which would have been widely shared:

> What a brilliant creature he is! But there is somehow a great gulf between him and me which I don't think I shall ever cross. I like him. I like his humour and vitality. I like his courage. . . . But not for all the joys of Paradise would I be a member of his staff! Mercurial! A much abused word, but it is the literal description of his temperament.[41]

As the 1930s went on Churchill further blotted his copybook and placed renewed question-marks over his judgement, even among those inclined to support him over his critique of Nazi Germany, by his continued opposition to the government's liberal policy towards India and his support for Edward VIII during the 1936 Abdication Crisis. A fortnight before the outbreak of war one veteran diplomat recorded:

> There are I believe a fair number of people who think and say that in these times Winston ought to be in the Government, but why? Look at his past history: give him credit for not having dismissed the fleet in August 1914, but after that: Antwerp, Dardanelles, Denikin Expedition, Treasury (change to Gold Standard), India Bill, and his attitude in the Abdication. Could anybody have a worse record?[42]

It was Churchill who largely excluded himself from the decision-making of the 1930s.

When it came to questions of foreign policy, Churchill was

never as consistent and virtuous as his later account in *The Gathering Storm* tended to suggest. On closer examination the image of Churchill as the resolute and unwavering opponent of the 1930s' dictators – a reasonable basis from which to launch an assault upon Neville Chamberlain – begins to dissolve. His contemporary criticism of the aggression of totalitarian regimes other than Hitler's Germany was at best muted. When Japan invaded Manchuria in 1931 Churchill declared that there would be a general unwillingness to fight or to 'make any special exertions in defence of the present government of China'.[43] Similarly, his record over Ethiopia and the Spanish Civil War failed in reality to place him in a distinctly different camp from Chamberlain and the National Government. Nor did Churchill rush to denounce the Anglo–German Naval Agreement of 1935. As late as 1937 he even seemed willing to give Hitler the possible benefit of the doubt. Accepting that history was full of examples of men who had risen to power by 'wicked and even frightful methods' but who had gone on to become great figures, enriching the 'story of mankind', he held out the possibility that 'so it may be with Hitler'.[44] That October he told the readers of the *Evening Standard* that there was a 'good chance of no major war taking place in our time'.[45] Before 1938 his most significantly outspoken criticism of government policy related to its failure to uphold Baldwin's pledge to maintain air parity with Germany. The government, however, had come to admit its failure in this respect and to begin to increase the pace of rearmament. As long ago as 1954, in a short and persuasive article (but one which had little impact upon popular perceptions), Richard Powers concluded that Churchill's stance in the mid-1930s was much closer to that of the majority of his party than had been generally recognized or than he had subsequently described it.[46] Not until May 1938 did Churchill begin consistently to withhold his support from the government over questions of foreign policy in the division lobby of the House of Commons.

As regards his contemporary attitude towards Chamberlain, it would be wrong to perpetuate the stark contrast of traditional historiography. Whatever his subsequent attitude towards Chamberlain's shortcomings in the diplomatic field, Churchill had suggested to Baldwin back in 1928 that Chamberlain would make a good Foreign Secretary. The two men had generally worked well together in government in the late 1920s and had never been seen as clear-cut antagonists. Open warfare between

them was largely restricted to a period of about six months
between the signing of the Munich agreement and the German
occupation of Prague. Indeed it was Churchill who seconded
Chamberlain's nomination for the Conservative party leadership
following Baldwin's retirement in May 1937. As the party's
senior Privy Councillor he may have felt obliged to do this; but
the fulsome manner in which he went about his task suggests
something more than the constraints of mere duty. He was
particularly complimentary about Chamberlain's contribution
to the rearmament policies of the Baldwin government. Later in
the year, when the cabinet appeared at the Nyon Conference to
be standing up to Mussolini's transgressions in the
Mediterranean, Churchill went out of his way to praise the
government's foreign policy during the Party Conference: 'His
Majesty's Ministers', he insisted, 'possessed the confidence of the
Empire in the sober and resolute policy which they were pursu-
ing.'[47] In a typical passage of purple prose in his memoirs
Churchill described his feelings of loss and devastation following Eden's resignation from Chamberlain's government in
February 1938. Yet he was quick to sign a round-robin in
support of the Prime Minister's policy and, when rumours circulated of a pro-Eden plot, he lost no time in emphasizing his
continued backing for the government. As the Chief Whip
recorded, Churchill

> wanted to assure me . . . that he had no hand whatsoever
> in any intrigue against the Government and he said that
> from his conversation with the Prime Minister in the
> Lobby a few days ago he felt sure that the Prime Minister's
> point of view on the present foreign situation and his own
> were not divergent.[48]

Policy towards Czechoslovakia in 1938 is usually taken as the
most striking contrast between Churchill and Chamberlain, but
even here there is scope for qualification. The former's starting
point was not all that different from that of the Prime Minister.
In the spring of 1938 Churchill seems to have been convinced by
the Sudeten German leader Henlein that a satisfactory settlement could be reached if Britain and France managed to
persuade the Prague government to make concessions to its
German minority. In late June he argued that the good offices of
Britain and France were likely to lead to a solution based on
home rule for the Sudetens within the Czech state. Then, in an

article in the *Daily Telegraph* on 26 July, he suggested that the Czechs owed it 'to the Western Powers that every concession compatible with the sovereignty and integrity of their state shall be made'. The German ambassador in London reported that Churchill's adherents did not shrink from the idea of the incorporation of the Sudetenland into Germany. Churchill may not have joined in the near hysterical show of enthusiasm which greeted Chamberlain's announcement in the House of Commons that he had accepted Hitler's invitation to talks in Munich at the end of September, but we do know that he shook the Prime Minister's hand as he left the Chamber, wished him 'God speed' and later announced in the press that he supported what Chamberlain was attempting 'from the bottom of my heart'.[49]

Churchill's critique of the actual agreement reached at Munich was trenchant and clear and there began a period in which he and Chamberlain were most clearly at odds. That said, there was always something slightly incongruous about the man who had spent so much time criticizing the government for its deficiencies in defence planning now advocating a line which might easily have led to a war, for which by his own estimation Britain was unprepared. Yet on 10 March 1939, in other words before the critical events usually taken to signal a change of direction in British foreign policy, Churchill declared that he found much to approve in the government's attitude. At the same time he expressed his admiration for the management of the Treasury through the 1930s – for which, of course, Chamberlain more than any other single individual could take the credit – which had enabled enormous rearmament to take place without damaging the country's financial stability.[50] Once the British guarantee to Poland had been issued at the end of the month, it is clear that Churchill's differences with Chamberlain were much reduced and that he would have been ready, had the invitation been delivered, to enter a government of which the latter remained the head. In the event Churchill had to wait until the war crisis in September before rejoining the cabinet. Chamberlain had always recognised that this would be a necessary consequence of the failure of his own policy to avoid war, but had regarded Churchill's inclusion before that point was reached as unnecessarily provocative from Hitler's point of view.

But it is the period when the two men served in government together – and not just the time up to the prime ministerial changeover of May 1940 but including also the months when

Chamberlain served as Lord President of the Council under Churchill's premiership – which offers the most effective rejoinder to the Churchillian version of events with its emphasis on the notion of a clear break and the start of better times once the new man moved into 10 Downing Street. What is particularly striking is the strength and effectiveness of the partnership which the two men formed in government, a development which Chamberlain's sister later attributed to 'Neville's extraordinary powers of patience and forbearance'.[51] As one recent writer has put it, 'it was only at the end of an often strained relationship that the two of them had really appreciated the talents possessed by each other'.[52] Churchill was impressed by Chamberlain's handling of cabinet discussions, and told him so and, when the Prime Minister rejected Hitler's suggestion of peace talks in the autumn of 1939, declared 'I'm proud to follow you'.[53] In February 1940 Churchill told Cecil King of the *Daily Mirror* that he would prefer Chamberlain to Eden as Prime Minister 'by eight to one'.[54]

It was an important element in the argument of *The Gathering Storm* that Chamberlain had been insufficiently vigorous in the prosecution of the war. At the time, however, Churchill took a rather different line. Like the Prime Minister he calculated on the war being a long one, in which Britain's chief strength would derive from the husbanding of her resources and those of the Empire over a period of years. He therefore opposed any steps by Britain which might escalate the conflict in Europe and precipitate German retaliation. Of the possibility of aerial attacks on German cities, Churchill wrote in the first days of the war: 'It is in our own interests that the war should be conducted in accordance with the more humane conceptions, and that we should follow and not precede the Germans in the process, no doubt inevitable, of deepening severity and violence.'[55] Chamberlain's ill-judged remarks about Hitler 'missing the bus' and his public statement in April 1940 that he was ten times more confident of victory than at the outbreak of hostilities provided Churchill with an easy target when he came to write his memoirs. But the views of the contemporary Churchill were not very dissimilar from those of his political chief. In his broadcasts the First Lord of the Admiralty offered an equally optimistic evaluation of Britain's prospects, telling his audience in November 1939 that 'if we come through the winter without any large or important event occurring we shall in fact have gained the first campaign of the war'.[56]

The circumstances of Chamberlain's replacement by Churchill in May 1940 also merit reconsideration. Historians have long been conscious of the paradox that, if it really was a parliamentary debate on the campaign in Norway which precipitated Chamberlain's downfall, then there was a strange irony that it should be Churchill, who as First Lord of the Admiralty was more directly responsible than any other minister for the mistakes of strategy and tactics which had led to military disaster, who emerged as the beneficiary of Chamberlain's misfortune. A.J.P. Taylor, whose understanding of this situation now seems less than complete, judged that 'public opinion ignored these niceties. It judged men by their spirit. Chamberlain paid the penalty for appeasement. Churchill reaped the reward for his years of solitary warning'.[57] To his credit Churchill did not try to distance himself from Chamberlain in the speech with which he wound up the parliamentary debate on the Norwegian campaign from the government front bench, even though opposition speakers, particularly Lloyd George, had encouraged him to do so. But many insiders would have been very annoyed if Churchill had followed this advice. According to John Colville, any attempt by the First Lord to disclaim responsibility would have created 'a first-class political crisis, because the country believes that Winston is the man of action who is winning the war and little realise how ineffective, and indeed harmful, much of his energy is proving itself to be'.[58]

More importantly, we are now conscious that the stark break with the past of Churchillian mythology did not extend very far beyond the pages of the new premier's memoirs. Early accounts, such as that given in *Your MP*, implied that the nation faced a stark choice in May 1940 between Winston Churchill and Neville Chamberlain. This was far from being the case. Churchill's emergence as Prime Minister in May 1940 may have been divinely ordained but, if so, the will of the Almighty was nearly thwarted by the acts of man. Chamberlain himself, the King and the vast majority of the Conservative party would undoubtedly have preferred to see Lord Halifax rather than Churchill assume Chamberlain's mantle, a succession which would clearly have indicated the main lines of continuity in British policy. A.L. Rowse, who later became an unequivocal scourge of the 'appeasers' in general and of Neville Chamberlain in particular, at the time wrote to the press in support of a Halifax premiership. The leaders of the Labour party, despite some later assertions to the contrary, would also have acquiesced in Halifax's elevation. In his contemporary diary entry Hugh Dalton, Labour's front-bench foreign affairs spokesman, declared that Attlee, the party leader 'agrees with my preference for Halifax over Churchill but we both think that either would be tolerable'.[59] With hindsight Churchill clearly stands out as the *right* choice for the premiership in the crisis of 1940. At the time, however, he was by no means the obvious choice. He owed his promotion essentially to the fact that the main parties were prepared to serve under him at a moment when all saw the need for a truly National Government.

There *was* a decisive change in May 1940, but largely because the nature of the war changed coincidentally with but independently of Churchill's assumption of the premiership. At the very moment that Chamberlain contemplated his future following the disappointing outcome of the parliamentary division on the Norwegian expedition, Hitler launched his western offensive and the Phoney War came to an abrupt end. In this situation Churchill showed qualities of leadership which Chamberlain would probably have lacked, but the fact remains that these were new circumstances of a type which the latter had not had to face while Prime Minister. Churchill inspired as Chamberlain never could. But while the latter's voice may have lacked the wonderful resonance of Churchill's, he was not incapable of expressing comparable sentiments. In a radio broadcast later in the year Chamberlain declared:

> We are a solid and united nation which would rather go down to ruin than admit the domination of the Nazis . . . If the enemy does try to invade this country we will fight him in the air and on the sea; we will fight him on the beaches with every weapon we have. He may manage here and there to make a breakthrough: if he does we will fight him on every road, in every village, and in every house, until he or we are utterly destroyed. . . . We shall be fighting for our hearths and homes, and we shall be fighting with the conviction that our cause is the cause of humanity and peace against cruelty and persecution, of right against wrong; a cause that surely has the blessing of Almighty God. It would be a faint heart indeed that could doubt of our success.[60]

Read with a Churchillian intonation, these words could easily have come from the mouth of Chamberlain's successor.

The construction of Churchill's government also indicated a continuity which was at odds with the way in which he later portrayed these events. Churchill was less ruthless as a politician than as a historian. Including Churchill himself there were twenty-one ministers, out of a total of thirty-four, who had also served under Chamberlain. Of the big four who had dominated the era of appeasement – Chamberlain, Halifax, Simon and Hoare – only the last was now cast into the political wilderness, being appointed ambassador to Franco's Spain. Most importantly, Chamberlain himself occupied a crucial position inside the new government. In part this reflected Churchill's appreciation of his own political predicament and his need to ensure the loyalty of the Conservative party machine. But it was also an indication of the value which he had come to place on Chamberlain's abilities and it is clear that he would have liked him to occupy a higher position in the new administration than Lord President of the Council, but had to back down in the face of Labour opposition. 'In these eight months we have worked together', wrote Churchill, 'I am proud to have won your friendship and your confidence in an ever increasing measure. To a very large extent I am in your hands – and I feel no fear of that.'[61] As it was, Chamberlain quickly emerged as an extremely important figure in Churchill's team, virtually a supremo on the domestic front and one in whom the new premier felt confidence in entrusting the chairmanship of the cabinet whenever the business of the war impelled his own absence. Chamberlain was also asked to chair a small committee which examined the consequences of a possible French collapse. He was, Churchill admitted to Cecil King, 'the best man he had – head and shoulders over the average man in the administration'.[62] Chamberlain took evident delight in reporting Churchill's words: 'I can't tell you what a help Neville is to me. I don't know what I should do without him.'[63]

Chamberlain had no complaints about his treatment by his new master and set about his duties with his customary industry and commitment. 'Winston has behaved with the most unimpeachable loyalty. Our relations are excellent and I know he finds my help of great value to him.'[64] Another member of Churchill's War Cabinet, Clement Attlee, who had no particular axe to grind on Chamberlain's behalf, later remembered that he 'worked very hard and well: a good chairman, a good committee man, always very businesslike. You could work with him.'[65]

Observers were struck by the courtesy, even deference, with which the new Prime Minister treated his predecessor. Churchill's loyalty to Chamberlain became important when, in the early summer of 1940, a campaign got underway with considerable support from junior ministers inside the government to remove Chamberlain and his associates from office. The Prime Minister told the House of Commons that an inquest into the recent past would be 'a foolish and pernicious process' and successfully urged the plotters to abandon their witch hunt. As Churchill explained, 'I owe something to Chamberlain, you know. When he resigned he could have advised the King to send for Halifax and he didn't. . . . Chamberlain works very well with me and I can tell you this – he's no intriguer.'[66]

If Chamberlain's replacement by Churchill represented some sort of expression of national will for a new and better beginning, it is not clear that the elite in Whitehall and Westminster fully shared in such sentiments. Recent research has shown how Chamberlainite the Conservative party remained after May 1940. Many Conservative MPs who had withheld their support in the crucial division of 10 May came to regret their decision in the light of the political outcome it had produced. Some had intended only to register their disquiet at the lack of progress in the war to date. Others had merely hoped to induce Chamberlain to reorganize his cabinet. Some could only bring themselves to support the new government because Chamberlain had led by example in doing so. If Churchill was good enough for Chamberlain, 'he must be good enough for us'.[67] The prevailing mood was well captured by the Chamberlain loyalist 'Chips' Channon when he described the scene in the House of Commons on 13 May:

> when . . . Neville entered with his usual shy retiring little manner, MPs lost their heads; they shouted; they cheered; they waved their Order Papers, and his reception was a regular ovation. The new PM spoke well, even dramatically, in support of the new All-Party Government, but he was not well received. And all the speeches that followed were mediocre. Only references to Neville raised enthusiasm.[68]

Many insiders greeted Churchill's premiership not just without enthusiasm but with undisguised dismay. The junior Foreign Office minister, R.A. Butler, spoke of a 'half-breed American whose main support was that of inefficient but talkative people of a similar type', while John Colville, a member of Chamberlain's secretariat who went on to serve – and later to admire – the new premier, confessed that at this stage 'the mere thought of Churchill as Prime Minister sent a cold chill down the spines of the staff at 10 Downing Street'. Their feelings were 'widely shared in the Cabinet Offices, the Treasury and through-out Whitehall'.[69] Even as late as November 1940, by which time Chamberlain was dead and Churchill had experienced his finest hour, Lord Woolton could still record that 'Chamberlain succeeded in getting a personal allegiance from members of his government because although he was not strong he was absolutely reliable and trustworthy. There is no allegiance to Churchill; there is nobody in the government whom the public would trust.'[70]

We must also question the extent to which May 1940 marked a distinct change in government policy towards the war. As has been argued, Churchill operated in a different environment from Chamberlain, but that was largely the consequence of develop-ments beyond either man's control. The first weeks of the new premiership coincided with the fall of France and the consequent transformation of the war itself. Churchill is renowned above all else for his absolute determination, which he succeeded in instill-ing into the British people, to continue the fight against Hitler no matter what the cost. As he told his junior ministers, 'if this long island story of ours is to end at last, let it end only when each one of us lies choking in his own blood upon the ground'.[71] Behind the scenes, however, we now know that a more hard-headed if less heroic debate was conducted inside Churchill's War Cabinet. Here, there was considerable support for at least investigating the possibility of opening talks to determine what terms Hitler might be prepared to offer. Though the debate grad-ually polarized into one between Churchill and Halifax (in which, ironically, Chamberlain's support for the former may have been the decisive factor in putting thoughts of negotiation to one side), it is now clear that, as David Dilks has argued, 'we do find [Churchill] prepared to contemplate a peace which would inevitably leave Germany master of Europe. The usual belief, namely that Churchill was from the moment of his acces-sion as Prime Minister determined to fight on until the whole of Europe was liberated, can no longer be sustained.'[72] In the light of such realities there is something to be said for John

Charmley's judgement on Churchill's rhetoric about 'never surrendering'. 'It was sublime – nonsense – but sublime nonsense.'[73] Churchill's thinking about the war in May 1940, and the way in which it might be won, was not in fact as far removed from Chamberlain's as the popular perception would suggest. This becomes clear in the arguments which he used to encourage the French to stay in the war in spite of their sudden military reverse in the late spring. His belief was that the German economy, and therefore the country's capacity to wage war, was overstretched and at breaking point. If, therefore, the Allies could hold on, victory would be theirs.

The Churchill–Chamberlain partnership did not, of course, last long. By the time that he gave up the premiership Chamberlain was probably already suffering from the cancer which would kill him before the year was out. But one cannot but be struck by the efforts Churchill made to retain his predecessor's services for as long as possible and the reluctance with which he accepted his final resignation. When Chamberlain died in November, Churchill delivered a suitably laudatory oration in the House of Commons, though some listeners already sensed a tendency to leave the dead man to shoulder the blame for what had gone wrong and to buttress his own deeds and standing:

> Whatever else history may or may not say about these terrible tremendous years, we can be sure that Neville Chamberlain acted with perfect sincerity according to his lights and strove to the utmost of his capacity and authority . . . to save the world from the awful, devastating struggle in which we are now engaged. This alone will stand him in good stead as far as what is called the verdict of history is concerned.[74]

Churchill's final prediction was not, of course, fulfilled, not least as this chapter has argued because of his own attempts to shape history's judgements. But it is worthy of note that his sympathetic statements about Chamberlain were not merely for public consumption. A government whip recalled Churchill saying, 'What shall I do without poor Neville? I was relying on him to look after the Home Front for me'.[75] To Halifax he remarked simply, 'I shall never find such a colleague again'.[76]

Clearly, all this is a long way from the Churchillian image of Neville Chamberlain which emerged in the longer term. On the day Chamberlain died, an unknown correspondent wrote to express her conviction that 'you saved the life of our Country and we always think of you with deep and everlasting gratitude'. The lady added as a postscript, 'I have a portrait of you and Mr. Churchill side by side on my mantelpiece'.[77] By the end of the war it seems unlikely that many Britons would have regarded this as an appropriate photographic juxtaposition, still fewer in the years which followed. Yet, as that war with Germany neared its conclusion, it is at least arguable that Churchill himself, conscious of the lack of options available to the British government, engaged in an act of appeasement comparable to those held against his predecessor. Historians continue to debate whether the western democracies 'betrayed' Eastern Europe at the Yalta Conference of February 1945 by handing it over to the totalitarian control of Soviet Russia. The rights and wrongs of this decision lie outside the scope of the present study, though it is worth pointing out that Churchill must have known that in negotiating with Stalin he was dealing with a dictator guilty of crimes against humanity on a scale which Hitler could not rival at the time of the Munich Conference in 1938. Some contemporaries were certainly struck by the historical parallel, arguing that Churchill had 'done to the Poles at Yalta exactly what Chamberlain did to the Czechs at Munich'.[78] And it is interesting to note Churchill's own comparison with his predecessor's predicament. A member of the coalition government recorded his words: 'Poor Neville Chamberlain believed he could trust Hitler. He was wrong. But I don't think I'm wrong about Stalin.'[79] It seems doubtful whether the verdict of history would concur with this judgement. At all events Churchill was certainly wise to omit from his speech in the House of Commons debate on the Yalta agreement – though only it seems as a last minute decision – a phrase to the effect that Stalin was only looking for 'peace with honour'. Yalta, however, never blighted Churchill's historical reputation as Munich had done Chamberlain's, in part no doubt because it did not prove to be the prelude to a third world war, but also in part because there was no one with Churchill's authority and literary talents to portray this episode in the way that he had done with the earlier conference.

Overall, the impact of *The Gathering Storm* upon Chamberlain's reputation was devastating, both at the time of its publication and in terms of its lasting impact upon subsequent historical writing and popular perceptions. Combined with the attack from the Left represented by *Guilty Men*, it formed the right wing of a pincer movement from which Chamberlain had little opportunity to escape, though interestingly one which the Labour party often seemed ready to appropriate by exaggerating the role it had played in ensuring Churchill's succession in May 1940. Yet as it becomes somewhat easier with the passage of time to subject Churchill's own record to critical examination and as his failings as an historian become ever more apparent, this seems a less than satisfactory basis upon which to judge Neville Chamberlain. The latter in his reticence deserves better than to be the victim of an over-articulate successor. Churchill was capable of misjudging situations just as grievously as Chamberlain ever did. Only a week before the Japanese attack on Pearl Harbor in December 1941 Churchill asserted that, should the Japanese go to war, they would 'fold up like the Italians'. As John Ramsden wisely reminds us, 'if such a phrase had ever been uttered by Neville Chamberlain, it would have been hanging round his neck as an historiographical albatross ever since, much as "Hitler has missed the bus" has done'.[80] It is not necessary completely to debunk Churchill's achievement as a war leader in order to recognize and accept his fallibility. Nor does his indispensable part in securing victory automatically condemn Chamberlain's efforts to preserve the peace.

Notes

1. Review of W.S. Churchill, *The Gathering Storm* by Preston Slosson in *American Historical Review*, vol.liv (1948), p.102.
2. A.J.P. Taylor, *English History 1914–1945* (Oxford, 1965), p.4.
3. C.L. Mowat, *Britain Between the Wars* (London, 1955), p.656.
4. R.R. James, *Churchill: A Study in Failure 1900–1939* (London, 1970), p.ix.
5. A.L. Rowse, *All Souls and Appeasement* (London,1961), p.15.
6. W.S. Churchill, *The Gathering Storm* (London,1948), p.157.
7. Halifax MSS, diary 6 June 1940.
8. Mowat, *Between the Wars*, p.657.
9. R. Blake, 'Winston Churchill as Historian' in W.R. Louis (ed.), *Adventures with Britannia* (London,1995), p.46.
10. I. Berlin, *Mr.Churchill in 1940* (London, 1964), p.27.
11. Churchill, *Gathering Storm*, pp.526–7.
12. A.J.P. Taylor *et al.*, *Churchill: Four Faces and the Man* (London,1969), p.123.
13. A. Roberts, *'The Holy Fox': A Biography of Lord Halifax* (London,1991), p.289.

14. *Ibid.*, p.308.
15. P.F. Clarke, *Hope and Glory* (Harmondsworth, 1997), p.195.
16. C. Brooks, *Devil's Decade: Portraits of the Nineteen-Thirties* (London, 1948), p.206.
17. Cecil MSS, Add.MS 51079, Cecil to A. Chamberlain 16 August 1927.
18. A.P. Herbert, *Independent Member* (London,1950), p.109.
19. J. Ramsden, 'How Winston Churchill Became "The Greatest Living Englishman" ', *Contemporary British History*, 12, 3 (1998), pp.1–40.
20. M. MacDonald, *Titans and Others* (London, 1972), p.89.
21. Taylor, *Four Faces*, p.148.
22. M. Gilbert, *Winston S.Churchill*, vol.8 (London, 1988), p.315.
23. N. Rose, *Churchill: An Unruly Life* (London, 1994), p.45.
24. Taylor, *Four Faces*, p.149. Emphasis added.
25. M. George, *The Hollow Men* (London, 1965), p.10 (foreword by A.L. Rowse).
26. D.C. Watt, 'The Historiography of Appeasement' in C. Cook and A. Sked (eds), *Crisis and Controversy: Essays in Honour of A.J.P. Taylor* (London, 1976), p.112.
27. George Ferguson in the *Montreal Star* 16 Dec. 1961.
28. Chamberlain MSS, NC11/1/425, Halifax to Annie Chamberlain 13 May 1948.
29. *Ibid.*, BC4/8/83, Hilda Chamberlain to Dorothy Lloyd 15 May 1948.
30. *The Listener* 7 Oct. 1948.
31. Churchill, *Gathering Storm*, p.33.
32. *Ibid.*, p.14.
33. *Ibid.*, p.173.
34. *Ibid.*, p.199.
35. *Ibid.*, p.257.
36. *Ibid.*, p.512.
37. *Ibid.*, p.458.
38. *Ibid.*, pp.526–7.
39. Lord Birkenhead, *Halifax: The Life of Lord Halifax* (London, 1965), p.410.
40. A. Duff Cooper, *Old Men Forget* (London, 1953), p.171.
41. R. Jenkins, *The Chancellors* (London, 1998), p.305.
42. Roberts, *Holy Fox*, p.187.
43. C.B. Pyper, *Chamberlain and his Critics* (London, 1962), p.19.
44. James, *Failure*, pp.291–2.
45. *Ibid.*, p.405.
46. R. Powers, 'Winston Churchill's Parliamentary Commentary on British Foreign Policy, 1935–1938', *Journal of Modern History*, 26, 2 (1954), pp.179–82.
47. R.A.C. Parker, *Chamberlain and Appeasement* (Basingstoke, 1993), p.323.
48. Chamberlain MSS, NC7/11/31/188, note by D. Margesson 17 March 1938.
49. G. Stewart, *Burying Caesar: Churchill, Chamberlain and the Battle for the Tory Party* (London,1999), p.324.

50. W.S. Churchill, *Step by Step* (London, 1939), pp.322–5.
51. Chamberlain MSS, NC1/15/5/4, Hilda Chamberlain to Annie Chamberlain 19 April 1955.
52. Stewart, *Burying Caesar*, p.441.
53. D. Dilks (ed.), *The Diaries of Sir Alexander Cadogan 1938–1945* (London, 1971), pp.252–3.
54. C. King, *With Malice Toward None: A War Diary* (London, 1970), p.21.
55. Chamberlain MSS, NC7/9/47, Churchill to Chamberlain 10 Sept. 1939.
56. J. Charmley, *Churchill: The End of Glory* (London, 1993), p.376.
57. Taylor, *English History*, p.472
58. J. Colville, *The Fringes of Power*, vol.1 (London, 1986), p.124.
59. B. Pimlott (ed.), *The Political Diary of Hugh Dalton* (London, 1986), p.344.
60. D. Dilks, 'The Twilight War and the Fall of France: Chamberlain and Churchill in 1940' in D. Dilks (ed.), *Retreat from Power*, vol. 2 (London, 1981), p.63.
61. K. Feiling, *The Life of Neville Chamberlain* (London, 1946), p.442.
62. King, *With Malice*, p.50.
63. Chamberlain MSS, NC1/23/80, Chamberlain to D. Lloyd 18 May 1940.
64. *Ibid.*, NC18/1/1162, Chamberlain to Ida Chamberlain 21 June 1940.
65. F. Williams, *A Prime Minister Remembers* (London, 1961), p.37.
66. A.J.P. Taylor (ed.), *W.P. Crozier: Off the Record* (London,1973), p.175.
67. Charmley, *End of Glory*, p.396.
68. R.R. James (ed.), *Chips: The Diaries of Sir Henry Channon* (London, 1967), p.252.
69. Colville, *Fringes of Power*, vol.1, p.142; J.Wheeler-Bennett (ed.) *Action This Day* (London,1968), p.48.
70. Woolton MSS, diary 20 Nov. 1940.
71. H. Dalton, *The Fateful Years* (London,1957), p.336.
72. D. Dilks, 'Appeasement Revisited', *University of Leeds Review*, 15,1 (1972), p.50.
73. Charmley, *End of Glory*, p.411.
74. House of Commons Debates, 5th Series, vol. 365, col.1618.
75. J. Stuart, *Within the Fringe* (London, 1967), p.87.
76. R.R. James, *Victor Cazalet: A Portrait* (London, 1976), p.278.
77. Chamberlain MSS, NC13/18/372, M.E. Hodges to Chamberlain 9 Nov. 1940.
78. D. Carlton, *Churchill and the Soviet Union* (Manchester, 2000), p.141.
79. B. Pimlott (ed.), *The Second World War Diary of Hugh Dalton* (London, 1986), p.836.
80. J. Ramsden, ' "That will depend on who writes the history": Winston Churchill as his own Historian', *University of London inaugural lecture*, 1996, p.14.

|5|

The growth of revisionism

I have no doubt what the verdict of history will be. As we recede from the range of hills we have crossed, and the mists of the present no longer blur their horizon, we shall see your husband's solitary endeavour as something titanic – a great peak standing alone in an age of confusion and darkness.[1]

The urge towards revisionism may well be intrinsic to the craft of the historian, equipped as he is with a sceptical and questioning eye as he evaluates the work of his predecessors. Even so, it is by no means easy to say precisely when a revisionist interpretation of Neville Chamberlain's career actually began. It was as late as 1965, a quarter of a century after Chamberlain's death, that Professor D.C. Watt wrote of the possible rise of a revisionist school. Many writers would now see clear evidence of such a growth from the mid-1950s onwards, while Max Beloff once appeared to lay claim to the origination of this trend by pointing to a series of reviews which he wrote of Sir Lewis Namier's books on appeasement as they were published in the late 1940s, one consequence of which was that Namier never spoke to him again. In all probability, however, the seeds of revisionism were present in 1940, at the very moment that Chamberlain's reputation reached its nadir, though few in the atmosphere of the time were ready to nurture those seeds in public, still less articulate an alternative interpretation of his career. After all, while many jumped on the bandwagon of the new orthodoxy, by no means all of Chamberlain's friends and advisers deserted and disowned him during the rapid demolition of his public renown. It is striking how many of those who wrote to him at the time of his resignation from the premiership and of his complete withdrawal from public life a few months later did so in terms of their confidence that history would one day judge him kindly. Beverley Baxter came away from Chamberlain's funeral having heard 'not once but a dozen times . . . from different voices: "History will say that he saved this country." '[2] Similar ideas were taken up – however guardedly – in many press obituaries. Of course, there was an element of ritualized inevitability about all of this. Chamberlain's retirement and death were not moments at which to display a complete absence of human charity. His illness and resignation were a time for words of encouragement and support; his death for condolence to his surviving family. But, importantly, many of the ideas expressed at this early date provided the basis for a later revisionist historiography which would portray Chamberlain in a very different light from that of the *Guilty Men* stereotype.

Many now paid tribute to Chamberlain's untiring efforts to preserve peace. *The Times*, in a leading article, praised a 'martyr to one of the greatest of human causes' who had failed only because he sought an integrity equal to his own in men for whom the word had no meaning.[3] 'If it be a sin to strive for peace', judged Wilson Harris writing in the *Spectator*, 'he was no doubt the most offending soul alive.' But his striving would never weigh in the balance against him.[4] The former Liberal leader, Herbert Samuel, suggested that Chamberlain's efforts to save Britain and Europe from war would live in history and that 'many of the criticisms of today will have been erased long before they reach posterity'. His handling of the situation at the time of Munich was one of the finest things ever done by a British Prime Minister.[5] Chamberlain had risked everything, concurred Joseph Ball, to avert the catastrophe of another world war, a conflict from which as he had once said there could be no winners.[6] According to Cuthbert Headlam, MP, history would come to appreciate the 'magnificent effort' Chamberlain had made through courage and resolution to save the peace.[7] It was, as the *Birmingham Post* noted, easier to criticize what he had done than to put forward a constructive alternative.

More specifically the argument was voiced that Chamberlain had performed an important service in postponing war in 1938 and allowing time for rearmament to proceed. Lord Midleton, a former Secretary of State for War, wrote of the 'many months of invaluable respite' which Chamberlain had secured without which 'we should now be at the feet of Germany'.[8] His work as a junior minister at the Admiralty had given Geoffrey Shakespeare an understanding of the immense value of the year that followed Munich. He trembled to think what would have happened if the country had been plunged into war in 1938. 'Historians will see more clearly than we do the value of this precious breathing space and his fame will grow with the years.'[9] The postponement of war for a whole year, insisted Malcolm MacDonald in a letter which arrived on the day that Chamberlain died, gave Britain time to make military preparations which would turn 'what would probably have been defeat into what will now, I believe, certainly be a victory for European civilization'. What Chamberlain had done represented a personal achievement without precedent in the history of statesmanship and long after 'all the scribblers who have attacked you are forgotten, your name will be amongst the most honoured in the dynasty of our Prime Ministers'.[10] The *Scotsman* developed the same theme:

> History, we are convinced, will vindicate Mr. Chamberlain's policy in striving to maintain peace in Europe, and will proclaim his wisdom in postponing the clash until we were better prepared to endure it. Appeasement and rearmament were the twin aims of his policy. . . . Taken all in all, however, the cautious policy of Mr. Chamberlain served this country better than the warmongering of his critics – euphemistically the 'firm stand' – would have done.[11]

Such embryonic revisionism was not confined to British shores. While majority opinion in the United States still held Chamberlain's policies to have been mistaken, tribute was paid to his obvious sincerity and the tirelessness with which he had worked for victory when Poland was invaded and he saw the collapse of all his hopes. Many American newspapers were at pains to point out that, as the *New York Sun* put it, appeasement represented the desires and aspirations of the vast majority of the British public. The *Herald Tribune* made the telling point that the world would never know whether a sterner policy towards Germany would have prevented war given the fact that Germany's military preparations were so vastly superior to those of Great Britain. A Canadian columnist tried to remind his readers that

Chamberlain's career was not restricted to the era of Munich. As Chancellor of the Exchequer he had rescued Britain from the financial morass into which she had sunk and his work was now enabling the country to sustain the greatest war in its history.[12] In South Africa the *Rand Daily Mail* drew attention to Chamberlain's integrity. It was his misfortune rather than his fault that he was called upon to deal with unscrupulous and deceitful men. From such a severe trial his own reputation emerged 'immaculate'.[13]

The scope for further revisionist analysis was obvious. Despite these initial stirrings Chamberlain's reputation stood at a very low base-line. It could only recover. As Gladstone had once remarked of Aberdeen, 'in the final distribution of posthumous fame Lord Aberdeen has nothing to forfeit, he has only to receive'. But while the war lasted few were those who were prepared to put their heads above the parapet to begin the slow process of Chamberlain's rehabilitation. 'If at any time his memory should require any defence', asserted one MP at the time of Chamberlain's death, 'I shall not fail to take up the cudgels wholeheartedly and to the best of my poor ability.'[14] Such promises were soon forgottten. Chamberlain's standing was now indissolubly tied to an understanding of pre-war British foreign policy whose reappraisal would seem in some way to challenge the current war effort and the heroic crusade of his successor in Downing Street. Moreover, it was not obvious from which direction a concerted defence of Chamberlain might emerge. The line of the political Left was firmly fixed in the thinking of the authors of *Guilty Men*. But the Conservative party too was moving on under the direction of a new leader who seemed in many ways the antithesis of Chamberlain and all he had stood for. Not surprisingly, only a few isolated individuals sought to challenge the orthodoxy that had been established in the spring and summer of 1940. Those who recalled the Chamberlain premiership in favourable terms were understandably disinclined to publicize this fact. Sir Herbert Williams, MP, Chairman of the Commons Select Committee on National Expenditure, argued that 'the days of Chamberlain were not too good from some points of view, but ... administratively Chamberlain's Government was infinitely better than this [Churchill] one'.[15] But such thoughts were unlikely to receive much publicity, at least as long as the war lasted.

Few of Chamberlain's ministerial colleagues now leapt to his

public defence. In any case the practice of former cabinet ministers rushing to make their contribution to the corpus of instant
history belongs to a later age. One Chamberlain loyalist,
however, did enter the fray. Lord Maugham, Lord Chancellor
from March 1938 until September 1939, determined to produce
a short defence of the Munich settlement. His declared purpose
was to make his 'contribution to History' in relation to an event
'which has elicited so much calumny of Neville'.[16] *The Truth
about the Munich Crisis* was published in 1944. Maugham
argued that it had been right to negotiate with Hitler. The full
enormity of his capacity for evil was by no means apparent in
September 1938, at which date, if his words inspired no great
confidence, he could still not simply be dismissed as a proven
liar. With the benefit of hindsight it was very easy to argue that
the country's defences should never have been allowed to fall
into the state of disrepair that they had by the autumn of 1938,
but this had been the reality with which Chamberlain had been
confronted. The feeling of almost universal relief with which the
Munich settlement had been greeted was too easily forgotten.
Those politicians who had applauded Chamberlain's decision to
visit Hitler for a third time, when it was clear that the preservation of peace would have to entail further concessions to the
Führer, but who turned on the Prime Minister only days later
following his return to Britain, were hardly worthy of comment.
In any case Munich had provided a breathing space during
which necessary military and naval preparations could be made.
'In particular, time was all important for the purpose of bringing into existence the aeroplanes which we did not then possess
and to train many of those supremely gallant young airmen who
in the autumn of 1940 enabled us to win the Battle of Britain.'[17]

What sort of impact Maugham's short book might have
would be determined by its circulation. Chamberlain's trusted
confidant, Horace Wilson, did what he could:

> With help from others I had arranged beforehand for
> copies to be ordered (and to be asked for at the libraries)
> so as to stimulate interest and I have sent a dozen or so
> copies to various people (including Ottawa, Washington,
> West Africa and Palestine!) with a request to 'pass on'
> when read. I hope one or two will be wiser as a result.[18]

But this first essay in revisionism had little positive impact.
Maugham was 'appalled' at some of the reviews he received and

at the contents of his postbag. He could not understand why so many people now seemed so certain that Britain should have gone to war with Hitler at the time of Munich, regardless of the consequences. It represented a 'species of insanity which precludes a sane judgement'.[19]

The Chamberlain camp placed more confidence in the literary efforts of W.W. Hadley, editor of the *Sunday Times*. His journalistic style was likely to create a bigger impact than that of the former Lord Chancellor. Hadley had been upset by the campaign waged against Chamberlain in the last months of the latter's life – 'I remember nothing worse of its kind' – but had bided his time out of the belief that nothing effective could be done in the way of rebuttal in the early stages of the war. By 1944, however, he sensed that the tide of opinion had begun to turn and that the moment was right to make his contribution to a process which would ultimately vindicate what Chamberlain had done. 'It will take a few years, but I have no doubt that the evil feeling against Mr. Chamberlain will disappear and his work be judged aright.'[20]

Hadley's *Munich: Before and After* (1944) reiterated many of the arguments contained in Maugham's book. But he also stressed that the events of the immediate pre-war years which had so shaped Chamberlain's reputation were in part the inevitable product of the conditions left at the end of the First World War, for which the ex-Prime Minister could bear no responsibility. Like Maugham, Hadley argued that Hitler's infamies had not made it any less desirable to seek to avoid war, providing this was done in a way that was consistent with Britain's honour and interests. He too was keen to remind his audience of the contemporary public reaction to the Munich settlement, at least as expressed in the national press, and he poured scorn on those MPs who had moved from praise to censure of Chamberlain by the time of the Commons debate in early October 1938. The crucial question had been posed – but not answered – in that debate by the Conservative MP, David Maxwell-Fyfe, when he challenged honourable members to say 'at what stage they think this country ought to have gone to war or threatened war'.[21] Also like Maugham, Hadley drew attention to the importance of the year's delay which the Munich settlement had brought about. It might be true that German production in the means of war was greater in 1938–9 than was Britain's. But that missed the central point. 'In some essential things, we had not got, in 1938, the barest minimum of military requirements. When war came a year later we were still at a big disadvantage, but the position was much better than in the autumn of 1938.'[22] Finally, Hadley tried tentatively to rehabilitate the reputation of Chamberlain, the man. The latter's shy and reserved nature easily caused misunderstanding, at least outside the circle of his close associates. Though widely thought of as hard and cold, he was sensitive to any human suffering and instinctively sympathetic. Nor was the image of a right-wing Tory, propagated by his political opponents, at all accurate. 'He cherished a good deal of the old Birmingham Radicalism, and his mind was forward-looking.'[23] Such remarks were meant as a preliminary to a fuller biographical study which, in the event, Hadley never wrote, though he did contribute an entry to the *Dictionary of National Biography* published in 1949.

But perhaps the most effective blow delivered on behalf of Chamberlain's reputation during the war years – precisely because it confronted the arguments of *Guilty Men* head on – came from the pen of the young Conservative MP, Quintin Hogg. Hogg's own early career serves as a commentary on Chamberlain's fluctuating fortunes. He was first elected to parliament in October 1938 in the celebrated Oxford by-election as an avowed supporter of the Prime Minister and, more particularly, of the recently negotiated Munich settlement. At that time he described the settlement as 'the greatest miracle of modern times performed by a single man'.[24] His faith in Chamberlain's policies soon waned, however, and, disillusioned with the latter's conduct of the Phoney War, he cast his vote in the opposition lobby in the key parliamentary division on 8 May 1940. Yet he did so in a curiously ambiguous way, reaffirming 'in spite of what I felt bound to do, my personal affection and loyalty towards [Chamberlain]'.[25] Hogg became more conscious than most of his political contemporaries of the extent to which the political climate shifted leftwards during the course of the Second World War and of the way in which the thesis of *Guilty Men* and similar publications had captured the moral highground. With one eye clearly fixed on the forthcoming General Election he sought to challenge the prevailing tide of Cato, Cassius, Gracchus *et al.*

The Left was Never Right was published in 1945 and was probably the most impressive piece of right-wing political propaganda published before the end of the conflict. The

author's starting point was that the pre-war record of the
Labour and Liberal parties was no fit basis from which to criticize the actions of Chamberlain and the National Government.
He 'charge[d] the authors of *Guilty Men* with using the agony
of Dunkirk as a means of vilifying a political party which could
not defend itself owing to the party truce, and of furthering a
domestic policy with which the war has admittedly nothing to
do'.[26] Hogg admitted the mistakes and shortcomings of the
Chamberlain government, only too apparent now that the reality of Hitler's crimes had been revealed to all, but argued that the
country would have been in an even worse situation in
September 1939 had its fortunes been entrusted to Labour.
Indeed, Labour's contradictory obsessions with disarmament
and collective security would have led to total disaster. To illustrate his point Hogg quoted the speech of Clement Attlee,
attacking Chamberlain's 1936 budget. The Labour leader had
argued that, because of its concentration on defence, there was
hardly anything in the budget to improve the education and
health services for the benefit of the British people. It was in fact
a War Budget. 'Everything was devoted to piling up the instru-
ments of death.'[27] Nor did Labour's attitude significantly change
before the outbreak of hostilities. When the government introduced a motion for compulsory military training in April 1939,
138 Labour MPs and seven Liberals voted against it. The seven
Liberals included Geoffrey Mander, author of *We Were Not All
Wrong*.

Hogg argued that the Left's image of Chamberlain as 'the
embodiment of dingy betrayal, of narrow middle-class compla-
cency, a Brummagem idol worshipped by the business men who
. . . are now supposed to be using [England] for their own
parochial purposes' was an 'appalling lie'. Chamberlain was a
'tragic' figure in the highest sense of that word. His efforts to
preserve the peace for as long as possible and his determination
that Britain should not take responsibility for starting war until
the last hope of averting it had vanished were symbolic of 'all
that is best, decent, orderly and faithful in a world about to
dissolve into battle, murder and sudden death'.[28] Hogg wrote
powerfully and persuasively. What impact his message had upon
Chamberlain's evolving reputation is difficult to assess. But at
least as a Conservative political polemic his book must be
judged a failure. Hogg himself later admitted that it 'was too
little and too late to counteract the impression made by the

earlier Gollancz publications'.[29] *The Left Was Never Right* appeared just before the 1945 General Election at which the Tories sustained their most crushing defeat since 1906.

While Left and Right engaged in these preliminary historiographical skirmishes from which the former emerged on points as the clear victor, Neville Chamberlain's surviving family, as the most committed guardians of his posthumous reputation, placed their confidence in the early publication of an authorised biography. After some hesitation, during which the name of Blanche Dugdale, niece and biographer of another Tory Prime Minister Arthur Balfour, was considered, the task was entrusted as early as 1941 to Keith Feiling. Feiling was a well-known historian of Conservative leanings, both in terms of personal conviction and of his historical interests. He was too good an historian to accept dictation from the Chamberlain family as to what he should write, but his initial disposition seemed favourable to the late Prime Minister's memory:

> So far I have always written my own books in my own way and should have to do so again; wherever what seemed to me the truth may lead me. Lord Baldwin has written of bias in history, and we all have it; on the last ten years mine leaned hard to an effort to reconciliation with Germany. Moreover, I could point you to a good many places where I have written one of my strongest feelings; on the unfairness of putting all responsibility on one man in our system.[30]

Nonetheless, the Chamberlain family was in no doubt about what it was looking for. Feiling was uncertain whether he would be able to produce a biography of the depth the family wanted so soon after his subject's death and in the absence of documentation outside Chamberlain's private papers. But if Chamberlain's surviving sisters did not like the idea of a provisional life, they disliked even more the thought of doing nothing for the next decade while Chamberlain's enemies continued to entrench their version of the past ever more firmly in the popular consciousness. There were also concerns about Feiling's somewhat idiosyncratic prose style which 'makes him difficult to read which is a great drawback in a book you would like to be popular'. But the most important point was that Chamberlain's 'reputation will not suffer at his hands'.[31] In the event Feiling based his work upon a combination of

Chamberlain's private papers, particularly his diary and weekly letters to his sisters Ida and Hilda, together with a series of interviews with his political contemporaries, or more particularly those likely to be favourable to him. Lloyd George was among those excluded as one 'capable of giving perfectly incorrect information'.[32] Churchill caused momentary hesitation, but Feiling was confident that he was 'a very big man with, as I know, a very affectionate side' who 'came to feel a very genuine respect and affection for Neville'.[33] Perhaps more typical of the interviewees was the junior Foreign Office minister, R.A. Butler, who told Feiling that Chamberlain was like Saul in one respect and like the younger Pitt in another. Like Saul he towered head and shoulders above the other members of his government; like the younger Pitt he was at root a man of peace and the husbander of the nation's resources.

Feiling worked fast and his book was completed by 1944. But the Chamberlain family, while quite clear that it would not be possible to avoid controversy if the prevailing orthodoxy were to be effectively challenged, judged that wartime publication would be counter-productive as the general public was too much absorbed in current issues to bother over much about past events. Publication of *The Life of Neville Chamberlain* was therefore delayed until 1946. The book represented a considerable achievement. It says much for the quality of Feiling's research and analysis that, more than half a century later, his remains the most impressive and persuasive single-volume biography of its subject. The author himself was modest about what he had been able to achieve in the absence of the official archives of Britain and of her friends and foes, and of the correspondence of contemporary politicians. Nonetheless, the Chamberlain who emerged from Feiling's pages was a sensitive, intelligent and perceptive actor on both the domestic and international stages, light years removed from the criminally negligent dupe portrayed in *Guilty Men*.

Though biography is by definition the most personal of all historical genres, Feiling placed an important marker for future revisionist writing in his insistence that the task of Clio, the muse of history, was to explain actions and events and not to attack individuals. He admitted that the whole period after 1931 had, in hindsight, proved disastrous, but this was something 'for which all sections of the nation must shoulder some responsibility'.[34] As regards the earlier part of the 1930s Feiling sought to rescue Chamberlain's reputation from four 'legends' – that he was always hostile to the concept of collective security, that he was biased by his inherent sympathy for Germany, that he completely ignored the Soviet Union, and that he impeded rearmament. Over the question of rearmament, in particular, Chamberlain's private correspondence provided some telling quotations. In February 1936 he had felt relatively satisfied that 'if we can keep out of war for a few years, we shall have an air force of such striking power that no one will care to run risks with it'. His rearmament strategy was based upon a clear appreciation of the development of military technology since the war of 1914–18. In a future conflict Britain's resources would 'be more profitably employed in the air, and on the sea, than in building up great armies'.[35] Far from starving the armed forces of necessary funds, Chamberlain as Chancellor of the Exchequer had shown a clear appreciation that military hardware would not be the only component of Britain's defensive capability. Feiling thus anticipated the argument that a strong economy represented Britain's 'fourth arm of defence', a thesis which would not become widespread for a further three decades. Chamberlain had put it to the Commons that, provided Britain could avoid a German knockout blow, 'wars are won not only now with arms and men, they are won with the reserves of resources and credit', in fact with economic staying power.[36]

Much, of course, had gone wrong in the years of Chamberlain's premiership. But Feiling reminded his readers how easy it was to be wise after the event. 'The man deceives himself who professes that in 1937 he foresaw the decrees of Providence for 1939–41.'[37] The same was true more specifically of the Munich settlement which, with hindsight, so many were ready to condemn. At the time, Feiling insisted, Czechoslovakia had not been seen as an issue that Britons should be asked to die for. If Chamberlain's public pronouncements after September 1938 now seemed wildly optimistic, this above all reflected the redoubled efforts that had been made to rearm. The Germans, Chamberlain claimed in February 1939, 'could not make nearly such a mess of us now as they could have done then, while we could make much more of a mess of them'.[38] By the spring of that year it was clear that the differences between the Prime Minister and his critics had been considerably narrowed. If there remained a significant difference of judgement it derived from Chamberlain's refusal to accept war as inevitable and his determination to work for the preservation of peace until all final hope had gone. Feiling did not attempt to whitewash his subject. 'There is nothing Neville would have hated more, with his soul of candour and integrity, than the "stained glass window" type of biography.'[39] Chamberlain and Halifax were, he admitted, 'too unwilling to look beyond what must immediately be done, too insular, not at all in their objective but in their code, too inelastic, both for good and ill, to adapt themselves to revolutionary situations'.[40] Such balance made Feiling's overall defence of his subject altogether more credible.

Contemporary reactions to Feiling's book were predictably varied. Following the sudden death of Ida Chamberlain in 1943, her sister Hilda was left as the leading custodian of the family's good name. She declared that Feiling had proved himself a much better writer than she had expected and had now produced a book which would always be a standard work and which did justice to Chamberlain's character and 'to a large extent to his work'. She liked the proportions of Feiling's biography and particularly applauded his decision not to give excessive prominence to the years of Chamberlain's premiership. 'Indeed, I feel that all that last piece could hardly be better, for he has allowed him to speak for himself, and the story is so moving that I found it difficult to read at all.' She might have wished for more emphasis on the fertility of Chamberlain's mind and on the originality of his work at the Ministry of Health, but overall 'you will see I am satisfied that it is the kind of life we wanted and one that your Father would, himself, have approved'.[41] But many reviewers were less enthusiastic, demonstrating the mountain of entrenched opinion which any process of long-term rehabilitation would need to overcome. Many argued that, in stressing Chamberlain's undoubted qualities, Feiling had merely thrown his equally obvious shortcomings into stark relief. According to Thomas Jones, writing in *The Times*, Chamberlain's eminently logical approach to situations had proved his undoing. He had viewed everything in a 'small and soluble way' but 'it is the imponderables that matter in politics'. Chamberlain was a 'straightforward character, a loyal colleague, a peace Prime Minister of the second rank, called to guide the ship of State in a gathering storm and then, as the darkness thickened, to make way for the greatest of our war pilots'. An unnamed reviewer in the *Financial Times* took up the same point. Chamberlain was singularly devoid of those extra powers of imaginative insight into affairs which mark the truly great leader. In the *Daily Telegraph* Harold Nicolson asserted that Feiling had written not a defence of his subject but an explanation. Chamberlain's integrity was not in question; but his intelligence was. Feiling's analysis of Munich and of Chamberlain's use of the supposed breathing space which the settlement offered did not convince all who read it. According to Richard Law in *Time and Tide* the evidence suggested that Chamberlain had seen Munich as the basis of a solid peace. Subsequent rearmament was in the nature of an insurance policy, but Chamberlain still had no conception of 'what, in the context, rearmament must mean'.[42]

The reception accorded to Feiling's biography was a clear indication of the difficulty which even the most persuasive advocate would have in rescuing Chamberlain's reputation from an historical climate dominated by the continuing impact of *Guilty Men*, reinforced in the immediate post-war years by the powerful writings of Winston Churchill and the first generation of professional historians of the 1930s. Some found the situation difficult to comprehend. 'It puzzles me', wrote Horace Wilson in 1948,

> to explain how people who went through the horrors of the war, the bombing, etc., and are now despondent and depressed by its consequences, can have anything but respect and admiration for the man who tried to prevent it. In none of the books and articles that I have read have I found a coherent answer to the question: given the circumstances of 1937 and 1938, what alternative was practicable?[43]

Other Chamberlain loyalists were annoyed, in the context of a worsening Cold War with the Soviet Union, that Yalta had not done the sort of damage to Churchill's reputation that Munich had to Chamberlain's. If Czechoslovakian democracy lay in ruins, Samuel Hoare (now Lord Templewood) told a radio audience in November 1948, the reason was not something that Chamberlain had done, but the disastrous policy pursued at the inter-allied conferences of the Second World War which had handed Central Europe over to communist domination and made Prague a Soviet garrison town.

Over the years which followed Chamberlain's defenders grew more numerous, but they were inevitably obliged to swim against the prevailing tide. If discussion and debate were now at least possible, it was still clear which side of the argument would come out on top. In the autumn of 1948 the BBC assembled a distinguished group of academics, politicians and diplomats to discuss the Munich settlement in a series of radio talks prompted by the publication of John Wheeler-Bennett's book on the same subject. But while Agnes Headlam-Morley presented a reasonably sympathetic account and Cyril Falls tried objectively to compare the advantages and disadvantages of war in 1939 as opposed to 1938, listeners were more likely to be swayed by Vansittart's denunciation of a 'morally indefensible agreement' or Duff Cooper's discussion of a 'cynical act of cold-blooded butchery'.

With hindsight certain landmarks in the growth of a revisionist school of thought stand out. In 1952 Norton Medlicott who, 'unlike the vast bulk of his contemporaries, did not abandon his devotion to historical method when he approached contemporary history',[44] published a short, sympathetic reassessment of Chamberlain's career in the popular journal *History Today*. In 1954 the youthful Donald Watt had the temerity to denounce the scholarship of Sir Lewis Namier, accusing him of behaving like a prosecuting counsel, judge and jury rolled into one rather than an impartial historian. Two years later Max Beloff sought to explain the mood of the 1930s to a generation which was in danger of forgetting the climate which had given birth to Chamberlain's policies:

> It does still seem to me that behind all this there lay in the democracies, and particularly in Britain, a conviction born of the [First World] war primarily that war itself was so horrible and unthinkable that all reasonable men would admit that it was not a thing which could be made use of to bring about purely political ends; and they assumed that the Germans must at bottom share this view and were encouraged by a great many Germans to believe this also.[45]

But at the time such contributions exercised only a limited impact. Their message was directed at a restricted audience and had little effect upon popular thought.

In the meantime the Chamberlain family remained hopeful that the tide of opinion would eventually turn. In anticipation of that moment evidence supportive of his case was assiduously collected. At a time, however, when it was constantly being stressed that the western world needed to show moral strength in its attitude towards Soviet Russia, it was galling to see Chamberlain's actions portrayed as 'a trampling of all moral standards under foot', while only such 'anti-appeasers' as Duff Cooper and Churchill were thought to have 'upheld the right'.[46] The family restricted access to Chamberlain's private papers to a small group of sympathetic authors. Some well-placed individuals such as Joseph Ball promised to publish their recollections, but in the event failed to deliver. Considerable hope was placed in the literary efforts of Samuel Hoare, probably Chamberlain's closest colleague within his own cabinet. Here was a man who could comment with authority both on Chamberlain's policies and on his personality, dispelling in the process many of the unflattering myths that had grown up around him. In the preparation of *Nine Troubled Years* Hoare was able to use several of the late Prime Minister's private letters, carefully selected for him by Hilda Chamberlain. The memoir, published in 1954, offers the most sympathetic portrait of Chamberlain written by a government insider. Its defence of the policy of appeasement was particularly effective.

Hoare did not seek to deny that British rearmament had been too long delayed. If the government had realised in 1933 that Hitler's advent to power had brought about a complete transformation in the European situation, it would no doubt have embarked upon a rearmament strategy which would have placed Britain in a very different position by the time of Munich from the one Chamberlain had to face. As it was, Chamberlain's guiding principle was that a world war would be an appalling disaster. Against this fundamental truth the satisfaction of German or Czech aspirations 'seemed altogether less important than the security of the peaceful families that were living and working in their own homes'.[47] Chamberlain believed that his dual policy of negotiation and rearmament had a fair chance of success, but he was never under any naïve illusions in his dealings with Hitler. Indeed, the latter's personality repelled him. ' "How terrible," as he said more than once, "that the fate of millions of simple and peaceful men and women should depend upon one man's whims, and that man a paranoiac." . . . From the first he was certain that the man was partially mad.'[48] At all events the rearmament strategy for which Chamberlain was primarily responsible was soundly based. Hoare's reading of the official history of British War Production had led him inexorably to the conclusion that it had required no substantial modification during the war years. He admitted that the Chamberlain government was not ideally suited to lead the country into war. 'We were essentially a peace-time Ministry, the successors of the first National Government that had been created to meet an economic crisis.'[49] Even so, the Phoney War threw up a situation in which any government would have found it difficult to prosper. The period of suspense seemed to many worse than an enemy attack, which would at least have served to stiffen the country's morale. Chamberlain could not benefit from the sense of immediate danger which worked to Churchill's advantage in the period after May 1940.

According to Hoare, Chamberlain was certainly an active Prime Minister. His reputation among Whitehall insiders was that of a premier who kept abreast of everything that was happening. His staff were amazed at his mastery of intricate detail. But the conclusion which Chamberlain drew from the unfortunate inheritance to which he succeeded was not his alone. Indeed, it was central to Hoare's argument that the whole policy of appeasement should be depersonalized:

> He was not an autocrat who imposed his views upon doubting or hostile colleagues. Appeasement was not his personal policy. Not only was it supported by his colleagues; it expressed the general desire of the British people. This is a fundamental consideration in judging his action.[50]

The Chamberlain family was hopeful that Churchill's final retirement from active politics in 1955 might serve to speed up the processes of historical revisionism. The Suez disaster of the following year, manufactured by his successor in Downing Street, scarcely suggested that unwavering opposition to appeasement was an immutable virtue. It was against this background that a rising young Conservative of the post-war era showed an interest in writing a new biography. That Iain Macleod felt drawn to Chamberlain was itself an encouraging sign. A progressive on the left of the party and the epitome of 'One Nation' Toryism, he shared many career experiences with his subject. Each man had risen to national prominence as Minister of Health; each served a period as Party Chairman. Macleod had both the potential and inclination to do justice to those more constructive aspects of Chamberlain's political life which had tended so far to be obscured by the all-pervading pall of Munich and appeasement. Granted also that Feiling had been discreet in his use of Chamberlain's private papers, omitting in particular some of his subject's more pointed criticisms of his predecessor, Stanley Baldwin, the opportunity clearly existed for fuller revelations about the difficulties which Chamberlain had encountered, especially before becoming Prime Minister. In the event the opportunity was largely missed and Macleod's book is significant for revealing the mountain of entrenched opinion which was still ready to resist any attempt at rehabilitating Chamberlain's historical reputation, rather than for any new insights into the latter's career.

Amidst the demands of his ministerial duties it seems unlikely that Macleod ever gave his new task the attention it merited. This book was, he once confessed, written as a pot-boiler to earn money for his daughter's 'social season'. Confronted by the aged Hilda Chamberlain with seven large boxes of papers, Macleod pondered whether it was really necessary to go through them all. In the event, much of the book was ghost written by Peter Goldman who had once worked with Macleod in the Conservative Research Department (in the origins of which Chamberlain had been closely involved). Published in 1961, *Neville Chamberlain* added little to the portrait already offered by Keith Feiling. As Esmond Wright put it,

> The man who emerges . . . is not greatly different from the accepted image. Alert, competent, efficient, the mainstay of an ineffective but shrewd and warm Prime Minister (Baldwin) and of a not greatly talented Administration (1931–37), the 'pack horse in our great affairs' as Churchill so tellingly called him: he was all of these.[51]

Reviewers with continuing axes to grind were rather less charitable. It left John Connell, 'who entered the war, I may say, as a Territorial A.A. gunner serving an antiquated, ex-naval, semi-mobile 3 inch veteran of World War One, quite unpersuaded'.[52] In like vein Robert Boothby could not understand

> why Mr. Iain Macleod, with laurels still fresh upon his brow and a career of dazzling promise ahead of him, has chosen this moment to dredge the evil-smelling political pond of the 'thirties. Some of us had to swim in it. He did

not. If his object was to rehabilitate Mr. Chamberlain, he has failed.[53]

By 1961 the aged Churchill was probably beyond voicing a protest, but the guardians of his version of the past, often protective also of their own anti-appeasement credentials, were not slow off the mark. Lord Avon, the former Anthony Eden, was deeply upset that such an apologia for Chamberlain should have been written by a serving cabinet minister, and thought fit to complain to the Cabinet Secretary. 'The mere fact that Mr. Macleod was a member of the Government now in office . . . would cause a good many people to think that the book had some sort of official authority.' Munich, Avon argued, was still an issue capable of dividing the Conservative party and the appearance of an apparent justification of appeasement during the course of a Cold War crisis in Berlin was particularly unfortunate.[54] A reviewer in the *New York Post* even suggested that the book had destroyed any chance Macleod may have had of ever becoming Prime Minister, a view which Macleod himself came in part to share.

For much of the post-war era the question of Chamberlain's reputation was inextricably bound up in the wider historical issue of the origins and causation of the Second World War itself. The latter was never quite subject to the complacent consensus that has sometimes been suggested, not least because there was always a striking paradox in the way that interpretations of the war's inevitability, based upon the simple assertion of Hitler's crimes and guilt, were often coupled with the insistence of Churchill and others that this was a war which could easily have been averted. Yet it is probably true to suggest that the origins of the Second World War never, at least before the 1960s, achieved the degree of historical and historiographical controversy which had so quickly enveloped the origins of the conflict of 1914. There was something comfortably reassuring about interpretations based on the verdict of the Nuremberg trials which inevitably relegated questions about issues such as British appeasement to a level of only secondary importance. Speaking in 1956 at an international conference of historians in Rome, Professor Mario Toscano could confidently assert that, compared with the sometimes torrid debate that had raged over the origins of the First World War, a more general agreement existed among historians of all nations concerning the causes of the second great conflict of the twentieth century. 'It is generally felt that . . . we already know the answers and do not need to ask further questions.'[55]

In British circles this certainty was shattered by the publication in 1961 of A.J.P. Taylor's *The Origins of the Second World War*. In the provocative style at which he was so adept, Taylor presented Hitler not as a demonic mastermind working out the inexorable processes of an ideologically-motivated masterplan, but as a Micawber-type figure who seized opportunities as they were presented to him. Taylor's Hitler was not much more than a typical German politician in pursuit of the same foreign policy goals which had motivated his 1920s' predecessor, Gustav Stresemann. This fundamental reassessment received reinforcement from a German historian, writing from a very different perspective and focusing on a rather different period of history. Fritz Fischer's *Germany's Aims in the First World War*, published in an English translation in 1967, further questioned the uniqueness of Adolf Hitler by pointing to an underlying continuity between Germany's war aims in 1914 and 1939.

Both writers provoked storms of historical controversy. Taylor's conclusions, in particular, failed to secure universal endorsement. But their writings served to ensure that the origins of the war of 1939 would become an area of intense academic debate in a way that had never been the case before. And inevitably revisionism about Hitler was bound to give rise to revisionism about Neville Chamberlain. If Hitler's foreign policy was to be interpreted as a series of clever improvisations rather than an ideological blue-print for aggression, then Chamberlain's well-meaning attempts to thwart what had hitherto been regarded as an inevitable conflict at least made better sense. Against the background of his more important conclusions about Hitler's motivation, Taylor concluded that Chamberlain's appeasement policy was both logical and realistic, though it had often been clumsily executed, and Taylor remained very critical of policy in 1939, especially the failure to secure an agreement with the Soviet Union. As regards the charge of leaving Britain unprepared for war – central to the thesis of *Guilty Men* – Chamberlain emerged largely exonerated. If Britain and France merely wished to defend themselves, insisted Taylor, quite a small increase in their land armaments would have been sufficient and such an increase was easily provided between 1936 and 1939. Only if they hoped to defeat

Germany in battle and restore the sort of position which had
existed in 1919 were their efforts inadequate. But to do this
would have required the quite impossible multiplication of existing rearmament levels by a factor of six or even ten. When it
came to the Munich settlement, still for many the most damaging blight upon Chamberlain's reputation, Taylor had little but
praise. It was

> a triumph for all that was best and most enlightened in
> British life; a triumph for those who had preached equal
> justice between peoples; a triumph for those who had
> courageously denounced the harshness and short-sighted-
> ness of Versailles.[56]

In the wake of Taylor's self-conscious iconoclasm there
emerged a new generation of scholars, less ready to accept the
certainties of their predecessors and more prepared to think
again about the British role in the coming of war in general and
Chamberlain's part in the process in particular. In many cases it
was simply the youth of these writers which served to free them
from the prejudices of their forebears. For them the 1930s were
an era of the historical past rather than a period of their own
conscious experience. Perhaps the most striking contribution
was made by Martin Gilbert, whose *Roots of Appeasement*
appeared in 1966, not least because the same author's *The
Appeasers*, published only three years earlier, had represented
one of the last significant reassertions of the orthodox school.
Gilbert now presented a subtle and thoughtful analysis of the
whole policy of appeasement which suggested that, far from
being the personal invention of Chamberlain's misguided thinking, it represented the mainspring of British foreign policy
throughout the inter-war years. Its origins lay in the outbreak of
war in 1914 and the determination of British statesmen of
'liberal' persuasion that the mistakes of that moment should
never be repeated. This in itself was a significant conclusion. In
suggesting that appeasement was not the creation of the political right, Gilbert helped to undermine the morally superior left-
wing critique which infused the 'Guilty Men' school. The
policy's primary aim became to satisfy legitimate German grievances which resulted from the errors and excesses of the peace-
makers of 1919. 'Appeasement was designed to perfect their
map, and thereby to lead Europe away from war.'[57]
Appeasement thus developed into an on-going corrective to the

injustices of the Treaty of Versailles. The liberal tradition refused to accept that human nature could be completely overcome by evil and maintained that all politicians could be satisfied if properly treated. With hindsight there was no doubt an argument that appeasement lacked meaning in the world that existed after Hitler's advent to power on 30 January 1933. But the fact that the policy failed when confronted by Nazism did not make the policy itself retrospectively mistaken. 'It was never a misguided policy, even if it became, by 1938, temporarily an unrealistic one.'[58] This was by no means a complete exoneration of Chamberlain's conduct as Prime Minister. But it was an important landmark in the transitional process of explaining his actions rather than simply condemning them. 'I have tried to explain and do justice to all opinions, and seek to malign none', insisted Gilbert. The 'Guilty Men' tradition had had its day 'and ought now to fade away', leaving the inter-war years to become 'the object of more reflective inquiry'.[59]

Keith Robbins' book, *Munich 1938*, written to mark the thirtieth anniversary of the celebrated conference, followed in the same vein. Robbins sought to discover the determinants of Chamberlain's policy. Like Gilbert he saw the issues involved in a long-term context. 'Munich must be considered in the light of fifty years of European history, not merely three or four years of British foreign policy.'[60] Chamberlain's correspondence showed that he was fully alive to the potential menace of Nazi Germany. His comments 'are not those of a gauche provincial who blissfully believed that the German Government was intent on mounting a huge trade fair for Birmingham businessmen to visit'.[61] But Chamberlain could not make policy as statesmen of an earlier generation had done. The bomber now meant that no civilized politician could regard war simply as the continuation of policy by other means. If the obliteration of defenceless women and children was what war now involved, then war itself could no longer be excused. But in any case, insisted Robbins, at the time that Chamberlain became Prime Minister in May 1937, very few 'had detected in Hitler an insatiable thirst for blood'.[62] Chamberlain seems to have concluded that Britain could look with no confidence for support from the Empire, the United States or the League of Nations. In such a situation his double policy of rearmament and the quest for better relations with the dictator powers seemed the only sensible option. Precisely what he believed he had achieved at Munich remained an open question which only the opening of all the relevant archives could finally resolve. On the one hand some of Chamberlain's pronouncements seemed to suggest that he had accepted Hitler's word without reservation. On the other he had insisted that future policy must combine the cultivation of friendly relations with Germany with a strategy of intensified rearmament. Robbins had not sought to 'replace the guilty men and dress them up as faultless seers as in a historical puppet-show'.[63] Rather, as the author later recalled, this was a 'transitional book' which broke free from the prejudices of the orthodox historiography while leaving open the direction in which future research might travel.[64]

*   *   *

The processes of revisionism which ultimately transformed our understanding of British foreign policy in the 1930s were paralleled by similar developments in the historiographical interpretation of Britain's economic fortunes in the same decade and in the inter-war period as a whole. Although such analyses were less personally focused on Neville Chamberlain himself, they inevitably allowed for a more sympathetic assessment of his stewardship of the Exchequer between 1931 and 1937, and of his contribution to economic and social policy throughout the inter-war years. C.L. Mowat, in his general history of this period published in 1955, was one of the first to argue that the record of the National Government was not one of unmitigated mismanagement and incompetence. 'Failure in the latter sphere [politics]', he suggested, 'darkened its reputation in the former [economics]; in retrospect it has been blamed for all the misfortunes of the time.'[65] But an almost entirely negative picture of the 1930s dominated the writings of economic historians until the 1960s. Then, it began to be argued that the overall picture had been distorted by an excessive concentration upon the phenomenon of unemployment. And rather as *Guilty Men* had exercised a baneful influence over much of the subsequent historiography of British foreign policy, so too a balanced assessment of the 1930s' economy was impeded by such contemporary tracts as George Orwell's *The Road to Wigan Pier* (1937) and Walter Greenwood's *Love on the Dole* (1933). Such works created a strong – indeed, for many, an indelible – monochrome image of mass unemployment, dole queues and hunger marches. Thus, 'the true impact of unemployment upon social conditions was often obscured by the more emotive and committed writings on the subject'.[66]

Yet there was clearly a paradox. As A.J.P. Taylor put it, 'at the same time, most English people were enjoying a richer life than any previously known in the history of the world: longer holidays, shorter hours, higher real wages. They had motor cars, cinemas, radio sets, electrical appliances. The two sides of life did not join up.'[67] Indeed, for those in work in the 1930s – and these were always the large majority – the decade was one of rising living standards and increased levels of consumption. Unemployment was essentially a regional problem whose localised severity tended to camouflage the underlying strength of the national economy. Revisionist historians began to point out that, notwithstanding high levels of unemployment which persisted until the coming of the Second World War, the domestic economy recovered quite quickly after 1932 and displayed some vigour at least until the recession of 1937–8. It is clear that industries such as house-building enjoyed something of a boom, while there was an impressive rate of growth in 'new' industries such as motor manufacture. As a result, income per head of the population may have grown by up to one third between 1920 and 1939. Overall, it became possible to suggest a favourable comparison between the performance of the British economy in the period 1929–39 and its record before 1914. According to D.H. Aldcroft, writing in 1967, 'it would be profitable if scholars in future devoted more attention to the factors underlying this growth pattern, rather than in discussing the economic disasters which characterised the period'.[68] Even for the unfortunate minority who were unemployed in the 1930s, Britain offered a relatively generous system of benefits which was among the best in Europe. For this it was difficult to deny to Neville Chamberlain a considerable share of the credit. As Bentley Gilbert concluded in 1971, Chamberlain was 'the most successful social reformer in the seventeen years between 1922 and 1939 . . .; after 1922 no one else is really of any significance'.[69]

It was always part of the full-blooded critique of the economic mismanagement of the 1930s to argue that the National Government's faults were largely those of omission. In the heyday of the post-war Keynesian consensus the Treasury was depicted as having done nothing, or nearly nothing, in the face of an economic crisis which had cried out for positive action. Such arguments added to the picture of unnecessary waste which characterized early writings on this subject. The Depression was something which, if it could not have been solved by government measures, could certainly have been greatly mitigated. Gradually, however, economic historians became less inclined than they once were to see the 1930s as a period in which the economy was left to the unrestrained mercy of market forces. Indeed, they came to see clear evidence of a movement towards a managed economy. Though sterling was forced off the Gold Standard in September 1931, its subsequent float was managed by the government through the Exchange Equalisation Account set up in April 1932, by which time Chamberlain had become Chancellor. This mechanism prevented the value of the pound from fluctuating too wildly against other currencies. The conclusion later that year of the Ottawa Agreements, for which Chamberlain acted as Britain's chief negotiator, involved the imposition of a far-reaching system of protective tariffs which significantly altered the pattern of British trade in the years which followed. Government intervention in the operation of British industry was by no means unusual in the 1930s. Revisionists noted the schemes of rationalization introduced in the steel and textile industries, the nationalization of mining royalties and civil aviation and government funding for London transport. The government had also shown signs of developing a regional policy through the setting up of four Special Areas in South Wales, North-East England, West Cumberland and Clydeside at the end of 1934. Chamberlain himself had, of course, grown up amidst traditions of protectionism and municipal socialism and was never an unreformed advocate of the free market. Indeed, it was possible to argue that his pragmatic interventionism went some way to anticipate the model of the Labour government's public corporations of the post-war era.

But perhaps the most important factor in the revision of the traditional view of the decade was the breakdown of the Keynesian consensus in the 1970s. This allowed for a more dispassionate assessment of the so-called 'locust years' than had been possible in the immediate post-war period, whose affluence and full employment seemed to stand as proof that much more could have been done to alleviate the misery of the thirties. Standard works had proclaimed that Keynes, largely ignored by the government before the outbreak of the Second World War, had the answer to unemployment.[70] According to the National Government, however, 'experience has taught us that they [government-funded relief works] do less good in the direct provision of work than harm in the indirect increase of unemployment by depleting the resources of the country which are needed for industrial restoration'.[71] Joan Robinson, writing in 1962 at the height of the Keynesian ascendancy, decreed that the Chamberlain Treasury's arguments in this field were 'simple' and 'laughable'.[72] The experience, however, of managing the British economy in an era of 'stagflation' in the 1970s called into question not only Keynesian prescriptions for that period but also the hitherto widely accepted assumption that a Keynesian solution could, without too much difficulty, have removed the scourge of unemployment four decades earlier. By 1976 a British Labour Prime Minister told his party conference that the option of spending one's way out of a recession no longer existed, and even questioned whether this solution had ever really been viable.

The ideological battles of the early Thatcher years were fought out against the mythology of the 1930s. At one point the TUC adopted the campaigning slogan 'forwards to the eighties not back to the thirties'. It soon became apparent, however, that a new economic orthodoxy, in many ways harking back to that which had existed in the 1930s, was forcing its way on to the centre stage. Not only in Britain, but throughout the capitalist world, price stability had become the most important goal of macroeconomic policy, relegating full employment to a poor second place. The advance of monetarist theory had inevitable consequences for interpretations of the 1930s. By 1981 N. von Tunzelmann could suggest that changes in economic thinking could well afford a new lease of life to the 'Treasury view' in histories of the inter-war years.[73] Keynesianism was losing its moral superiority. Two years later Glynn and Booth were more emphatic. The 'much proclaimed "End of the Keynesian Era" has cast doubts on the ability of established theories to explain not only the problems of the contemporary world but also, by extension, those of the interwar period'.[74] Historians began to conclude that Chamberlain's Treasury had been right to question the efficacy of schemes of large-scale public investment as advocated by figures such as Lloyd George and Keynes. At best, such remedies would have required a time-lag of up to three years before their full effects were apparent, during which time the impact on financial confidence could have re-created the crisis situation of 1931. Furthermore, economic historians started to place more emphasis on the structural aspects of 1930s unemployment. It now seemed unlikely that Keynesian reflation would have had much impact on those industries where the central problem lay in a deficiency of world demand and/or a permanent loss of markets. Unfortunately, the new industries were, on the whole, not located in the same areas as the industries in decline. Thus 'the majority view appears now to be that fiscally induced expansion could not have broken the back of the depression'.[75] Economic orthodoxy turned full circle. 'Most governments', concluded Lord Skidelsky in 1996, 'believe that Keynesian remedies for unemployment will be either ineffective or mischievous, much as they did when Keynes first started advocating them.'[76]

Finally, from the perspective of the monetarist 1980s, it became readily apparent that many of the preoccupations and priorities of Mrs Thatcher's Britain had their resonances in Chamberlain's stewardship of the 1930s. The importance accorded to the control of inflation (even at the expense of continuing high levels of unemployment) was the most obvious. Indeed, it seems unlikely that a revisionist interpretation of the 1930s economy could ever have gained credibility if Britain had not again become accustomed to the spectre of large-scale unemployment. But the Thatcherite focus on balanced budgets, debt repayment, low rates of direct taxation and the ideas of 'sound money' and 'living within one's means' also placed the economic history of the 1930s in a new perspective. The 1980s saw a general collapse in the belief in the state's beneficent capabilities in terms of managing the economy. What had once been dismissed as the complacent indifference or fatalism of the Chamberlain era in awaiting the processes of natural recovery – as Chancellor in 1933 he had suggested that Britain might have to accept ten years of large-scale unemployment – seemed less culpable in the light of a growing acceptance of the notion of natural economic cycles and the belief that governments cannot 'buck the market'.

Historians still debate the precise contribution of government policy to the processes of economic recovery after 1932. But it now appears that the most important long-term benefit of the pound's managed 'float' was the policy of cheap money. Between 30 June 1932 and 24 August 1939 bank rate remained at just 2 per cent. Monetary policy was allowed to determine the exchange rate rather than the other way around. Granted the important part which the housing market played in the recovery of the domestic economy, the ability to borrow at low rates of interest was of considerable significance. But revisionist writers also saw the need to judge Chamberlain's stewardship of the national finances according to the priorities and preoccupations of his own age rather than the differing values of what now appeared to be a Keynesian interlude. It was noted that Chamberlain achieved surpluses on the government's accounts in 1933, 1934, 1935 and 1937. The standard rate of income tax in 1937 was five shillings (25p) in the pound, just as it had been in 1931. During 1934–6 it was actually lower. The Board of Trade wholesale price index (1930=100) stood at 106.6 in 1936 and was under 100 in 1931–4. Only under the impact of rearmament did inflation start to become a problem in 1937. The balance of payments, though in deficit for most of the decade, showed considerable signs of improvement after 1932. Over the decade as a whole the average rate of economic growth hardly altered, notwithstanding some loss of output during the depression. Business confidence never again collapsed after the crisis of 1931. It was not an outstanding record, but it could now be presented as a creditable one, just as it had been judged by Chamberlain's contemporaries.

Thirty years after his death – or perhaps a little later in relation to his economic policy – a revisionist interpretation of Chamberlain's career had secured a firm foothold, though not yet a dominant one, in the historiography of inter-war Britain. But it is important to stress that this process had only really affected Chamberlain's reputation within a relatively restricted academic environment. The dominant popular image remained what it always had been since the summer of 1940. When evidence of revisionist thinking crept into some of the articles in a multi-part history of the Second World War, published in the 1960s and designed for the general public, the editor was deluged with letters of protest conveying a 'note of deep indignation and outrage'.[77] Critics of Thatcherism may have drawn unflattering parallels between the 1930s and the 1980s. But in response the lady herself – always a skilled populist among politicians – sought not to rehabilitate the 1930s but to find historical justification in an altogether earlier era, in the values of Victorian Britain. As late as 1984, by which time the revisionist trickle had swollen into a torrent, a reviewer of David

Dilks's new biography of Chamberlain could still write in terms
more appropriate to the era of *Guilty Men:*

> However much revisionist historians may chip away at the
> record, the stench of Munich still wafts down through the
> years. There have been other misjudgements, other betray-
> als, but Munich will always occupy a notably unhappy
> niche in British history, and the task of rehabilitating
> Chamberlain will inevitably be the work of Sisyphus . . . It
> was a period of almost unmitigated disaster, presided over
> by a bunch of second-rate politicians most of whom would
> barely deserve a paragraph in the DNB let alone a two
> volume biography.[78]

The battle to restore Chamberlain's reputation, then, would not
be easily won. By the 1970s, however, revisionist writers
believed that they had a crucial ally on their side – the historical
record itself.

Notes

1. Chamberlain MSS, NC11/1/164, A.Bryant to Annie Chamberlain
   14 May 1954.
2. *Daily Sketch* 15 Nov. 1940.
3. *The Times* 13 Nov. 1940.
4. *Spectator* 15 Nov. 1940.
5. Chamberlain MSS, NC7/11/33/146A, Samuel to Chamberlain 14
   Oct. 1940.
6. *Ibid.,* NC7/11/33/19, Ball to Chamberlain n.d. [Aug. 1940]
7. *Ibid.,* NC13/17/122, Headlam to Chamberlain 15 May 1940.
8. *Ibid.,* NC13/17/161, Midleton to Chamberlain 17 May 1940.
9. *Ibid.,* NC13/19/2/524, Shakespeare to Annie Chamberlain 13 Nov.
   1940.
10. *Ibid.,* NC13/18/879, MacDonald to Chamberlain 8 Nov. 1940.
11. *Scotsman* 11 Nov. 1940.
12. *Toronto Telegram* 14 May 1940.
13. *Rand Daily Mail* 13 Nov. 1940.
14. Chamberlain MSS, NC13/19/2/549, J. Stuart to Annie
    Chamberlain 27 Nov. 1940.
15. C. King, *With Malice Toward None: A War Diary* (London, 1970),
    p.114.
16. Chamberlain MSS, NC11/1/613, Maugham to Annie Chamberlain
    30 Sept. 1943.
17. Lord Maugham, *The Truth about the Munich Crisis* (London,
    1944), p.63.
18. Chamberlain MSS, NC11/1/615, Wilson to Annie Chamberlain 22
    March 1944.

19. *Ibid.*, NC11/1/617, Maugham to Annie Chamberlain 13 April 1944.
20. *Ibid.*, NC1/15/5/10, Hadley to H. Chamberlain 14 May 1944; NC 11/1/369, Hadley to Annie Chamberlain 15 May 1944.
21. W. Hadley, *Munich: Before and After* (London, 1944), p.117
22. *Ibid.*, p.153.
23. *Ibid.*, p.28.
24. G. Lewis, *Lord Hailsham: A Life* (London, 1997), p.56.
25. Chamberlain MSS, NC7/11/33/108, Hogg to Chamberlain 9 May 1940.
26. Q. Hogg, *The Left was Never Right* (London, 1945), p.75.
27. *Ibid.*, p.73.
28. *Ibid.*, p.186
29. Lord Hailsham, *A Sparrow's Flight* (London, 1990), p.230.
30. Chamberlain MSS, NC11/15/129, Feiling to H.Wilson 31 July 1941.
31. *Ibid.*, BC4/7/9a, Ida Chamberlain to Dorothy Lloyd 24 Oct. 1942.
32. *Ibid.*, NC1/16/4/18, I. Chamberlain to Annie Chamberlain 7 Jan. 1942.
33. *Ibid.*, NC11/15/2, Feiling to Annie Chamberlain 27 Oct. 1941.
34. K. Feiling, *The Life of Neville Chamberlain* (London, 1946), p.198.
35. *Ibid.*, p.314.
36. *Ibid.*, p.319.
37. *Ibid.*, p.320.
38. *Ibid.*, p.394.
39. Chamberlain MSS, NC11/15/2, Feiling to Annie Chamberlain 27 Oct. 1941.
40. Feiling, *Chamberlain*, p.398.
41. Chamberlain MSS, BC4/8/62, H. Chamberlain to D. Lloyd 21 Dec. 1946.
42. *The Times* 10 Dec. 1946; *Financial Times* 23 Dec. 1946; *Daily Telegraph* 13 Dec. 1946; *Time and Tide* 1 Feb. 1947.
43. Chamberlain MSS, NC11/1/925, Wilson to Annie Chamberlain 18 July 1948.
44. D.C. Watt, 'The historiography of appeasement' in C. Cook and A. Sked (eds), *Crisis and Controversy: Essays in Honour of A.J.P. Taylor* (London, 1976), p.115.
45. 'The Policy of Appeasement', BBC Home Service 8 Aug. 1956.
46. Chamberlain MSS, BC4/8/91, H. Chamberlain to D. Lloyd 29 Oct. 1948.
47. Viscount Templewood, *Nine Troubled Years* (London, 1954), p.323.
48. *Ibid.*, p.378.
49. *Ibid.*, p.341.
50. *Ibid.*, p.375.
51. *Glasgow Herald* 27 Nov. 1961.
52. *John O'London's* 30 Nov. 1961.
53. *Punch* 13 Dec. 1961.
54. R. Shepherd, *Iain Macleod: A Biography* (London, 1994), p.272.

55. A.J.P. Taylor, *The Origins of the Second World War* (London, 1961), p.9.
56. *Ibid.*, p.189.
57. M. Gilbert, *The Roots of Appeasement* (London, 1966), p.159.
58. *Ibid.*, p.187.
59. *Ibid.*, p.xiii.
60. K. Robbins, *Munich 1938* (London, 1968), p.3.
61. *Ibid.*, p.154.
62. *Ibid.*, p.133.
63. *Ibid.*, p.3.
64. K. Robbins, *Appeasement* (Oxford, 1988), p.7.
65. C.L. Mowat, *Britain Between the Wars 1918–1940* (London, 1955), p.413.
66. J. Stevenson and C. Cook, *The Slump: Society and Politics during the Depression* (London, 1977), p.76.
67. A.J.P. Taylor, *English History 1914–1945* (London, 1965), p.317.
68. D.H. Aldcroft, 'Economic growth in Britain in the inter-war years: a reassessment', *Economic History Review*, 20,3 (1967), p.325.
69. B.B. Gilbert, *British Social Policy 1914–1939* (London, 1970), p.195.
70. See, for example, D.H. Aldcroft, *The Inter-war Economy: Britain 1919–39* (London, 1970) and M. Stewart, *Keynes and After* (London, 1972).
71. Public Record Office, CAB 27/490, cited Stevenson and Cook, *The Slump*, p.63.
72. J. Robinson, *Economic Philosophy* (London, 1962), p.73.
73. N. von Tunzelmann, 'Britain 1900–45: A Survey' in R. Flood and D. McCloskey (eds), *The Economic History of Britain since 1700* (Cambridge, 1981), vol.2, p.249.
74. S. Glynn and A.E.Booth, 'Unemployment in Interwar Britain: a case for re-learning the lessons of the 1930s?', *Economic History Review*, 36, 3 (1983), p.329.
75. M. Thomas, 'The macroeconomics of the inter-war years' in Flood and McCloskey (eds) *Economic History* (2nd edn, 1994), vol.2, p.356.
76. R. Skidelsky, *Keynes* (London, 1996), p.106.
77. Watt, 'Historiography of Appeasement', p.112.
78. *The Guardian* 22 Nov. 1984. The reviewer was Richard Gott, joint author of *The Appeasers*.

|6|

The importance of evidence

*It is a pretty safe prediction that with the fuller disclosure of
the truth which time will bring the stature of Neville
Chamberlain will increase rather than diminish.*[1]

By the mid-1960s Chamberlain's reputation had at least become
a topic of legitimate, and sometimes lively, academic debate
rather than a matter of received wisdom. But both sides in this
debate recognized that they were working with a limited body of
documentary material. It is true that as early as 1944 the British
government had decided to prepare for publication a series of
volumes of *Documents on British Foreign Policy* covering the
years 1919–39. This followed the precedent of the earlier series
of *British Documents on the Origins of the War* of 1914
published between 1926 and 1938. The editorial decision to
divide the process of publication into three series meant that the
Third Series, covering the crucial years 1938–9, had begun to
appear as early as 1949. The task was entrusted to respected
professional historians, although there was some suspicion that
some documents were included with the specific intention of
discrediting appeasement.[2] In addition, and also with the experience of the documentary history of the First World War's
origins in mind, the Allies had taken the decision to publish for
themselves the captured foreign policy archives of the Nazi
regime to preclude any possibility that a post-war German
government might use such documentation to the same effective
propaganda purposes as had been employed by the Weimar
Republic in the 1920s. To this very significant collection of
published documents could be added an ever growing number of

memoirs of the inter-war years together with the readily available record of the proceedings of parliament and of the contemporary press. Chamberlain's private papers had of course also been made selectively available to sympathetic authors. But beyond this corpus of material, and apparently out of reach, lay the full record of British governments of the 1920s and 1930s, including the papers of such policy-making bodies as the cabinet, cabinet committees and the Committee of Imperial Defence. As long ago as 1940 both Chamberlain's critics and his admirers had believed that this hidden archive would offer confirmation of their own point of view. Joseph Ball, planning to counteract the effects of *Guilty Men*, was convinced that the documentary record would eventually provide the vindication of Chamberlain's premiership. In the opposing camp Cecil King was fearful that incriminating documents might be destroyed, but still doubted whether 'the destruction of all the paper ever made would mislead future generations to the extent of approving Chamberlain's policies'.[3]

But if the opening of government archives would offer the possibility of resolving the debate over Chamberlain's career one way or the other, that prospect lay some way in the future. Under the Public Records Act of 1957 a general closure period of fifty years was confirmed on all government papers with provision being made for the Lord Chancellor to exclude particularly sensitive documents from the public domain for an even longer period of time. It was therefore likely to be only in the 1990s that historians would have anything like full access to the records of the Chamberlain government. In 1967, however, Harold Wilson's Labour government gave support and parliamentary time to a private member's bill which reduced the normal closure period to thirty years. At a stroke, therefore, a vast quantity of papers, minutes and memoranda became available to historians, covering almost the entire inter-war period. Inevitably, it was the record of the final years preceding the outbreak of the Second World War which attracted most attention, a fact which served to accentuate an existing trend whereby Chamberlain was judged on the basis of his premiership rather than his entire career.

In broad terms this legislative change opened the floodgates of revisionism. Judgements of Neville Chamberlain became steadily more sympathetic. The emphasis was now placed much more squarely on asking why British governments behaved as they did in the 1930s, leaving behind the old issue of the morality of British foreign policy and at the same time greatly reducing the focus upon personality, although those who still wished to concentrate their attention upon Chamberlain himself were greatly helped by the formal opening of his private papers for research in 1975. In this way it became possible to view Chamberlain – perhaps for the first time – in a true historical perspective. By analysing the strategic, economic and political factors which influenced British foreign policy, it became apparent that he had had to operate within extremely narrow parameters. In this process of explaining appeasement, many historians effectively justified it, for they presented a picture in which Britain had few, if any, alternative options. Chamberlain no longer appeared cowardly or inept. Rather he stood as someone who had managed Britain's difficult affairs with considerable skill and, if he ultimately failed, it seemed unlikely that anyone else could have done much better. For some historians appeasement began to seem as obviously 'right' – at least in practical terms – as it had once appeared indubitably 'wrong'. As one writer put it:

> If one begins to tot up the plausible motivations for appeasement . . . one sees that these are far more than enough to explain it. It is massively over-determined . . . any other policy in 1938 would have been an astounding, almost inexplicable divergence from the norm.[4]

Yet if Chamberlain's reputation was to be an ultimate beneficiary of the introduction of the Thirty Year Rule, such a development was by no means immediately apparent. The first two significant works to be published after an examination of the recently opened archives seemed close to confirming the verdict of *Guilty Men* thirty years after its publication. Ian Colvin's *The Chamberlain Cabinet* was an historiographical curiosity. Unlike most of the writers who now set to work at the Public Record Office, Colvin was a veteran of the 1930s. Indeed he himself had played a small part in the drama which he now sought to analyse and explain. As a correspondent for the *News Chronicle* he had been expelled from Berlin at the end of March 1939 and had brought back to London information – incorrect as it turned out – of an imminent German invasion of Poland. This false intelligence had then been a factor in persuading the British cabinet to issue its guarantee to that country. In many ways, therefore,

Colvin would have fitted more easily into the school of Namier and Wheeler-Bennett, struggling to find a balance between historical judgement and personal experience. He had already published a study of Sir Robert Vansittart, written in conventionally heroic, anti-appeasement terms. He now saw the 1967 act as affording an opportunity to 'those whose work or experience associated them intimately with a period . . . [to] study it in full depth with the advantage that later historians cannot share, that of human memory'.[5] Significantly, *The Chamberlain Cabinet* appeared under the imprint of the same left-wing publisher, Victor Gollancz, who had produced *Guilty Men* three decades earlier.

Colvin's book appears hurried and somewhat crudely constructed. Much of it reads as an ill-digested transcript of the minutes of the cabinet and its foreign policy committee over the years of Chamberlain's government. But his conclusions are trenchant and unequivocal. Colvin charged the government with a failure to rearm in time, with an unnecessary surrender over Czechoslovakia in 1938 and with entering war a year later weaker than need have been the case because of its failure to secure an alliance with Soviet Russia. Chamberlain himself is presented as a vain autocrat, unduly susceptible to praise and flattery, who completely dominated his cabinet and frequently by-passed it in a way which threatened to undermine constitutional convention. The Prime Minister was reluctant to take advice except from people who were like-minded to himself. His approach to foreign affairs was 'one of sustained astonishment that some formula could not be found to suit all parties, as if some deep-rooted dispute had never existed'.[6] Colvin's scrutiny of the newly opened records had revealed 'no example in two and a half years of Cabinet meetings in which the discussion in Cabinet altered his mind on a subject, though he was known to alter it between Cabinets'.[7] While few would have expected *The Chamberlain Cabinet* to remain the last word on the subject, Colvin provided valuable ammunition for the still strong forces of orthodoxy.

The work of Keith Middlemas, *Diplomacy of Illusion*, published in 1972, was an altogether more serious matter. The author used a far wider range of documentation than had Colvin, including the private papers of some of Chamberlain's ministerial contemporaries such as Samuel Hoare and Thomas Inskip. He was also granted privileged access to Chamberlain's

own diaries and letters. Middlemas set out to offer 'a preliminary comment on British policy in the light of the new documents available about the process of policy formulation itself'.[8]
As with some earlier works the very title of his book gave an
indication of the thrust of his conclusions. He was convinced
that Chamberlain, on becoming Prime Minister, had initiated a
radically different foreign policy from that of his predecessor in
which a key change was the abandonment of a strategy of deterrence in favour of one of defence designed only to repel a
German attack on Britain. This led, logically enough, to a
'heightened sensitivity to possible causes of European war'.[9]
Middlemas conceded that earlier accounts of British foreign
policy in this period had paid insufficient attention to such
determinants as the limits of British power, the restraints
imposed by a combination of military weakness and extensive
commitments and the lack of support available from the
Dominions and the United States. Nonetheless, the 'illusion' of
British policy lay in its unwillingness to face the stark question
of whether war was inevitable and in the persistence with which
policy makers, especially Chamberlain, believed that they could
secure co-existence with Germany on British terms. Granted
that the form of appeasement which Chamberlain pursued could
neither protect Britain from attack nor deter Hitler from acts of
aggression, the policy was, in Middlemas's view, fundamentally
flawed. Once more, therefore, the key to the situation was found
in the inadequacy of Britain's political leadership.

Middlemas's Chamberlain was no 'helpless innocent, shuf-
fling sheeplike among the crooked leaders of the Third Reich'.[10]
But this seasoned politician suffered from a 'strategic blindness'
because of his unwillingness to contemplate the deliberate
launching of a war. This 'led directly to blackmail by leaders
who did not acknowledge Chamberlain's standards and used
them as weapons against him when they could'.[11] The Prime
Minister was an autocrat not because he failed to consult but
because he believed that other ministers, once consulted, were
bound to follow his own processes and line of thought. For
Middlemas the key period was the six months between the
Munich agreement and the guarantee to Poland, a time when
Chamberlain dominated his government and its foreign policy
as never before. During this period, charged Middlemas, the
Prime Minister should have carried out a comprehensive policy
review in the light of the Munich settlement. Instead, he

persisted with the view that Munich had opened the way for a lasting Anglo-German understanding. Only the stunning events of March 1939 made him think again. Appeasement was then abandoned, while 'rearmament and the new diplomacy represented a conscious revival of the policy of deterrence and containment'.[12]

The publications of Colvin and Middlemas thus suggested that the opening of the archives might merely confirm the image of Neville Chamberlain which, notwithstanding the efforts of some revisionist writers, had dominated both the historiography and the popular perception since 1940. One reviewer of Middlemas's book commented on 'the familiarity of the theme' and concluded that 'the road to Munich cannot any longer be a voyage of major discovery for British historians'.[13] Yet these works failed to anticipate the general trend of historical writing in the 1970s and 1980s. This literature is best analysed in terms of the key arguments and themes which now emerged.

In the first place, and contrary to one of Middlemas's main arguments, historians became increasingly sceptical of the idea that 'appeasement' was in any sense an invention of Chamberlain himself. It was perhaps best seen as a tradition which had been inherent in British policy since the mid-nineteenth century, 'the "natural" policy for a small island state gradually losing its place in world affairs, shouldering military and economic burdens which were increasingly too great for it, and developing internally from an oligarchic to a more democratic form of political constitution in which sentiments in favour of a pacific and rational settlement of disputes were widely propagated'.[14] Britain's circumstances as a satisfied power after the First World War merely confirmed this underlying attitude. An often quoted Foreign Office memorandum of 1926 encapsulated the British position:

> We . . . have no territorial ambitions nor desire for aggrandisement. We have got all that we want – perhaps more. Our sole object is to keep what we want and live in peace. . . . The fact is that war and rumours of war, quarrels and friction, in any corner of the world spell loss and harm to British commercial and financial interests. . . . [S]o manifold and ubiquitous are British trade and British finance that, whatever else may be the outcome of a disturbance of the peace, we shall be the losers.[15]

The appeasement of Germany in the 1920s was further encouraged by those who felt a sense of guilt about the imposition of the Treaty of Versailles. Furthermore, by this time of universal suffrage the majority of the population were asking more of their governments than ever before in terms of improved social services, narrowing the scope for extensive spending on foreign policy and defence.

When it came to the 1930s, though a debate would later develop as to whether Chamberlain's version of this traditional policy was distinctively different, most detailed analyses served to overthrow the once clear distinction between appeasers and anti-appeasers. As Oliver Harvey had noted in his diary in 1941, 'the truth is everybody was an "appeaser" of Germany at one time or another'.[16] Indeed, it was striking that for much of the decade Chamberlain's thinking on Germany and other international problems was not dissimilar to that of men who later numbered among his most vociferous critics including Churchill and Vansittart. Norton Medlicott, seeing an essential continuity in British policy towards Germany throughout the decade, argued that Chamberlain and Vansittart were both 'Thirty-Niners', policy-makers who saw the need to postpone war until such time as Britain had a realistic chance of winning it. Overall, the notion that Chamberlain had conducted a personal foreign policy from No. 10 Downing Street in defiance of the considered professional advice of the Foreign Office ceased to be tenable. Though the doubters increased in number after 1938, 'even then distinctions between those who continued to support appeasement and those who came to oppose it are not always easily drawn'.[17] Then, as historians placed Chamberlain's policies increasingly in the mainstream, so too his style of government appeared more conventional. Christopher Hill's study of the Chamberlain cabinet's decision-making processes did much to dispel Colvin's image of an autocrat who had undermined the traditions of cabinet government and sought refuge in the endorsement of a small group of like-minded ministers. 'The crucial decisions during September 1938 were, in the end, cabinet decisions, and not those of the inner cabinet or one man . . . The same was true of the Russian negotiations in 1939.'[18] Some writers even suggested that, after the autumn of 1938, Chamberlain's was no longer the controlling voice in his own cabinet and that Halifax as Foreign Secretary was increasingly able to determine government policy.[19]

Perhaps the most compelling new perspective afforded by the archives was the opportunity to examine the full range of British commitments and concerns in the 1930s. This provided a necessary corrective to the idea, encouraged by the thematic editorial arrangement of the volumes of *Documents on British Foreign Policy* that policy towards Nazi Germany could be viewed in narrow isolation. Back in 1965 Donald Watt had complained that, with one or two exceptions, existing discussions of British foreign policy in the 1930s failed to view the problem as the Chamberlain government had been obliged to do, 'as part of a concurrent though rarely concerted attack on Britain's position in Europe, in the Mediterranean and the Middle East, and in East Asia and the Pacific'.[20] Watt believed that it was in the failure to see British policy in relation to the three aggressor states of Germany, Italy and Japan as a unity that the orthodox school was most vulnerable to challenge. Historians now had the chance to prove him right. David Dilks's analysis proved particularly persuasive. He argued that it was impossible to understand British foreign policy in the 1930s unless it was realized that policy makers had to give as much attention to the Mediterranean and the Far East as they did to Europe. Thus 'there could never be a British policy towards Germany alone; it could be reached, and therefore it can be appreciated, only in relation to the other potential enemies'.[21] If Britain had become embroiled in war in Europe, this might have given Japan a favourable moment to attack British interests in the Far East. On the other hand the outbreak of war with Japan might have encouraged Germany to embark upon aggressive adventures in Europe.

It became apparent that Chamberlain himself had been among the first British ministers to appreciate this strategic dilemma and to try to formulate a policy to cope with it. As early as February 1934, only a year after Hitler had come to power, the cabinet's Defence Requirements Committee had identified Germany as Britain's ultimate potential enemy against whom the country's long-term defence planning should be directed. As Chancellor of the Exchequer Chamberlain seems to have accepted this finding and to have tried to take it to its logical conclusion. As he explained to his sister, in a letter in which he wrote of his loathing for Nazism, 'If we are to take the necessary measures of defence against [Germany] we certainly can't afford at the same time to rebuild our battlefleet. Therefore we ought to be making eyes at Japan.'[22] He thus became the leader of a faction within the government which sought, unsuccessfully as it turned out, an accommodation with Japan in order to concentrate the country's defence effort against Germany. Convinced that Britain did not have adequate resources to fight Germany and Japan together, he argued against those of his colleagues who wished for Imperial reasons to focus on defence against the latter. Furthermore, Chamberlain believed that Britain's limited funds should be concentrated upon building up the RAF even if this meant abandoning any pretence to participate in a future continental land war.

By the following year, as Mussolini cast covetous eyes upon Abyssinia, it had become necessary to add Italy to the list of Britain's potential enemies. The nightmare scenario of a war on three fronts – even though this was not what materialized in September 1939 – was the everyday possibility which informed policy makers from the mid-1930s onwards. By 1937 the Air Staff considered that the chance of a 'unilateral war' with any one of those possible enemies was 'extremely remote'. Even if hostilities broke out in the first instance with just one opponent, Britain would 'very quickly find all three of these Powers arrayed against us'.[23] In November 1935 the Defence Requirements Committee pointed out what the country's strategic vulnerability implied for British foreign policy:

> We consider it to be a cardinal requirement of our national and imperial security that our foreign policy should be so conducted as to avoid the possible development of a situation in which we might be confronted simultaneously with the hostility, open or veiled, of Japan in the Far East, Germany in the West, and any Power in the main line of communication between the two.[24]

It thus appeared that appeasement was a response to this unwelcome situation, a means rather than an end in itself. Essentially it meant 'enforced negotiations from a position of relative weakness; an ignoble failure but unavoidable'.[25] While Chamberlain might have been able as Prime Minister to devise a particular response to the country's predicament, he could not fundamentally change it. As he noted in September 1937, 'the proposition that our foreign policy must be, if not dictated, at least limited, by the state of the national defence, remains true'.[26] It became the cardinal task of Chamberlain's foreign policy to buy time and to reduce the number of Britain's potential enemies.

Such thinking explains Chamberlain's determination in the early months of his premiership to investigate the possibility of an accommodation with Italy – a strategy which ultimately brought him into collision with his Foreign Secretary, Anthony Eden. In 1935 Chamberlain had favoured the imposition of sanctions against Italy because of the latter's aggression in Africa. Two years later, however, the on-going process of German rearmament had convinced him that the attempt to uphold the League in areas where British vital interests were not at stake was a luxury which the country could not afford. As the Prime Minister explained, 'in view of the enormous interests involved . . . and the frightful cost of rearmament, the burden of which has not by any means been fully felt as yet, we should be gravely wanting in our duty if we failed to make every effort to reach a favourable understanding'.[27] Under the guidance of Sir Thomas Inskip, the Minister for the Co-ordination of Defence, the government embarked upon a wide-ranging strategic review, whose reports at the end of 1937 and the beginning of 1938 were of fundamental importance in shaping Chamberlain's subsequent policies. The Chiefs of Staff advised that, notwithstanding the assistance which Britain might hope to obtain from France and, possibly, other allies, it was impossible to foresee the time when the country's forces would be strong enough to safeguard Britain's territory, trade and vital interests against three major enemies in three different theatres of war. World war would almost certainly destroy Britain's empire and any continuing pretensions to Great Power status.

It had always been part of the original indictment of Neville Chamberlain, especially as expressed by Winston Churchill, that he had not only failed in his assessment of Britain's potential enemies but also that he had been negligent in rallying potential allies, in other words that some form of Grand Alliance such as ultimately came into being during the Second World War was available in the 1930s and could have stopped Hitler and his fellow aggressors in their tracks. Newly opened documents offered fresh insights into the reality or otherwise of this notion and into Chamberlain's thinking on the matter. He was clearly doubtful whether British participation in such an alignment of powers would have made the preservation of peace more likely. The existence of the Triple Alliance had certainly not prevented war in 1914 and, like most of his generation, Chamberlain subscribed to the view that the division of Europe into opposing camps before 1914 had actually contributed to the outbreak of hostilities. As he told the House of Commons in April 1938:

> To all intents and purposes the real effect of this proposal [for an alliance with France and the Soviet Union] would be to do what we, at any rate, have always set our faces against, namely to divide Europe into two opposing blocs or camps. So far from making a contribution to peace, I say that it would inevitably plunge us into war.[28]

When it came to the various component parts of any Grand Coalition Chamberlain felt further cause for doubt.

The starting point in the Churchillian vision of a bloc of states which could have thwarted the fascist threat was a close association between Britain and France. But Chamberlain always nurtured grave misgivings about French reliability. As he wrote to Lord Weir, the government's adviser to the Air Ministry, 'I wish the French Government did not collapse every time we get to a critical point when we want their firm and continuous support. But that is I suppose a phenomenon of Nature which we must just accept.'[29] Research in French archives seemed to show that this lack of confidence was largely justified. France pursued a policy of appeasement as a result of her own domestic considerations, rather than being forced into it by a bullying British ally as had often been suggested and as the French themselves sometimes had good cause to imply. This was never more true than at the time of the Czechoslovakian crisis in 1938 when Prime Minister Daladier was only too conscious of France's unpreparedness, both material and psychological, for war. In the view of the Chief of the French Air Staff the country's air force would be defeated within a fortnight. Indeed, the French seem to have sent a secret formal notification to the Czech government in July 1938 that they were not going to fight on their behalf. If a solid basis for resistance to German aggression existed, it was not to be found in an Anglo–French military alliance.

It also became clear that Chamberlain held a long-term conviction that isolationist sentiment in the United States was too strong to allow the Americans to intervene actively in the diplomacy of the European powers. Indeed, he belonged to a generation which had come to accept American isolationism as a given fact of the international scene. His scepticism was confirmed by American conduct during the Far-Eastern crisis of

1931–3 when the United States had managed to give a very misleading impression of a country ready and willing to take action but thwarted by British caution. Like many other policy makers of this era he found the American combination of moralizing words and empty gestures uniquely irritating. The 'real trouble with Yanks', he complained in 1934, was that they 'never can deliver the goods'.[30] Chamberlain seems to have been convinced that only the entirely unpredictable eventuality of a direct attack on American possessions would persuade the United States to fight, a proposition which Roosevelt's failure even to try to persuade Congress to declare war when Germany invaded Poland, notwithstanding the considerable Polish–American population, does much to substantiate.

Chamberlain was unimpressed by Roosevelt's 'quarantine' speech of 5 October 1937, even though it appeared to indicate a greater American readiness to become involved in world affairs. He feared that it might have the effect of consolidating links between the aggressor powers when his policy was directed towards keeping them apart and he was particularly concerned about the possible impact in the Far East. 'In the present state of European affairs', he insisted, 'we simply cannot afford to quarrel with Japan and I very much fear, therefore, that after a lot of ballyhoo the Americans will somehow fade out and leave us to carry all the blame and the odium.'[31] He found the American performance the following month at the Brussels Conference on the Far East unimpressive and was understandably cautious about Roosevelt's celebrated 'peace initiative' the following January upon which Churchill later heaped such significance. If the United States had been ineffective in the Far East where she had obvious interests at stake, what likelihood was there of any tangible assistance in the European theatre? In the aftermath of Munich it was easy enough for the Americans to advocate a tougher stance towards Germany, but Chamberlain understood that it was the British people and not they who would be in the front line should Hitler be provoked to attack. Even after war had broken out Chamberlain remained wary about the prospect of American intervention, fearing that the consequence would be their economic domination of the British Empire. 'Heaven knows', he admitted to his sister in January 1940, 'I don't want the Americans to fight for us – we should have to pay too dearly for that if they had a right to be in on the peace terms.'[32]

Such thinking may seem misplaced, even perverse, in the light of the United States' vital assistance to the British war effort during Churchill's premiership and her overall contribution to victory over the Axis powers. But it is necessary to place Chamberlain's ideas in the context of the situation as it appeared in the 1930s when, stripped of Churchillian sentimentality about American selflessness, the attack on Pearl Harbor lay, unforeseeably, in the future. Furthermore, many historians have now shown that the wartime Special Relationship was an altogether more competitive alignment than Churchill portrayed in his war memoirs. Writers such as Gabriel Kolko have argued that the reduction of British power was indeed, as Chamberlain had perhaps foreseen, a fundamental American war aim.[33] At the far end of the revisionist spectrum John Charmley and others have even been ready to challenge the Churchillian version of history head on, painting Churchill rather than Chamberlain as the villain of the piece. By focusing on the price Britain paid for victory over Germany and the fact that the country was substantially weakened after five years of Churchill's premiership, it is the war hero rather than the much derided Chamberlain who emerges as Charmley's 'Guilty Man'. Thus it has been suggested that Chamberlain's policy of appeasement 'offered the only way of preserving what was left of British power; if 1945 represented "victory", it was, as Chamberlain had foreseen, for the Soviets and the Americans'.[34]

The fact that it was not possible to look with any confidence to the United States for support in relation to Britain's diplomatic and strategic problems made the position of the Empire more important than might otherwise have been the case. But the constitutional status of the Dominions was no longer what it was in 1914 when George V had declared war on behalf of all his realms. Under the Statute of Westminster of 1931 the full independence of the Dominions in international affairs had been confirmed. The dream of Chamberlain's father, among others, that a process of consultation would lead to the construction of a single foreign policy for the whole empire had faded into memory as the Dominions made it increasingly clear throughout the inter-war years that they preferred to develop separate foreign policies appropriate to themselves. Ritchie Ovendale concludes that the Dominions were not responsible for appeasement, but that their support for the policy provided one more good reason for it. The message which reached the new Prime Minister from the Imperial Conference of May 1937 that South

Africa, Canada and Australia were unlikely to give Britain even
qualified support in the event of a continental war convinced
him that 'his policy of preserving peace in Europe was the right
one'. Yet 'over Czechoslovakia, Chamberlain saw the reluctance
of the Dominions to fight, and the consequent break-up of the
Commonwealth as decisive'.[35] Malcolm MacDonald, the
Dominions Secretary, later recalled that it was for this reason
that he supported the Prime Minister throughout the crisis. The
views of the High Commissioners had 'considerable though not
decisive, influence on Ministers' thinking'.[36] Paradoxically,
though, it was Chamberlain's policy of appeasement, argues
Ovendale, which by exhausting all peaceful alternatives 'ensured
that when war came in 1939 the Commonwealth was united'.[37]

The final component in Churchill's Grand Alliance was of
course the Soviet Union. Chamberlain's deep suspicion of the
Stalinist regime was well known and easily confirmed by the
historical record. The Prime Minister was virtually the last
member of his own cabinet to be won round in the spring of
1939 to the necessity of a Russian alliance in order to give meaning to the British guarantee of Polish independence. Churchill
too was no enthusiast for Bolshevism but he at least – or so the
orthodox interpretation would have it – had had the vision to
recognize the need to sup with the devil in the face of the even
greater threat posed by Adolf Hitler. Chamberlain, on the other
hand, had embarked upon negotiations with the Soviet Union in
a manner almost calculated to ensure their failure, in A.J.P.
Taylor's stinging phrase, 'the most incompetent transactions
since Lord North lost the American colonies'.[38] Historians who
unravelled the complicated diplomatic tangle surrounding the
Anglo–Soviet negotiations in the spring and summer of 1939
were at least increasingly conscious of the weakness of the
British bargaining position, especially when compared with the
seductive hand held out to Stalin by Nazi Germany. But no final
judgement seemed possible in the absence of Soviet records. The
true intentions of Soviet diplomacy remained impenetrable,
though some historians were always ready to regard
Chamberlain's doubts as wholly justified, notwithstanding
Stalin's enormous contribution to the allied war effort (or was it
merely the Soviet war effort?) after the German invasion of June
1941.

The opening of the archives, and particularly of his private
papers, confirmed the depth of Chamberlain's loathing of

warfare – something which he shared with a large majority of the British population. Throughout his life he abhorred war because of the waste which it involved and, from a personal point of view, the way it diverted resources away from what he wanted to do in politics in terms of improving the lot of his fellow man. Chamberlain's personal experience of the First World War, in which his cousin Norman to whom he was particularly close had been killed on the Western Front, had of course been mirrored across the land. It was eerily calculated that, if Britain's war dead were to march down Whitehall four abreast, three and a half days would elapse before the end of the procession reached the Cenotaph. What the evidence revealed, however, was that it was something even worse than a repetition of the catastrophe of 1914–18 which haunted the minds of British policy makers in the 1930s, Chamberlain included. Recapturing the mood of the decade was less a matter of uncovering hitherto secret documentation – though government papers offered plenty of confirmation – but more a readiness to examine long ignored sources already in the public domain.

Attitudes towards the morality and utility of war as an extension of the diplomatic dealings of nation states, one with another, have of course varied greatly in the course of the last hundred years. At the end of the Second World War there seemed little scope for doubt. 'There can have been very few people in the Western World', writes Sir Michael Howard, 'who did not believe in 1945 that the war which they had fought and won had been not only necessary but in every sense "just".'[39] But this judgement was essentially reached only when the course of the war had revealed precisely what was at stake in that conflict and that its cost was – just about – endurable. Such a realization came much easier in 1945 than it would have done in 1939; easier still than in 1938 when the mood had been very different. That modern warfare proved somewhat less awful than had been widely predicted is not something for which Chamberlain can be legitimately criticized. As Harold Macmillan recalled thirty years later, 'we thought of air warfare in 1938 rather as people think of nuclear warfare today'.[40]

The development of the bomber was widely believed to have transformed the very nature of armed conflict, in the process largely denying to Britain what had hitherto been her greatest geographical asset in warfare, her island status. 'The belief in the Luftwaffe's potency', writes Benny Morris, 'was probably the single most important determinant of appeasement in the 1930s.'[41] The apocalyptic science fiction of earlier decades seemed by the 1930s to have become the reality of modern war. Popular fiction conditioned the thinking of the British public. Air Commodore L.E.O. Charlton's *War Over England* published in 1936 pictured the country being defeated in the space of two days. An attack on the annual Hendon Air Show kills two-fifths of Britain's pilots along with 30,000 spectators. Subsequent raids on London badly disrupt the capital's water and electricity supplies before a gas attack prompts immediate surrender. Writers who believed that they were describing reality rather than fiction confirmed such predictions. The pacifist Bertrand Russell presented a frightening picture of a future war:

> London for several days will be one vast raving bedlam, the hospitals will be stormed, traffic will cease, the homeless will shriek for help, the city will be a pandemonium. What of the Government at Westminster, it will be swept away by an avalanche of terror. Then will the enemy dictate its terms.[42]

This, of course, was fantasy, but fantasy which found its echo in the official mind in Whitehall. The limited experience of civilian bombing in the First World War when taken in conjunction with advances in aircraft technology led to the extrapolation of alarmist statistics. If just 300 tons of bombs dropped on London in the earlier conflict had produced 4820 casualties, then it seemed reasonable for the CID to suggest that more than half a million deaths could be expected in the first few weeks of a German aerial assault. Britain, and London in particular, was seen as defenceless in the face of the bomber which, as Baldwin had said, 'will always get through'. In reality Britain's total civilian casualties nationwide during the Second World War barely exceeded the figure predicted for London alone during the first week of German aerial bombardment. Not even the Blitz of 1940 justified the fears that had been held throughout the previous decade. But such calculations were made in good faith and Chamberlain's actions must be judged with them in mind. 'If Ministers took literally all that was recommended to them by the best expert opinion', writes David Dilks, 'they would have had to expect from concentrated air bombardment something like the effects which we should now anticipate from limited nuclear warfare.'[43]

The concept of the 'knockout blow', 'the bolt from the blue', had become embedded in the thinking of military advisers and strategic planners by the mid-1930s. Ministers were terrified, recorded General Ironside, 'of a war being finished in a few weeks by the annihilation of Great Britain. They can see no other kind of danger than air attack.'[44] Apart from enormous casualties such an eventuality would break civilian morale, prompt panic evacuations from Britain's cities, undermine law and order and bring government and administration to a halt. In February 1935 Chamberlain warned the CID of the 'new danger' that a country might think it could settle a conflict with a single knockout blow on a vital target. His thinking had scarcely changed at the time of the Czech crisis in 1938. 'You know', he told Horace Wilson as the two men flew back from Godesberg over the dense conurbation of South-East England, 'it is a terrible thing to be responsible for the decision as to peace or war, knowing that if it is war there is very little we can do to save all these people.'[45] The fact that we now know that Germany was in no position to launch a significant bombing offensive against Britain in September 1938 in no way reduces the weight of the burden under which Chamberlain had to decide policy at this time.

With the attitude which he had towards war, it can be no surprise that Chamberlain was a reluctant rearmer. Yet the records reveal that he was nonetheless a committed one. As Chancellor of the Exchequer in a government whose *raison d'être* was the restoration of the national finances, Chamberlain's influence in all areas of public expenditure was bound to be strong. He believed that the level of defence spending recommended by the Defence Requirements Committee was unsustainably high and set about persuading the government that available resources should be concentrated on the RAF as the one area which could provide Britain with a genuine deterrent. Air power was, he asserted in October 1936, 'the most formidable deterrent to war that could be devised'.[46] The public would also be readier to accept expenditure on arms which they associated with the nation's defence. It was largely as a result of Chamberlain's intervention that the Ministerial Committee on Disarmament submitted proposals in July 1934 to construct 75 squadrons for the RAF rather than the originally suggested 52. He thus emerged as 'the strongest single force in the shaping of British defence policy between 1934 and 1939'.[47]

But Chamberlain's emphasis on defence and deterrence had clear implications for the future role of the British army and any idea of a continental commitment. Seen in this light the Inskip Report of 1937, with its relegation of 'cooperation in the defence of the territories of any allies we may have in war' to a final place 'which can only be provided after the other objectives [of defence policy] have been met', represented a considerable triumph for the newly elevated Prime Minister. 'What was generally termed a policy of "limited liability" in continental warfare', comments Michael Howard, 'had now shrunk to one of no liability at all.'[48] In terms of foreign policy, the defence strategy which Chamberlain had engineered clearly implied isolation from continental Europe. As Inskip reminded his colleagues at the beginning of the Czechoslovakian crisis, 'we had based our rearmament programme on what was necessary for our own defences. We had concentrated on the navy and the air.'[49] A report by the Chiefs of Staff in March 1938 did no more than reflect the realities of power in Europe as they existed at that time:

> No pressure that we and our possible Allies can bring to bear, either by sea, or land or in the air, could prevent Germany from invading and overrunning Bohemia and from inflicting defeat on the Czechoslovakian Army. We should then be faced with the necessity of undertaking a war against Germany for the purpose of restoring Czechoslovakia's lost integrity and this object would only be achieved by the defeat of Germany and as the outcome of a prolonged struggle.[50]

Chamberlain clearly saw the need to carry public opinion with him in support of a policy of rearmament. From 1934 onwards he frequently spoke in public of the need to plug the gaps in the nation's defences. Despite evidence – real and im-agined – of the passivity of the electorate, he was keen to place rearmament at the forefront of the National Government's elec-toral campaign in 1935. The government 'should take the bold course of actually appealing to the country on a defence programme'. He explained his thinking in the pages of his diary in a way that gives the lie to any suggestion that he was blind to the German menace:

> Germany is said to be borrowing over £1,000 millions a year to get herself rearmed, and she has perfected a wonder-ful industrial organisation, capable of rapid expansion for

the production of the materials of war. With Mussolini hopelessly tied up with Abyssinia and Gt. Britain disarmed, the temptation in a few years' time to demand territory etc. might be too great for Goering, Goebbels, and their like to resist. Therefore we must hurry our own rearmament, and in the course of the next 4 or 5 years we shall probably have to spend an extra £120m or more in doing so. We are not yet sufficiently advanced to reveal our ideas to the public, but of course we cannot deny the general charge of rearmament, and no doubt, if we tried to keep our ideas secret till after the election we should either fail or if we succeeded lay ourselves open to the far more damaging accusation that we had deliberately deceived the people.[51]

In 1936 Chamberlain led calls inside the cabinet to give priority to building a bomber force which would deter German aggression. Britain would soon possess 'an air force of such striking power that no one will care to run risks with it'.[52] His thinking was logical enough. If Britain was fearful of the impact of a German aerial assault then it was reasonable to suppose that Germany too would fear retaliatory British action and that Hitler, however fanatical in his ambitions, would draw back from provoking a British counter-attack. The problem was, however, that Britain had fallen increasingly behind Germany in terms of rearmament in the first years of the Third Reich. It has been estimated that Germany spent something like three times as much as Britain on military equipment between 1933 and 1938. Predictions of the future growth of the Luftwaffe began to convince Chamberlain that a policy of numerical parity in bombers was unattainable. In short, the notion of deterrence began to lose credibility. During 1938, therefore, he helped bring about a major reorientation in British strategic policy whereby emphasis was shifted, contrary to the advice of the air staff, away from the deterrent of the bomber and towards the purely defensive capabilities of fighter aicraft. By the time of the Czechoslovakian crisis the new policy was still only theoretical. Britain as yet lacked the defensive capacity to thwart a German attack. In such a situation General Ironside was convinced that Chamberlain was, 'of course, right. We have not the means of defending ourselves and he knows it ... *We cannot expose ourselves to a German attack. We simply commit suicide if we*

do.'[53] On 7 November 1938 the cabinet approved the whole of
the Air Ministry's proposals for fighter aircraft under Scheme
M, while stating that orders for bombers should only be placed
to a level which would avoid plant and labour being left idle. As
a single bomber cost the equivalent of four fighter aircraft
Chamberlain, whose thinking remained that of the Treasury
long after he had moved to 10 Downing Street, was convinced
that the new policy would make the most effective use of available resources.

Chamberlain thus emerges as a key figure in determining both
the scale and the type of British rearmament in the 1930s. But
insofar as the first of these functions involved the traditional role
of the Exchequer in limiting government expenditure, did the
opening of government archives do anything to dispel the orthodox image of one who had short-sightedly placed the preservation of financial stability before the imperative needs of national
survival? Did the mass of documentation now available to historians overturn the verdict of Duff Cooper who, only three weeks
after his resignation from Chamberlain's cabinet over the
Munich settlement, had written of the 'paralysing hand of the
Treasury'?[54] In answering these questions historians in the
1970s and 1980s were greatly assisted by a shift in the focus of
their enquiries into appeasement towards the archives of the
Treasury and the Board of Trade, a process encouraged not only
by a sense of 'diminishing returns' in relation to the holdings of
the Foreign Office but also by an increasingly broad understanding of the sorts of source material which are relevant to the
diplomatic historian. Historians came to argue that
Chamberlain's Treasury had a much more complex and thoughtful attitude towards rearmament than those who simply clamoured for more defence spending without regard for its effect on
the national economy. As the Chancellor charged with avoiding
a repetition of the near economic catastrophe of 1931,
Chamberlain may, understandably enough, have begun by
considering 'the financial risk greater than the war risk', but he
soon came to appreciate that there was no simple alternative
between defence spending and a sound economy, indeed that the
latter should be regarded as the 'fourth arm of defence'.[55]

The central problem for the British government in the 1930s
was not to choose between strong armed forces and a strong
economy but to strike the appropriate balance between the two,
a desperately difficult task granted prevailing uncertainties

about the intentions of Britain's enemies and the date at which a future war might break out. All defence planning, at least in terms of how victory might be secured, was based on the assumption of a long war. Such a war could only be sustained by a strong economy, one in which sterling kept up its purchasing power, not least in order to maintain and service the country's armed forces. Thus 'the more prepared the defence services were, the less able the country would be to support them'.[56] Politicians in the 1930s were well aware that it had only been the financial support of the United States which had enabled Britain to sustain her war effort after 1916. But the Johnson Act of 1934 had forbidden any country which had defaulted on its debts to America from raising further loans in that country. Britain numbered among such states. With American neutrality legislation preventing the export of arms to countries in a state of war, future prospects looked bleak indeed. As Vansittart noted: 'We scrambled through the last war by importing in its early stages some 500 million dollars' worth of American munitions. Today, in the event of war, we can count on getting nothing. Our own supplies will therefore have to be more plentiful and *timely*.'[57] It thus seemed that Britain's armed forces would have to rely on home production and the country's capacity to export to earn foreign exchange in order to purchase raw materials.

If Britain's strength was seen to lie in a long war, it was widely assumed that the German position was the exact reverse. Providing Britain could survive an attempted German knockout blow at the beginning of hostilities, then it was anticipated that the enemy would slowly run out of raw materials and foreign exchange. While Britain and France would be able to draw upon the resources of their vast colonial empires, the Nazi regime would gradually weaken under the impact of an economic blockade as had happened in the First World War. As Warren Fisher, the Permanent Head of the Treasury, put it in February 1938, 'If we can survive the first two or three weeks, i.e. air attacks, we can win with our long range weapon – the Navy'.[58]

If, however, the long-term health of the national economy were to be damaged by profligate short-term expenditure on rearmament, all such calculations would be thrown into disarray. R.P. Shay's study of British rearmament in the 1930s showed how determined the government was to maintain a balanced budget. Running a deficit would destroy confidence and spark inflation. The latter would make it more difficult to pay for those materials which would be essential to victory in war, which Britain had to import. It was calculated that the price of imported raw materials made up more than a quarter of the cost of armaments produced in British factories. Inflation might also bring about the fall of the government and the onset of socialism and pacifism, leaving the country an easy target for a foreign enemy.

As Shay concludes, 'the reconciliation of safety with solvency was a task of considerable difficulty'.[59] Chamberlain's statement to the cabinet shortly after Munich that, ever since his appointment as Chancellor, he had been 'oppressed with the sense that the burden of armaments might break our backs' was thus a more complex assertion than it appears on the surface.[60] Early in 1939 the Treasury was still warning that

> defence expenditure is now at a level which must seriously call into question the country's ability to meet it, and a continuance at this level may well result in a situation in which the completion of our material preparations against attack is frustrated by a weakening of our economic stability, which renders us incapable of standing the strain of war or even of maintaining those material defences in peace.[61]

Not surprisingly Chamberlain continued to regard the peaceful settlement of Germany's claims in relation to Poland as the best option from a British point of view. Even in the period of the Phoney War the Prime Minister remained concerned to husband the country's resources and to avoid a transition to a war economy. Such a policy may have provoked anger and criticism of his war leadership, but it made sense in terms of Whitehall's understanding of Britain's strengths and weaknesses.

It had of course always been part of the orthodox critique of the 1930s that there had existed a Keynesian alternative to the government's policies as spearheaded by Chamberlain and the Treasury. Criticism of the country's preparedness for war in 1939, and more particularly in 1940, was based upon the implicit premise that Britain could have been as strong as the Third Reich had different policies been pursued. Yet the documents placed considerable doubt over such assumptions. It emerged that, notwithstanding the slack within the economy resulting from continuing high levels of unemployment, concern over the dangers of inflation was widely shared. By 1937 the balance of payments deficit was back to the level it had been at in 1932. Keynes himself suggested in 1937 that more rapid rearmament than that upon which the government had embarked would have run the risk of sparking off an inflationary spiral. The government did borrow for defence spending, without the need for prompting by Keynes, but regarded this as an emergency measure, undesirable and indeed unsustainable in the long term. 'Defence loan expenditure was seen as a temporary expedient, to be followed by a return to a balanced Budget after the completion of the rearmament programme, which was planned for the end of the financial year 1941.'[62] Keynes believed that the balance between financing rearmament by borrowing and out of current revenue was about right. 'Broadly speaking, and with all the benefit of hindsight, it is impossible to say that the limit set by the Treasury upon rearmament was unreasonable or unnecessary.'[63] Detailed research also showed that there were further limitations on the scale of British rearmament which were not determined purely by the availability of finance. Structural weaknesses in industry and the labour market made it impossible to move easily to the manufacture of weaponry. Furthermore Chamberlain believed that trying to run the sort of command economy which underpinned the German war machine was impossible in Britain in peacetime, not least because it would threaten the economic stability upon which, as has been seen, so much else rested.

Overall, then, it was a very different picture of Chamberlain's role in preparing Britain for war which emerged from the archives from that presented in the vitriolic pages of *Guilty Men*. The National Government's rearmament drive began, of course, from a very low base-line. In 1932 the Ten Year Rule which had structured defence planning on the assumption that Britain would not have to face a major war for ten years was finally scrapped. By that stage, however, 'Britain ranked fifth in air strength, anti-aircraft defences were under half complete, coastal defences twenty-five years obsolete, the Army unable to fulfil treaty obligations and the Navy not capable of carrying out its tasks if a major war should break out'.[64] In such circumstances the government's achievement was considerable. By 1936 £186 million was being spent on defence out of a total central government income of £797 million. It is true that for much of the period after Hitler came to power Britain fell, relatively, further

behind Germany, but a policy to equal the military spending of
the Third Reich would surely have required a conviction of
inevitable war, shared probably with the British electorate,
which few if any genuinely held until the decade was well
advanced. As it was, writes George Peden, 'when the test of war
came Britain was able to contribute to the Allied cause the
world's largest navy, an aircraft industry which out-produced
Germany's in 1940, and an army which was just large enough to
deny the German army any decisive advantage in men or quality of equipment'.[65]

Even the image of the ignominious collapse of the
Anglo–French military effort in the spring of 1940 which did so
much long-term damage to Chamberlain's reputation has not
gone unchallenged. 'A consensus has emerged', writes Martin
Alexander, 'that the Allies were, on a material calculation alone,
sufficiently equipped to have avoided defeat – if not yet sufficiently to have tried to win the war.'[66] Modern scholarship has
shown that the rapid German advance was not the result of
material superiority but of the way in which the two sides
deployed their respective forces. 'Superior doctrine and tactics,
not superior technology, decided the battle for France.'[67] Such
arguments ran roughshod over the central contention of *Guilty
Men* and of so much else that had been said and written in the
succeeding decades.

As historians analysed the governmental archives made available to them under the Thirty Year Rule, most were conscious
that there was one category of documents potentially of enormous importance to them, which remained unavailable. The
papers of the country's intelligence services were not subject to
the conventions governing ministerial archives. Indeed, all the
records of the services themselves remained completely closed.
They were, as Alexander Cadogan once described them, 'the
missing dimension of most diplomatic history'.[68] Many historians had tended to accept that they simply had to live without
such evidence. But fragments had made their way into the ministerial archives and in the 1980s some writers began to piece
together the available material. The result was surprisingly valuable. 'The source material now available, for all its many gaps
and defects is sufficient to fill in both the general outline of the
missing intelligence dimension and much of its operational
detail.'[69] The picture which emerged offered another important
determinant of British foreign policy in the 1930s.

Broadly speaking it appeared that, prior to 1936, intelligence assessments had tended to underrate the military threat posed by Nazi Germany. The expanding German army was regarded as a legitimate instrument of the German state and violations of the armaments provisions of the Treaty of Versailles were seen as merely satisfying the needs of German national security. Such interpretations offered no incentive at this time for the National Government to convert the British economy to a programme of intensive rearmament. By the autumn of 1936, however, intelligence sources in the War Office and the Air Ministry began to change their tune and concede that German rearmament did in fact pose a serious threat to the peace of Europe. There followed a period of about two years in which the intelligence services tended now to exaggerate the capacity of the Nazi regime to wage war on land and in the air. 'Worst-case' assessments suggested that there would be little advantage in planning to send a British army to continental Europe. The balance of power was assumed to be stacked heavily in Germany's favour and helped convince the British government that an attempted policy of deterrence was intrinsically dangerous and ought to be avoided. In short, the assumed efficiency of the German economy and its war machine were important underpinnings of the policy of appeasement, especially at the time of the Czechoslovakian crisis in 1938.

On the basis of the intelligence information available, General Ismay judged that 'from a military point of view time is in our favour and, if war with Germany has to come, it would be better to fight her in say 6–12 months' time, than to accept the present challenge'.[70] An SIS paper drawn up as the Czechoslovakian crisis reached its crescendo recommended that the Sudeten German area should be peacefully separated from Czechoslovakia and incorporated in Germany. In the longer term Britain should build up her armaments and maintain them at the highest possible level. Little confidence could be placed in external support. 'In respect of allies we cannot really trust any foreign country, but at least France is bound to us (as are we to her) by ties of necessity and we should maintain these ties on the firmest possible basis.' As regards the Soviet Union, 'we can never bank on this country but, to keep on the right side of this devil, we must sup with him to some extent, adapting the length of our spoon to circumstances at any given moment'. Furthermore, the policy of appeasement should be actively pursued. The SIS recommended a colonial adjustment in Germany's favour, not dependent on that power's good behaviour, together with an attempt to find out what legitimate grievances Germany had and how they could be addressed, before her claims reached a critical stage. 'This document', comments David Dilks, 'does show beyond dispute that the policy of 1938–9 was not followed because British ministers preferred their own intuition, or soothing and convenient advice, to that of a well-informed intelligence service.'[71]

By 1939, however, the mood had changed again. On the basis of reports of difficulties in the German economy and rearmament programme, the British became more confident of their own military capability and less fearful of a German knockout blow. Increased production of British fighter aircraft and the development of radar suggested that the country was less vulnerable to air attack than hitherto. Rising optimism contributed to Chamberlain's perception that Hitler had 'missed the bus'.[72] The feeling that the arms gap between the two countries was beginning to close 'helped to foster that unreal atmosphere of confidence which was the background to the fateful British guarantees to the states of Central and Eastern Europe'.[73] A comment by General Pownall, the Director of Military Operations and Intelligence, shortly before the outbreak of war, illustrates how far opinions had changed over a period of twelve months. 'Last September we might have lost a *short* war. Now we shouldn't, nor a long war either.'[74] Though Chamberlain's underlying desire was still to avoid conflict if he possibly could, 1939 saw a greater readiness on his part to contemplate it in certain circumstances.

Overall, of course, the performance of the intelligence services in the 1930s in assessing the German problem and its implications for Britain was lamentable. Many of their key evaluations were quite simply wrong. The mood swung from optimism to pessimism and back to relative optimism again as the decade progressed. None of these phases was really justified. British intelligence failed to comprehend the dynamic expansionist thrust of Nazi ideology in the first years after Hitler came to power. It exaggerated Germany's military capability in the middle years of the decade both in terms of its capacity to launch a knockout blow against London and its preparedness to overrun Czechoslovakia. And most of the optimism of 1939 was sadly misplaced. Germany still possessed twice as many front-line aircraft as Britain and more than twice as many long-range bombers. The gap in numerical strength between the two countries actually widened in the months after Munich. But Chamberlain had little if any control over the quality of intelligence information available to him. The important point was that the foreign policy which he and other British ministers pursued was fully in step with the secret assessments made at this time. 'What emerges from this pattern', writes a leading authority in this field, 'is the mutual support that operated between intelligence assessments and appeasement policy.'

At no stage during the 1930s were there any fundamental contradictions between intelligence reporting and the foreign policy of the government. In fact, the intelligence picture tended, if anything, to provide the strongest possible support for the government's efforts to maintain pacific relations with the Third Reich.[75]

Writing in the early 1960s A.L. Rowse had declared that the policies of the appeasers, especially Chamberlain, were totally inexplicable. The main achievement of two or three decades of sustained revisionist historiography, firmly grounded in archival sources, was to make those policies entirely understandable. Not all who contributed to the process approved of what Chamberlain had done; but all believed they now understood why he had done it. Some writers offered particularly individualistic appraisals. According to Simon Newman appeasement cannot be said to have failed because it was in fact never seriously attempted. He argues that, while Chamberlain was not prepared to fight over Czechoslovakia, neither was he willing to offer Hitler a free hand in Eastern and South-Eastern Europe. Indeed, he tried to erect political and economic barriers to further German expansion in these areas.[76] Maurice Cowling, extending his thesis on 'High Politics' to the 1930s, sought to interpret British foreign policy in a context of domestic party politics. He suggested that Chamberlain's underlying concern was that a future large-scale war would lead to major advances by the Labour party and the Trade Union movement on the pattern of 1914–18. Appeasement therefore offered the Conservative party the opportunity of retaining power while preserving both the British Empire and the sort of society of which it approved. Chamberlain's mistakes, as far as Cowling was concerned, began with the Munich settlement which ended

hopes that an isolationist Britain could steer clear of involvement in central and eastern Europe.[77]

Yet the tide of revisionism, powerful though it was, never
carried everyone along with it. Almost inevitably it sparked a
reaction and, by the end of the century, there existed a significant post-revisionist literature on Chamberlain and appeasement which in some cases even tried to resurrect the essential
message of the original orthodox school. Such writers suggested
that the revisionists, in stressing the objective factors which
determined British policy in the 1930s, had gone too far to
remove the impact of individual views and personality.
'Chamberlain was as important to appeasement in Great
Britain as Hitler was to Nazism. The mentality of the man – his
prejudices, motivations, thought and behaviour patterns – is
vital to assessing policy formulation and execution.'[78] The most
persuasive analysis of this kind came from the pen of the
Oxford historian, R.A.C. Parker. He believed that historians
had so successfully dissected the determinants of Chamberlain's
policy as to make it seem that there had been no possible alternatives. But Parker was sure that such alternatives did in fact
exist and that Chamberlain and his colleagues had made
conscious choices from among available options. 'After the
Anschluss in March 1938 Chamberlain could, the evidence
suggests, have secured sufficient support in Britain for a close
alliance with France and a policy of containing and encircling
Germany, more or less shrouded under the League covenant.'[79]
He was particularly critical of the Prime Minister's conduct
after Munich, completely rejecting the notion that he had
consciously gained time for rearmament through the postponement of war in September 1938. Chamberlain had accepted
Hitler's demands as a means of averting war altogether rather
than postponing it, of making increased armaments unnecessary rather than winning time to manufacture them. As the
usually reticent Horace Wilson had once confessed in his years
of retirement, 'our policy was never designed just to postpone
war, or enable us to enter war more united. The aim of appeasement was to avoid war altogether, for all time.'[80] Only a month
after the Munich settlement Chamberlain had dismissed the
'false emphasis' placed on rearmament, as if 'one result of the
. . . agreement had been that it would be necessary for us to add
to our rearmament programme. Acceleration of existing
programmes was one thing but increases in the scope of our

programme which would lead to a new arms race were a different proposition.'[81]

Parker was too good an historian to dismiss Chamberlain's policy out of hand as one of total surrender and unlimited retreat. Nonetheless he showed that the historical record placed serious question-marks over the Prime Minister's judgement. After the meeting at Godesberg he told the Inner Cabinet that Hitler's objectives were limited to the incorporation of the Sudeten Germans in the Reich. Immediately afterwards he assured the full cabinet that the Führer 'would not deliberately deceive a man whom he respected and with whom he had been in negotiation and he was sure that Herr Hitler felt some respect for him'.[82] Chamberlain seemed to grow more hopeful of peaceful German intentions when the available evidence should have pointed him in the opposite direction. After the Prague coup he became somewhat cautious, but remained 'the most hopeful, the most credulous of British statesmen'.[83]

The somewhat sinister element in Chamberlain's reputation, never far beneath the surface of the early historiography, reappeared as a result of Richard Cockett's research into the Prime Minister's efforts to control the press. The veteran journalist, James Margach, had already suggested that Chamberlain was the 'first Prime Minister to employ news management on a grand scale'.[84] Cockett went much further, showing that through the 'insistent courting of the proprietors, editors and political journalists' the Chamberlain government was able to give an impression of national unity in support of its policies which was far removed from reality. The famous headline of the *Daily Express*, 'There Will Be No European War', was, its proprietor Lord Beaverbrook later confessed, inserted at the request of the government. In terms of the present discussion these findings implied that Chamberlain may have enjoyed a lower approval rating, especially at the time of Munich, than a reading of the national press would suggest. By the summer of 1938 'large sections of the press had . . . quite clearly abandoned their role of articulating public opinion in favour of a religiously partisan support for Chamberlain'.[85] Beyond the mainstream press Joseph Ball, acting as the Prime Minister's intelligence and propaganda agent, used the journal *Truth* to discredit Chamberlain's political opponents and continued to propagate a Chamberlainite point of view through its columns even after his master's death. Similarly, Nick Crowson's study of local

Conservative parties suggested that a far larger section of Tory opinion was uneasy about Chamberlain's strategy towards the dictator powers than previous concentration upon Westminster opinion had implied.[86] All of this placed searching question-marks over what had always been one of the main justifications of Chamberlain's policies – that he had been in line with public opinion and had done what the vast majority of the population wanted.

But perhaps the most striking contribution to the post-revisionist school came from the Canadian historian, Sydney Aster. Just when it seemed safe, at least in academic circles, finally to inter *Guilty Men* in the graveyard of historiographical curiosities, Aster sought to resurrect the majority of Cato's original charges. Strikingly, he did so on the basis of an examination of Chamberlain's private papers, a source which, ever since it was first used by Keith Feiling, had generally worked to Chamberlain's advantage. What emerges from these papers, argued Aster, was 'misplaced trust, unwarranted optimism and erroneous judgements'.[87] Chamberlain showed a disregard for the aggressive dynamism of the totalitarian states, a loathing of war which was so strong as to distort his perspective, a blind conviction that there was no alternative to the policy he had decided upon and an implacable opposition to full-scale rearmament. He was taken in by Hitler and never saw appeasement as an opportunity to buy time for rearmament – at least not until the months following his resignation from the premiership when he tried to rationalize his earlier actions. 'In essence, the letters [to his sisters Ida and Hilda] confirm that the accusations spelled out by "Cato" in 1940 were in fact largely justified.'[88]

The historiography of appeasement thus completes a somewhat bizarre full circle, returning in the minds of at least some scholars very much to the point of departure in 1940. While the present book was being written, R.A.C. Parker added a further significant volume to the shelves of post-revisionism with a study of *Churchill and Appeasement*. Its 'tentative conclusion' is that the Second World War was, as Churchill had famously described it, 'the Unnecessary War' – in other words that the Churchillian alternative of an anti-fascist coalition of powers around a Franco–British axis could have prevented the catastrophe which Chamberlain's policies failed to avert. Despite, then, a quarter-century in which revisionism held the upper hand, Chamberlain's reputation faced a renewed challenge from resurgent exponents of the two-pronged assault – 'Cato' and Churchill – which had assailed him in 1940 and the years that followed. This situation suggests above everything else that the historical record will never provide a definitive interpretation. A distinction may be drawn between what 'the evidence' can demonstrate incontrovertibly and what a reasonable interpretation of that evidence can sustain. Indeed, it is striking that precisely the same documentation – in particular Chamberlain's private papers – has been used as the basis of radically different analyses. It is unlikely that as yet untapped British sources hold significant keys to this story (though Soviet archives may yet reveal important new information). The varying interpretations of historians, shaped by their particular generation, perspective, preoccupations and prejudices, will ensure that a lively debate on the reputation of Neville Chamberlain will continue into the foreseeable future.

Notes

1. *The Times* 11 Nov. 1940.
2. T.D. Williams, 'The Historiography of World War II' in E. M. Robertson (ed.), *The Origins of the Second World War* (London, 1971), p.43.
3. C. King, *With Malice Toward None: A War Diary* (London, 1970), p.54.
4. P. Schröder, 'Munich and the British Tradition', *Historical Journal* 19 (1976), p.242.
5. I. Colvin, *The Chamberlain Cabinet* (London, 1971), p.9
6. *Ibid.*, p.263.
7. *Ibid.*, p.265.
8. K. Middlemas, *Diplomacy of Illusion: The British Government and Germany 1937–39* (London, 1972), pp.3–4.
9. *Ibid.*, p.2.
10. *Ibid.*, p.339.
11. *Ibid.*, p.449.
12. *Ibid.*, p.441.
13. P. Rolo in *English Historical Review* , vol. LXXXIX (1974), p.468.
14. P. Kennedy, 'The Tradition of Appeasement in British Foreign Policy, 1865–1939' in Kennedy, *Strategy and Diplomacy 1870–1945* (London, pb. edn, 1984), p.38.
15. W.N. Medlicott, D. Dakin and M. Lambert (eds), *Documents on British Foreign Policy 1919–1939*, Series1A, vol.1 (London, 1966), pp.846–81.
16. J. Harvey (ed.), *The War Diaries of Oliver Harvey 1941–1945* (London, 1978), p.61.
17. W. Rock, *British Appeasement in the 1930s* (London, 1977), p.54.

18. R. Ovendale, *Appeasement and the English Speaking World* (Cardiff, 1975), p.317; C. Hill, *Cabinet Decisions on Foreign Policy: the British Experience, October 1938–June 1941* (Cambridge, 1991), passim.
19. See, for example, A. Roberts, *'The Holy Fox': A Biography of Lord Halifax* (London, 1991), chapters 13–18.
20. D. Watt, 'Appeasement: The Rise of a Revisionist School?', *Political Quarterly* (1965), p.208.
21. D. Dilks, 'Appeasement Revisited', *University of Leeds Review*, 15 (1972), p.38.
22. Chamberlain MSS, NC18/1/881, Chamberlain to H. Chamberlain 28 July 1934.
23. S. Greenwood, ' "Caligula's Horse" Revisited: Sir Thomas Inskip as Minister for the Co-ordination of Defence, 1936–1939', *Journal of Strategic Studies*, 17, 2 (1994), p.32.
24. R. Shay, *British Rearmament in the Thirties: Politics and Profits* (Princeton, 1977), p.90.
25. P. Bell, *Chamberlain, Germany and Japan 1933–4* (Basingstoke, 1996), p.175.
26. Public Record Office, PREM 1/210, note by Chamberlain on Eden to Chamberlain 9 Sept. 1937.
27. D. Dilks, ' "The Unnecessary War"? Military Advice and Foreign Policy in Great Britain, 1931–1939' in A. Preston (ed.), *General Staffs and Diplomacy before the Second World War* (London, 1978), p.120.
28. House of Commons Debates, 5th Series, vol.334, col.61.
29. Chamberlain MSS, NC7/11/31/283, Chamberlain to Weir 15 Jan. 1938.
30. *Ibid.*, NC18/1/893, Chamberlain to Ida Chamberlain 27 Oct. 1934.
31. *Ibid.*, NC18/1/1023, Chamberlain to H. Chamberlain 9 Oct. 1937.
32. *Ibid.*, NC18/1/1140, Chamberlain to I. Chamberlain 27 Jan. 1940.
33. G. Kolko, *The Politics of War: the World and United States Foreign Policy, 1943–1945* (New York, 1968).
34. J. Charmley, *Churchill: The End of Glory* (London, 1993), p.2.
35. Ovendale, *English Speaking World*, pp.319–20.
36. C. Sånger, *Malcolm MacDonald: Bringing an End to Empire* (Liverpool, 1995), p.140.
37. Ovendale, *English Speaking World*, p.320.
38. A.J.P. Taylor, *The Origins of the Second World War* (London, 1961), p.229.
39. M. Howard, *War and the Liberal Conscience* (Oxford, 1981), p.115.
40. H. Macmillan, *Winds of Change 1914–1939* (London, 1966), p.522.
41. B. Morris, *The Roots of Appeasement: The British Weekly Press and Nazi Germany During the 1930s* (London, 1991), p.181.
42. B. Russell, *Which Way to Peace* (London, 1936), p.37.

43. Dilks, 'Unnecessary War', p.117.
44. R. Macleod and D. Kelly (eds), *The Ironside Diaries 1937–1940* (London, 1962), pp.42–3.
45. D. Dilks, 'Appeasement and "Intelligence" ' in Dilks (ed.), *Retreat from Power 1906–1939* (London, 1981), p.143.
46. *The Times* 3 Oct. 1936.
47. Dilks, 'Unnecessary War', p.108.
48. M. Howard, *The Continental Commitment* (Harmondsworth, pb. edn, 1974), p.118.
49. C. Barnett, *The Collapse of British Power* (London, 1972), p.519.
50. B. Bond, *British Military Policy between the Two World Wars* (Oxford, 1980), p.277.
51. Chamberlain MSS, NC2/23A, diary 2 Aug. 1935.
52. Ibid., NC18/1/949, Chamberlain to H. Chamberlain 9 Feb. 1936.
53. Macleod and Kelly (eds), *Ironside Diaries*, p.62. (emphasis in original).
54. G. Peden, *British Rearmament and the Treasury* (Edinburgh, 1979), p.1.
55. PRO, CAB 23/75, Cabinet 15 Feb. 1933.
56. Peden, *British Rearmament*, p.103.
57. W.N. Medlicott and D. Dakin (eds), *Documents on British Foreign Policy 1919–1939*, Second Series, vol. XVII (London, 1979), p.792, memorandum by Vansittart 31 Dec.1936. (emphasis in original).
58. U. Bialer, *The Shadow of the Bomber: the Fear of Air Attack and British Politics 1932–1939* (London, 1980), p.127.
59. Shay, *British Rearmament*, p.165.
60. PRO, CAB 23/95, Cabinet 3 Oct. 1938.
61. Shay, *British Rearmament*, p.243.
62. Peden, *British Rearmament*, p.88.
63. Dilks, 'Unnecessary War', p.126.
64. Bell, *Chamberlain, Germany and Japan*, p.4.
65. Peden, *British Rearmament*, p.184.
66. M. Alexander, 'The Fall of France, 1940', *Journal of Strategic Studies* 13,1 (1990), p.33.
67. C. McInnes and G. Sheffield (eds), *Warfare in the Twentieth Century: Theory and Practice* (London, 1988), p.69.
68. D. Dilks (ed.), *The Diaries of Sir Alexander Cadogan 1938–1945* (London, 1971), p.21.
69. C. Andrew and D. Dilks (eds), *The Missing Dimension: Governments and Intelligence Communities in the Twentieth Century* (London, 1984), p.5.
70. W. Wark, *The Ultimate Enemy: British Intelligence and Nazi Germany 1933–1939* (Oxford, pb.edn, 1986), p.208.
71. D. Dilks, 'Flashes of Intelligence: The Foreign Office, the SIS and Security before the Second World War' in Andrew and Dilks (eds), *Missing Dimension*, pp.119–22.
72. Chamberlain MSS, NC18/1/1084, Chamberlain to H. Chamberlain 5 Feb. 1939.
73. W. Wark, 'British Military and Economic Intelligence: Assessments

of Nazi Germany before the Second World War' in Andrew and Dilks (eds), *Missing Dimension*, p.98.

74. B. Bond (ed.), *Chief of Staff: The Diaries of Lt-General Sir Henry Pownall 1933–1940* (London, 1972), p.221. (emphasis in original).
75. Wark, *Ultimate Enemy*, p.235.
76. S. Newman, *March 1939, the British Guarantee to Poland* (Oxford, 1976).
77. M. Cowling, *The Impact of Hitler* (Cambridge, 1975).
78. G. Weinberg, W. Rock and A. Cienciala, 'The Munich Crisis Revisited', *International History Review* xi, 4 (1989), p.683.
79. R.A.C. Parker, *Chamberlain and Appeasement: British Policy and the Coming of the Second World War* (London, 1993), p.346.
80. M. Gilbert, 'Horace Wilson: Man of Munich?', *History Today*, 32 (1982), p.6.
81. PRO, CAB 23/96, Cabinet 31 Oct. 1938.
82. Parker, *Chamberlain and Appeasement*, p.169.
83. *Ibid.*, p.205.
84. J. Margach, *The Abuse of Power: the War between Downing Street and the Media from Lloyd George to James Callaghan* (London, 1978), p.50.
85. R. Cockett, *Twilight of Truth: Chamberlain, Appeasement and the Manipulation of the Press* (London, 1989), pp.83, 65.
86. N.J. Crowson, *Facing Fascism: The Conservative Party and the European Dictators 1935–1940* (London, 1997).
87. S. Aster, ' "Guilty Men": The Case of Neville Chamberlain' in R. Boyce and E. M. Robertson (eds), *Paths to War: New Essays on the Origins of the Second World War* (London, 1989), p.262.
88. *Ibid.*, p.241.

|7|

Chamberlain: an assessment

No man can fairly be judged till fifty years after he is dead.[1]

'All political lives', argued Enoch Powell, 'unless they are cut off in midstream at a happy juncture, end in failure, because that is the nature of politics and of human affairs.'[2] In writing these words Powell had Neville Chamberlain's father, Joseph, primarily in mind. But they also seem particularly appropriate in the case of Joseph Chamberlain's second son. After a ministerial career of considerable success and distinction, Chamberlain failed in his supreme trial – he failed in his self-appointed task of avoiding another war with Germany. For many, indeed, this is enough to damn his career as a whole and to determine the overall reputation which he should have. According to Lord Blake, for example, the verdict of history *must* be against him, because he 'risked the whole existence of the nation'.[3] Chamberlain himself hoped that it might be otherwise: 'on the whole, although I have in a sense failed in everything I set out to achieve, I do not believe that history will blame me for that and I don't regard my public life as a failure.'[4]

This study of Chamberlain's evolving reputation has thrown up some interesting general points – whether a man should be judged on the basis of his whole life or simply in relation to the most prominent events with which he was associated; whether such a judgement should be made in the light of the values and ideas of his own time, those of the later writer, or according to some transcendent measures which are valid throughout the ages; and the contrast between and relative importance of the popular image of a man and the assessments of scholarly authors, written by and largely shared among a narrowly academic community. None is easily resolved, but something may be said in relation to each and the case in question of Neville Chamberlain.

There is of course something rather perverse in the idea that Chamberlain's reputation should rest on the last three years of his life with the first sixty-eight years written off as a largely irrelevant prelude. But history does tend to associate an individual with one or two key developments, policies or ideas and it is upon these that, however unfairly, a reputation tends to be based. In Chamberlain's case this is particularly so. In his first two decades in public life he had considerable achievements to his credit, but he never emerged as a truly popular or charismatic figure in British politics. His very personal handling of British diplomacy after 1937, however, brought him to the centre of not only the national but the world stage. The stakes were enormous and the consequences of his actions potentially beyond calculation. In terms of his reputation he was taking, consciously or not, a tremendous risk – and one that did not of course come off. Thus, however much historians may strive for a more balanced approach, Chamberlain's standing at the bar of history will, in the last resort, inevitably depend upon assessments of his conduct of British foreign policy between 1937 and 1940 or, more particularly, upon popular interpretations of such shorthand symbols as 'appeasement', 'Munich' and the 'Phoney War' and of all the images which these words conjure up. 'If his policies had succeeded', reflected a cabinet colleague, 'he would have been acknowledged as the wisest statesman of his generation. Because they failed so tragically his Premiership is treated by history as a disaster.'[5]

As has been shown in these pages, assessments of Chamberlain have certainly varied according to the time and circumstances in which a particular judgement was made. An historical figure tends to be constantly remoulded to serve the needs and preoccupations of each succeeding generation and the final verdict of history (if such a thing truly exists) is not easy to anticipate. After all, Chamberlain has only been dead for sixty years, little more than a transient moment in the annals of the historical past. Over an extended period of time, 'heroes can become villains, the wise can be made to look foolish, and the innocent can be saddled with guilt for events which they did not live to see'.[6] Churchill at least got this right in words he delivered as part of his valediction at Chamberlain's death. 'In one phase men seem to have been wrong. Then again, a few years later, when the perspective of time has lengthened, all stands in a different setting. . . .'[7] Chamberlain's stewardship of the Exchequer in the 1930s assumed a very different image once the ideas – real and supposed – of John Maynard Keynes had been removed from the economic pedestal which they occupied for a generation after 1940. Rationally, indeed, it had always seemed harsh to judge Chamberlain by the standards of economic theories which only became truly fashionable after his death. Likewise, his scepticism about the Soviet Union seemed altogether more reasonable at the height of the Cold War than it had when that country was being presented as Britain's loyal and indispensable ally in the common struggle against Nazi Germany. 'We must pay him a carefully assessed tribute', wrote Robert Sencourt in 1954, 'for keeping his eye on the dark monster at the horizon.'[8] Perhaps the lesson of all this is that it is not really the role of the historian to pass judgement at all. His task is to explain the past and not to condemn or praise those who shaped it. If this is the case then Chamberlain can only be understood as a man of his particular generation, severely scarred by the experience of the Great War and subject to most of the prevailing views and assumptions of his own time.

The popular image of Neville Chamberlain is deeply ingrained, and it may well be that the historian is engaged in a losing battle if he thinks he is capable of changing it. That image is of 'the ineffective umbrella, the futile waving of a scrap of paper, "peace in our time", the lack of any effective preparations for the inevitable war, the ignominious dismissal by the House of Commons in 1940 after the Norway fiasco'.[9] These words were written forty years ago but the point remains valid today. Just how hard a task the academic historian faces was perhaps revealed by a full-page article in the *Independent on Sunday* in March 2000. Notwithstanding three decades of revisionist literature, the opening of a much-hyped but largely inconsequential box of papers belonging to Sir Walter Monckton, close friend and legal adviser to the Duke of Windsor, provided an excuse to analyse the attitude of the Royal Family towards Chamberlain's policies. (Plenty of relevant evidence was, in fact, already in the public domain.) But, according to the journalist Sean O'Grady, 'the revelation that the Queen Mother was an enthusiastic supporter of appeasement in the 1930s is a sharp jolt to the national psyche'.[10] It seems reasonable to suggest that the academic world is unlikely to have lost much sleep over this disclosure. The gap between the layman's preconceptions of Neville Chamberlain and the views of most professional historians must probably be accepted as an unbridgeable divide. Indeed, the former has become an historical phenomenon in its own right and it has been part of the purpose of this book to analyse and explain it.

Almost certainly Chamberlain himself would have wished to be remembered as a domestic reformer. Had his career been cut short at any time before 1937 this is almost certainly how things would have turned out. The human sacrifices of the First World War had left him with a deep loathing of armed conflict and a determination that the enormous cost involved should not have been in vain. 'Nothing but immeasurable improvements', wrote Norman Chamberlain in May 1917, 'will ever justify all the waste and unfairness of this war – I only hope that those who are left will *never, never*, forget at what sacrifice those improvements have been won.'[11] Chamberlain took his cousin's sentiments very much to heart. Though he could not, he confessed, expect journalists in the autumn of 1940 to deal with anything other than the affairs of the moment, it had been

> the hope of doing something to improve the conditions of life for the poorer people that brought me at past middle life into politics and it is some satisfaction to me that I was able to carry out some part of my ambition, even though its permanency may be challenged by the destruction of war.[12]

It was obvious, noted John Simon the recipient of this letter, 'that he looked back, as he was entitled to look back, on what he had done at the Ministry of Health as really the thing in his career in which he felt he had served the people well'.[13]

Chamberlain's legislative record at the Ministry of Health between 1924 and 1929, enshrining the principle of national policies locally implemented, remains, as Feiling described it more than half a century ago, 'massive and unquestioned, the chapter of his public life least controverted'.[14] The reform of public health, the extension of national insurance, and the reshaping of local government and the poor law represented considerable achievements by any standards. But these years should not be seen as a compartmentalized entity removed from the rest of Chamberlain's career. Rather they tell us much about the authentic Chamberlain, a man who was throughout his life on the progressive left of the Conservative party, a committed believer in social progress and in the power of government, at both the national and local level, to do good. Indeed, in 1923 he described himself to Samuel Hoare as a socialist and eight years later hoped that the existence of the National Government would afford the opportunity to dispense with the 'odious title of Conservative which has kept so many from joining us in the past'.[15] His first years in the House of Commons showed that he did not rule out nationalization where, as in the case of the inland waterways, the practical case for it seemed strong. In the last year of his life he still insisted that he had 'no prejudice against land nationalisation. With me it is merely a matter of expediency. . . . In the public interest I would have no hesitation in handing over to public ownership any particular piece of land if that would give better results.'[16]

By the new decade Chamberlain was established as a consummate politician, though his role in orchestrating the outcome of the 1931 crisis was probably less crucial, indeed less machiavellian, than has sometimes been suggested.[17] The much maligned National Government, of which he was of course a prominent member throughout, had a perfectly respectable record of social reform, though this fact has tended to be obscured by the differing preoccupations of later historiography and the persistent image of a 'low, dishonest decade'.[18] Notwithstanding opposition from the colliery owners Chamberlain's own government nationalized the royalties from coal mining in 1938. Further legislation related to factories, housing, slum clearance and physical training, while plans were drawn up to raise the school leaving age to fifteen. A scheme to provide pensions for former MPs reached the statute book on the eve of war in 1939. Drafts for the government's manifesto for the General Election projected for 1940 suggested

> commitments to advances in education, mainly in the technical field (so foreshadowing one of the legs on which the Butler Act of 1944 was to stand), and plans for family allowances and the inclusion of the dependants of insured persons in health and pensions cover.[19]

For most of the lifetime of the National Government, of course, Chamberlain was firmly ensconced at the Exchequer, a post which he only agreed to take 'when I had carried out my programme' at the Ministry of Health.[20] Freed from the Keynesian prism through which it was so long viewed, this period of Chamberlain's career now appears in a far more favourable light than was once the case. It cannot be ignored that many contemporaries regarded him as the most successful Chancellor since Gladstone. Indeed, if his stewardship of the national finances over a period of five and a half years had not been judged a success at the time, it seems unlikely that he would ever have succeeded to the premiership. Yet both as Chancellor and Prime Minister Chamberlain in a very real sense was diverted from his chosen path. Taking office at the height of the depression he 'rejoiced' at his opportunity even though 'the burden is heavy'.[21] Then 'after some hard years during which I had to stand up to a lot of criticism I thought my reward had come and that with reduced taxation and overflowing revenue I could enter on a new era of social improvement'.[22] The perceived need for rearmament in the face of an ever more threatening world threw his plans off course.

If therefore the most important part of Chamberlain's career came to focus on his role in foreign and diplomatic policy, this was not a matter of his own choosing. Equipped perhaps to be a great peacetime Prime Minister, fate decreed that he had to concentrate on diplomacy and preparations for war. 'I wish it was not so', he told an audience in June 1939, stressing again that he had gone into politics 'to do something to make things a bit better for the people'.[23] He felt enormous disgust at the idea of the nation's resources being diverted to armaments and away from the elevation of living standards. He had held it against the Kaiser in the First World War that he and his advisers had 'stayed the march of progress and had set back for an indefinite period reforms that might have bettered the lot of generations to come'.[24] Two decades later his thinking had not perceptibly changed:

> To me the very idea that the hard-won savings of our people, which ought to be devoted to the alleviation of suffering, to the opening out of fresh institutions and recreations, to the care of the old, to the development of the minds and bodies of the young – the thought that these savings should have to be dissipated upon the construction of weapons of war is hateful and damnable.[25]

At the end of his life his main regret was that, with the coming of war, he had failed 'to steer this country into calmer water and gradually to raise the standards of life among the people'.[26] Much perhaps depends upon the temperament of the individual commentator but, at the end of a century of Total War, there is something attractive about Chamberlain's scale of priorities.

It seems reasonable to conjecture that Chamberlain's background is important here. He himself once attributed any success he had in national politics 'largely to my experience of local government'.[27] His training on the Birmingham City Council was a more obvious preparation for his ministerial career before 1937 than for the tasks which faced him as Prime Minister. In Britain's post-imperial age we should probably applaud a premier who, like Chamberlain, had studied engineering, physics and chemistry and who had a practical knowledge and experience of the workings of manufacturing industry. But to many critics both during his lifetime and since his death this was but a manifestation of a fatal flaw in the make-up of Chamberlain the Prime Minister – his provincialism. Memorably, Clement Attlee once described him as a radio set 'tuned to Midland Regional'.[28] In consequence, he was 'a great municipal administrator, a good Minister of Health, a competent Chancellor and the most disastrous Prime Minister in British history'.[29] The bigger the task the less well equipped he was to deal with it. 'The world he understood', insists the author of one popular history of the 1930s, 'was a world of business men, where contracts were sacred and enforceable without violence, and difficulties could be ironed out round the conference table.'[30] Addressing an audience in Birmingham, suggested A.J.P. Taylor, Chamberlain was 'among his own people – jewellers, locksmiths, makers of pots and pans'.[31] First relayed by Anthony Eden, the story is still repeated without comment or qualification, of a dinner party at which Austen Chamberlain reminded his brother, 'Neville, you must remember you don't know anything about foreign affairs'.[32] Coming only months before Chamberlain assumed supreme responsibility for questions of war and peace, this seems damning indeed, even though we have long had the assurance of the soon-to-be Prime Minister's son that his uncle meant the remark humorously.

Like most well-ingrained myths the idea of Chamberlain's provincialism will not easily be dispelled. Yet far from being ignorant of the wider world Chamberlain had probably travelled more extensively than any Prime Minister before him. Apart from his ill-fated sojourn in the Bahamas his trips abroad had taken him to Africa, India, Burma, Canada and many of the countries of continental Europe. David Dilks's detailed study of his ministerial career in the 1920s reveals a man who, notwithstanding his departmental brief, followed foreign and imperial affairs with close attention. Even as a city councillor in Birmingham he had striven to invigorate the local Navy League and had opposed reductions in the size of the regular army. As a high-ranking minister in the National Government Chamberlain was among the first to recognize the dangers posed by Hitler's Germany and to seek to focus Britain's defensive resources on that threat. He was by temperament opposed to all forms of dictatorship whether of the Right or Left, telling an audience at the Albert Hall in May 1938 that both fascism and communism were 'utterly inconsistent with our democratic notions of equality and liberty'. While conceding that his understanding of the Nazi regime was defective, we can surely dismiss the more extreme interpretations which suggest that the innocent Chamberlain was completely fooled by the German dictator. Harold Nicolson was one who overstated his case. In the early days of the war he compared the visit of Chamberlain and Horace Wilson to Germany in September 1938 to 'two curates entering a pub for the first time':

> they did not observe the difference between a social gathering and a rough-house; nor did they realize that the tough groups assembled did not either speak or understand their language. They imagined that they were as decent and as honourable as themselves.[33]

Neither is it clear that, to the extent that Chamberlain did misjudge Hitler, this was the inevitable consequence of his narrow provincial background. Lloyd George, whose experience of international affairs and breadth of mind were considerable, showed perhaps even less insight than Chamberlain after his visit to the Führer in 1936. Indeed, very few of the procession of Britons who made the trip to Germany in the 1930s came away without some feeling of admiration for that country's leader.

Where Chamberlain's understanding was at fault was in his failure to grasp the importance of the ideological dynamic of the Nazi regime. With hindsight, it has often been said that there was no reason for ignorance about Hitler's true intentions. He himself had set them out in his own writings. But we need not concern ourselves as to whether Chamberlain ever actually read *Mein Kampf*. If he did not, there were plenty of people around him in Whitehall who must have done so. The problem was not so much reading Hitler's words as knowing how seriously to take them. Maurice Hankey, the long-serving cabinet secretary, well captured the dilemma:

> Are we still dealing with the Hitler of *Mein Kampf*, lulling his opponents to sleep with fair words in order to gain time to arm his people, and looking always to the day when he can throw off the mask and attack Poland? Or is it a new Hitler, who has discovered the burden of responsible office, and wants to extricate himself, like many an earlier tyrant, from the commitments of his irresponsible days?[34]

In practice, the majority of those who dealt with Hitler 'believed that there must be a distinction between ideology and practical politics, between drama and reality'.[35] After all, British policy makers already had considerable experience of dealing with one fascist regime. Mussolini had been in power in Italy since 1922. At least until 1935 he had behaved in a reasonably statesman-like manner. At times, as for example at Locarno in 1925, he had made a genuine contribution to European peace. Certainly he had done nothing to suggest that his ideological baggage somehow rendered him different in kind from the rest of the international community.

Many accepted, without condoning, the violence of the Nazi regime as the inevitable consequence of the 'revolution' that had taken place in Germany in 1933. The regime would in time probably settle down and Hitler reveal himself as no more than the lineal successor of Bismarck and Stresemann. The *Manchester Guardian*, no friend of the political far right, drew comfort from the conduct of Wilhelm Frick, the first Nazi to hold state office as Interior Minister in Thuringia, concluding that in office Nazis behaved as ordinary politicians. In part what had happened in Germany was seen as the Allies' own fault:

> It has been impossible to talk to a German in these years without realising how deeply the defeat of 1918, and the subsequent treatment of Germany by the Allies, have scarred the national consciousness. The Nazi Revolution is

the latest outcome of the feverish sense of defeat and disgrace which has plunged the mass of the German people through all these years in never-ending brooding over the wrongs of Germany, the woes of Germany and, latterly, the rights and the might of Germany.[36]

It now seems logical to suggest that appeasement, in the sense of removing legitimate German grievances, should have come to an end on 30 January 1933. But there was an alternative logic which at the time seemed to many equally compelling – that the sting could be removed from Nazism by righting those injustices which had brought it into existence in the first place. Nor, some thought, should the militarism of the Nazi system necessarily be taken at face value:

> Hitler talked in military metaphors because they are the favourite metaphors in Germany, but his actions were much more pacific and conciliatory, at any rate in the sphere of foreign policy. It may even be maintained that his movement has served the cause of international peace by sublimating the militaristic complexes of his people. He supplied brown shirts instead of battles and diverted the violent impulses of his fellow countrymen from the Polish frontier on to the Jews and Marxians in their midst.[37]

There were, of course, those (Chamberlain's brother Austen was one) who judged from the outset that the nature of the Nazi regime in the domestic arena was such as to require the country to be placed beyond the diplomatic pale. But Neville Chamberlain belonged to the large majority who adopted the opposite point of view, that the internal affairs of a country were its own concern (Hitler had after all come to office by democratic means) and that it was its conduct in the international arena which mattered. According to Lord Londonderry, who served as MacDonald's Secretary of State for Air, the German system was 'wrong both from the moral and practical points of view, but it is no use our standing on one side and looking down our noses because the system of government in Germany differs from the free-and-easy system of this country'.[38] This of course was, and remains, the traditional line of British diplomacy, the approach which dictated cooperation with Tsarist Russia in the First World War and with Stalin's Soviet Union in the Second. It is still the attitude which determines British policy towards Communist

China in our own day. Thus Chamberlain refused to accept that British foreign policy should be influenced by ideological considerations. 'After all', he told an audience at the Albert Hall,

> we have to live with these countries, we have to trade with them, we have to work with them in all matters which require international cooperation. Surely in those circumstances it is only common sense to try to make our relations with them as amicable as possible instead of nagging at one another until we all lose our tempers.[39]

As it was, the full extent of Nazi ambitions was not wholly apparent at any point before the outbreak of war in September 1939. For each of Hitler's foreign policy initiatives up to that time, with the exception of the Prague Coup, there was some sort of justification available in terms of legitimate German national aspirations or righting the injustices of the Versailles settlement. Even someone with the impeccable anti-appeasement credentials of Harold Macmillan could tell his constituents as late as March 1938 that Germany's existing violations of the Treaty of Versailles were not 'in principle of a kind to which objection could be made'. Indeed he believed that there was 'a good deal of reason' behind German rearmament, the remilitarization of the Rhineland and the Anschluss.[40] Certainly, at the time Chamberlain became Prime Minister in May 1937, there was little evidence that Hitler's foreign policy was markedly different, at least in its intentions, from that of his predecessors.

Chamberlain of course was wrong in his assessment that Nazism was little more than extreme nationalism and that German foreign policy was about the rectification of finite grievances, capable of resolution through the normal give and take of traditional diplomacy. Nazi ideology was about far more than that – though, in Chamberlain's defence, it is worth mentioning that precisely *what* it was about has not been entirely resolved by the historical profession over the last six decades. In his error, however, he was far from standing alone. The failure to come to grips with the ideological factor in German policy was almost universal. Benny Morris's exhaustive search through the weekly newspapers of the 1930s – one place where scope for reflection might logically have located them – revealed that of the thousands of articles written on Germany no more than two dozen set out specifically to define or analyse Nazi ideology. Prevailing opinion refused to believe that a civilized nation of seventy million people could possibly subscribe to a fanatical set of beliefs, 'let alone base domestic and foreign policies upon it'.[41]

Rather than being the product of a narrow provincial training Chamberlain's fundamental beliefs epitomized the liberal attitudes of a generation which believed that the lessons of the Great War spoke for themselves. That conflict was interpreted not as the consequence of human wilfulness or evil, but as a dreadful accident, in which opposing alliance systems and the remorseless build-up of huge armaments were probably component parts. Far from destroying faith in man's essential reasonableness, the War had by its sheer enormity reinforced the conviction of all civilized men that, in the modern age, armed conflict had reached the stage of technological development where it could no longer be regarded as an acceptable form of international conduct. Here perhaps was Chamberlain's true blindspot – though by no means unique to him.

The policy of appeasement was based upon the notion that there must be a point, and a not too distant one, at which those being appeased would become satisfied and where a new status quo could be constructed on the basis of lasting peace. Chamberlain rejected absolutely the notion that Hitler and Mussolini were incapable of being appeased, not because he found them attractive personalities – he did not – but because he could not understand how men in comparable positions to his own in countries renowned for their civilizations could be so completely consumed by evil as to welcome the waging of war as a conscious act of policy. The fact that they were and that they did ultimately rendered his own policy completely futile. As he told the Cordwainers Company in 1937, 'there is always some common measure of agreement if only we will look for it'.[42] The dictators were, he believed, 'too often regarded as if they were entirely inhuman. I believe this idea to be quite erroneous.'[43] He was convinced that the 'aim of every statesman worthy of the name, to whatever country he belongs, must be the happiness of the people for whom he is responsible'. Logically, therefore, no government would deliberately deny to its people 'their plainest and simplest right', to live in peace rather than the nightmare of war. 'I do not believe that such a Government anywhere exists among civilised peoples.'[44] As the international situation darkened in 1938 he still urged a Birmingham audience not to forget that we are all members of the human race and subject to the like passions and affections and fears and desires. There *must* be something in common between us, if only we can find it.[45]

Even when Hitler shattered his illusions by marching into Prague in March 1939, Chamberlain believed that the German people would be able to hold him back from the ultimate catastrophe of war for 'the desire of all the peoples of the world still remains concentrated on the hopes of peace'.[46] That belief still remained in place after the formal declaration of hostilities: 'there is such a widespread desire to avoid war and it is so deeply rooted that it surely must find expression somehow'.[47] Only perhaps after his retirement from the premiership did he come to realize that his hopes had been doomed to failure in the face of 'the insatiate and inhuman ambitions of a fanatic'.[48]

Chamberlain's mindset affords an important determinant of the foreign policy upon which he embarked on becoming Prime Minister. To it must be added first, his conviction that Germany, even Hitler's Germany, did have legitimate grievances resulting from the Versailles settlement of 1919, and second, the overall diplomatic situation which he inherited in May 1937. Chamberlain's readiness to consider treaty revisions and his belief that peace would remain unstable until this was done were widely shared. As a Foreign Office memorandum of 1935 put it, 'from the earliest years following the war, it was our policy to eliminate those parts of the Peace Settlement which, as practical people, we knew to be untenable and indefensible'.[49] Soon after becoming Prime Minister he spoke to the Spanish ambassador of his desire to sit round a table with the Germans and 'run through their complaints and claims with a pencil'.[50] Granted his view of warfare and his belief that it was all but universally shared, he found it difficult to understand the way in which the Germans insisted on going about their task of securing revision: 'They are such an efficient people that they could have almost anything they liked peacefully. But they cannot be satisfied unless they are perpetually rattling the sabre and consequently they can keep no friends.'[51]

At the same time Chamberlain recognized that his negotiating position was a weak one and that the world was in a more dangerous condition than for many years past. The rapid transformation of the international scene which had left the British

Empire under simultaneous challenge from three potential
enemies was one which could not have been predicted. With
hindsight it became clear that Britain had started to rearm too
late and too slowly and for this Chamberlain, as a senior
member of the National Government, must bear his share of
responsibility. ('Responsibility' would seem a far more appropriate word than 'blame'.) As Samuel Hoare later conceded, 'If,
in 1933, we had realized the complete change that had come
over Europe after Hitler's advent to power, and had at once
embarked upon a bigger and quicker programme, and in particular, upon an intensified expansion of the Air Force, the Chiefs
of Staff would have had a very different story to tell . . .'.[52] But
the fact was that virtually no one had made this leap of imagination in 1933 and, even if Chamberlain and other members of
the government had done so, their capacity to effect a conse-
quential change of policy must remain open to question. 'Given
the prevailing non-interventionist climate of public opinion in
the 1930s . . . was it certain that any government with any hope
of retaining office could have carried a really intensive rearmament or a resolute policy of armed intervention in Europe?'[53] In
addition, ministers had in their minds contemporary assumptions about the impact of massive expenditure on the national
economy – so soon after the near-disaster of 1931 – and a clear
perception that bankrupting the state would make little contribution to defence against a potential aggressor.

There is then a certain logic, if nothing else, about the broad
outlines of Chamberlain's foreign policy. It had taken an enormous coalition of powers to defeat Germany in 1918. The recre-
ation of anything like that alignment seemed a mere pipe-dream
in 1937, whereas Germany might very well be reinforced by
Italy and Japan, both of which had fought on Britain's side in the
First World War. Chamberlain clearly did have some idea, even
before Munich, of gaining time, not in the sense of preparing for
an inevitable war, but in order to reach a point where Britain
would be sufficiently strong to deter any aggressive thoughts
(difficult though he found it to contemplate or understand them)
on the part of any other power. In essence therefore, as the
government's Chief Whip once put it, Chamberlain's foreign
policy was 'far simpler than those who love to discover recon-
dite motives would suppose'.[54] It was not, as some more fanciful interpretations would have it, the product of an
Establishment conspiracy variously located at Cliveden or

Printing House Square. It was not simply a policy of cowardice or surrender. But neither was it a particularly heroic policy. In a private letter Chamberlain admitted that 'in the absence of any powerful ally and until our armaments are completed, we must adjust our foreign policy to our circumstances, and even bear with patience and good humour actions which we would like to treat in a very different fashion'.[55] But with no obvious alternative Chamberlain believed that his policy was the best that could be devised.

The new Prime Minister did not effect a dramatic change of direction to British foreign policy in 1937, though he strongly believed that a much clearer emphasis needed to be given to it than had been evident under the easy-going Baldwin and that it was his responsibility as head of the government to provide this new sense of purpose. Nor can it be argued that Chamberlain as Prime Minister in any sense acted unconstitutionally, usurping powers that were not rightly his or subverting the normal processes of democratic government. As chairman of the cabinet Chamberlain was decisive rather than dictatorial. It was his style to give a lead to discussions rather than simply sum up the thinking of his ministerial colleagues. He was certainly a strong premier, on top of his job, particularly in comparison to his predecessor, but his interference in the concerns of his departmental ministers has probably been exaggerated. 'He certainly never interfered with me', reflected Edward Halifax, 'and I fancy that what Anthony [Eden] thought was interference with him was in part well-intentioned stupidity.'[56] Similarly, his use of advisers was never as sinister as the authors of *Guilty Men* among others portrayed. Horace Wilson was little more than a loyal and efficient civil servant carrying out the Prime Minister's bidding to the best of his ability.

To his credit Chamberlain never lost sight of the priority of Germany within British strategic thinking, which he had first recognized in 1934, even though the surface manifestation of his diplomacy seemed at times to place a disproportionate emphasis upon Mussolini's Italy. As he explained to his adviser, Lord Weir:

> we ought to be able to get the F.O. to play up in such a way as to get our relations with Italy on to a better footing. That will reduce our anxieties in the Mediterranean but I still feel that the key of the situation is in Berlin and that is not so easily handled.[57]

There is no evidence to suggest that, in seeking a wide-ranging agreement with the dictator powers, Chamberlain was prepared to pursue a policy of peace at any price. There were always strict limits to the concessions which he was prepared to entertain. 'I think it very possible', he later reflected, 'that at Munich [Hitler] was under the impression, quite without justification, that I should agree with him about [leaving Germany a free hand to do what she liked in the East]. Hence his fury and bewilderment on finding that this was not the case.'[58] The basis for a genuine historical debate about the policy of appeasement should probably focus not on the policy itself, but on the lengths to which it was taken, whether it was pursued too long and whether Chamberlain did enough to develop alternative policy options to extricate himself from a strategy which, as has been suggested, had largely been forced upon him. In any such discussion, upon which Chamberlain's historical reputation continues to depend, the Czechoslovakian crisis and resulting Munich settlement of September 1938 will always occupy centre stage.

Granted that Chamberlain was inclined to see the Czechoslovakian problem on its intrinsic merits and not as part of Hitler's Grand Design, his reasoning is easy to follow. The claims of the Sudetendeutsch were not worth resisting at the cost of a European war. There was a widespread conviction that the existing frontiers of the Czech state were untenable and would remain so, even at the end of a victorious war fought to uphold them. This was the message which came from Sir Basil Newton, the British minister in Prague, as early as March 1938:

> having regard to her geographical situation, her history and the racial divisions of her population, Czechoslovakia's present position is not permanently tenable [and] it will be no kindness in the long run to try to maintain her in it.[59]

One contemporary writer, in a metaphor which would have appealed to much Conservative sentiment, compared the predicament of the Sudetendeutsch to Ulstermen 'forcibly united with Nationalist Ireland and expected to settle down comfortably as a subject minority'.[60] Though much has been written of the immorality of British participation in the dismemberment of a sovereign state, there was a strong feeling that what was being proposed was no more than putting right a mistake committed by the peace-makers of 1919. In 1945 the victorious Allies took a rather different approach, driving out the German-speaking inhabitants of the Sudentenland, but their understanding of the problem seemed essentially the same.

Throughout the spring and summer of 1938 Chamberlain pursued a policy based not on the idea of peace at any price but on the conviction that this particular issue was not worth a war and all the awful consequences this would entail. His radio broadcast on the evening of 27 September got to the heart of the matter:

> Armed conflict between nations is a nightmare to me; but if I were convinced that any nation had made up its mind to dominate the world by fear of its force, I should feel that it must be resisted. Under such a domination life for people who believe in liberty would not be worth living; but war is a fearful thing, and we must be very clear, before we embark on it, that it is really the great issues that are at stake, and that the call to risk everything in their defence, when all the consequences are weighed, is irresistible.[61]

The phrase about dominating the world by force was of course one which he would take up again in his Birmingham speech of March 1939 in the very different situation created by the Prague Coup. But as he contemplated the Czechoslovakian situation Chamberlain, like the newly-appointed Permanent Under-Secretary at the Foreign Office, Sir Alexander Cadogan, could not 'look on the Reich's absorption of Germans with much horror . . . I shan't be able to work up much moral indignation until Hitler interferes with other nationalities'.[62] Even Churchill, despite his later criticism of the settlement actually arrived at, believed that there was scope for negotiations between the Prague government and its German minority to agree upon revised frontiers for the Czech state. In any case it was by no means clear to Chamberlain that Britain could easily come to Czechoslovakia's aid, were she in a mind to do so:

> You have only to look at the map to see that nothing that France or we could do could possibly save Czecho-Slovakia from being overrun by the Germans if they wanted to do it. The Austrian frontier is practically open; the great Skoda munition works are within easy bombing distance of the German aerodromes, the railways all pass through German territory, Russia is 100 miles away.

Therefore, we could not help Czecho-Slovakia – she would simply be a pretext for going to war with Germany. That we could not think of, unless we had a reasonable prospect of being able to beat her to her knees in a reasonable time and of that I see no sign.[63]

Chamberlain's real problems arose when, at his second meeting with Hitler at Godesberg on 22 September, the Führer stepped up his demands. It was at this point that his lack of understanding of the true nature of the Third Reich placed him in difficulties. Yet, having accepted the general principle of cession, he did not believe that he would be justified in risking war over the detailed implementation of an agreed strategy. In this he was by no means alone. 'Surely the world can't be plunged into the horrors of universal war', wrote the Canadian High Commissioner Vincent Massey, 'over a few miles of territory or a few days one way or other in a time-table!'[64] The Prime Minister's priority was now to agree upon an orderly and non-violent way of implementing the transfer of Sudeten German territory to the Reich. This was bound to involve a detailed agreement somewhat less favourable to the Czechs than that outlined at Berchtesgaden, as must have been apparent to MPs when, almost without exception, they endorsed the Prime Minister's announcement that he was flying out to Germany for a third meeting with Hitler at Munich. Indeed, the speech of the Liberal leader, Archibald Sinclair, made it abundantly clear that the House understood that the Sudetenland would have to be ceded to Germany. Attlee too, in welcoming Chamberlain's statement that 'even at this late hour' the opportunity had arisen for further discussions 'which might lead to the prevention of war', cannot have believed that Hitler was about to withdraw his demands and leave the frontiers of Czechoslovakia unchallenged. Against this background some of the attacks made upon the Munich settlement in the Commons debate in early October appear less than fair. As Chamberlain reminded his critics, 'We did not go [to Munich] to decide whether the predominantly German areas in the Sudetenland should be passed over to the German Reich. That had been decided already.'[65]

Chamberlain's contemporary opponents offered no answer to the question posed in that debate by the Conservative backbencher, David Maxwell-Fyfe, who wondered at what point the country ought to have gone to war over the Czech issue. More

recently the Prime Minister has been criticized for the government's failure at any moment during the crisis to draw up a
balance sheet of the arguments for and against fighting Germany
in 1938 in conjunction with the not inconsiderable assets of the
Czech army and airforce, rather than allowing those assets to
fall under ultimate German control.[66] Recent assessments have,
on the whole, suggested that Munich altered the military
balance in Germany's and not Britain's favour, thus undermining
the argument about a year's breathing-space, even supposing
this can be shown to have been Chamberlain's real intention.[67]
But his calculations were based less upon the overall military
balance than upon Britain's perceived vulnerability to a German
aerial attack. The Chairman of the Aircraft Manufacturers'
Association later recalled sending the Prime Minister figures on
the country's aircraft production at this time:

> the intensive rearmament programme that the Prime
> Minister had authorised had not had time to take effect at
> the time of Munich, with the result that the figures I sent
> to Downing Street showed how terribly weak we still were
> in the air, and it is my opinion that when Mr.Chamberlain
> went to Munich he had not a single solitary card in his
> hand: that he went there with the full knowledge that if
> war was declared the equipment available to the RAF, both
> in types and numbers, was far, far below that of the
> German Air Force. It would be true to say that at that time
> we should have been almost defenceless in the air because
> of the superiority of the Germans.[68]

Such dire assessments were, we now know, wide of the mark.
Germany did not have the capacity in late 1938 to launch the
sort of assault from the air on British cities which dominated
contemporary thinking. But Chamberlain has often been criticized – without much justification – for defying the expert opinion of his own Foreign Office. It would be perverse if in this
instance he were also to be condemned for failing to go against
the prevailing advice which led him to believe, not only that the
balance of advantage would move in Britain's favour if war was
postponed, but also that the country was currently at the mercy
of an aerial attack. He could do no more than rely upon the
information available to him, flawed though it was.

If Britain had gone to war in September 1938 it seems unlikely
that she would have done so with the unity and resolution which

were present a year later. Geoffrey Dawson, the editor of *The Times* who remained a convinced supporter of Munich to the end, recalled the atmosphere at the time of the Czechoslovakian crisis:

> No one who sat in this place, as I did during the autumn of '38, with almost daily visitations from eminent Canadians and Australians, could fail to realise that war with Germany at that time would have been misunderstood and resented from end to end of the Empire. Even in this country there would have been no unity behind it.[69]

If the improvement by 1939 was a largely unlooked-for bonus from the Munich settlement, it deserves nonetheless to be put in the balance on Chamberlain's behalf. If the British people did not want to fight in September 1938 the responsibility for the outcome of the crisis is in some sense a collective one. In a democracy leaders must lead and Chamberlain has often been accused of being too ready to use prevailing opinion as an excuse for his own weakness and inertia. Perhaps so, but there is a corresponding danger that the leader who marches too many paces ahead of his followers will find himself completely out on his own.

Even if we accept that Munich was, in all the circumstances of September 1938, the best outcome that Chamberlain or any one else could have hoped for, controversy still rages over precisely what the Prime Minister believed he had achieved by his agreement with Hitler, the piece of paper publicly flourished as 'peace for our time'. From assessments of this issue have grown two diametrically opposed images of the same man. Chamberlain is either the far-sighted statesman who had successfully postponed war until a supposedly more advantageous moment in the future or Hitler's dupe who, in the face of all evidence to the contrary, continued to trust the German dictator and who failed even now to abandon appeasement in favour of some new policy option. Indeed, his lingering reputation, reinforced by recent post-revisionist writers, as a foolish old man who had been taken in by the Führer derives less from the Munich settlement itself than from the indications which he gave that he really believed he had secured a lasting peace. Those historians from Feiling onward who have championed the case for 'buying time' are, asserts R.A.C. Parker without hesitation or qualification, quite simply 'all wrong'.[70]

The evidence in this matter is contradictory; much of it is also anecdotal. According to Lord Swinton, Chamberlain impatiently brushed aside his proffered endorsement of Munich as 'worth while buying a year's grace' with the confident declaration, 'But I have made peace'. Yet both Alec Dunglass, Chamberlain's Parliamentary Private Secretary, and Patrick Donner, MP, recalled the Prime Minister being far more sceptical of Hitler's word: 'if he signs it and sticks to it that will be fine, but if he breaks it that will convince the Americans of the kind of man he is'.[71] In the same vein Chamberlain's cousin recalled a now lost letter in which

> Neville wrote that he found Hitler unstable, if not mad – that he didn't believe a word he said and that he hoped he had won a year to rearm before Hitler's lust for conquest overtook him. He thought it dangerous for these beliefs to be public knowledge, for that might tempt Hitler to move before we could do anything to protect ourselves. As near as I can remember, the last sentence was 'Pray God that what I have done will give us time to prepare'.[72]

Nor are we helped by Chamberlain's propensity to utter ill-considered remarks of the sort which a modern spin-doctor would be quick to repress. 'The very midsummer of madness', 'Hitler has missed the bus', 'I have my friends in the House' and above all 'Peace for our Time' have clung to Chamberlain and continued to shape his reputation long after his more thoughtful utterances were forgotten. Yet we do at least know that in the case of the last of these unfortunate phrases he quickly regretted what he had said, explaining to the House of Commons that it was the product of 'a moment of some emotion, after a long and exhausting day'.[73]

In all probability Chamberlain himself was unsure exactly what Munich had achieved. Over the following months his mood wavered between optimism and despair. His private letters reveal periods of mounting confidence punctuated by moments of anxiety and foreboding. His overall attitude is probably best encapsulated in a sentence addressed to Lord Halifax to which Professor Dilks has drawn attention: 'Edward, we must hope for the best while preparing for the worst'.[74] In the first instance Chamberlain did believe that the Munich agreement had made war less likely. 'A lot of people', he complained just a month after the settlement, 'seem to be losing their heads and talking and thinking as though Munich had made war more instead of less imminent.'[75] But this optimism was not the result of some supposed rapport and mutual confidence established with Hitler. It grew from the judgement that the longer war was postponed the less likely Germany would be to risk an encounter with a country which would become increasingly capable of defending itself and of inflicting an unacceptable degree of damage upon a potential enemy. Little more than a month before the outbreak of hostilities he could still write:

> Unlike some of my critics I go further and say the longer the war is put off the less likely it is to come at all as we go on perfecting our defences, and building up the defences of our allies. . . . You don't need offensive forces sufficient to win a smashing victory. What you want are defensive forces sufficiently strong to make it impossible for the other side to win except at such a cost as to make it not worth while.[76]

Over a period of time postponing a war and averting it altogether would become more and more synonymous. 'As always', stressed Chamberlain, 'I want to gain time, for I never accept that war is inevitable.'[77]

His critics have argued that it was only with hindsight and in the final months of his life that Chamberlain began to rationalize Munich as an unfortunate necessity from which an extra year's rearmament had been gained. In late May 1940, for example, he wrote that he had 'realised from the beginning our military weakness and did my best to postpone, if I could not avert the war'.[78] But the change of emphasis was inevitable once war had come about granted Chamberlain's earlier perception that a war postponed was more likely to be a war avoided. He had always realized that war might yet break out and a key part of his post-Munich strategy was to place Britain in a stronger position to engage in it. As he had reminded the Commons soon after the Anschluss, 'neither this nor any other Government can frame any policy which will prevent some other Government going to war if it has made up its mind to act in that direction'.[79] So while British rearmament remained geared primarily to a policy of deterrence and the strengthening of the country's bargaining position in any future negotiations with Germany, Chamberlain never excluded the possibility of conflict from his mind, much as he would have liked to be able to do so. Graham

Stewart's recent assessment seems the most balanced: 'Postponing war was, of course, not the ultimate goal of Chamberlain's policy. . . . Nevertheless, at worst, he believed that a possible war fought later would be more likely to be successful than a certain war fought [at the time of Munich].'[80]

Chamberlain found it difficult to give appropriate emphasis to the rearmament side of his policy for fear that he would thereby arouse the renewed hostility of those he still hoped to placate. His widow remembered asking him whether he could not give some indication of the doubt which she knew he felt about Hitler's good faith. But he believed that to do this 'might well wreck any chance there might be of a better understanding with Germany'.[81] In Germany and Italy, the Prime Minister warned the cabinet in late October 1938, 'it was suspected that this rearmament was directed against them, and it was important that we should not encourage these suspicions'.[82] Chamberlain was

> like a doctor who was called in to a very serious case but not an altogether hopeless one: what he endeavours to do is to try and reassure the patient that he will recover, in the hope that by creating confidence it will be helping towards the desired recovery. Mr. Chamberlain could hardly have come back from Munich and told the House of Commons that he had talked to Hitler but he did not believe a word Hitler had said and that he thought war would come, as this could have precipitated the very thing he was trying to avoid.[83]

As Samuel Hoare recalled, the double policy of peace and rearmament needed both skilful handling and subtle presentation. The two aims were difficult and at times almost impossible to reconcile.[84]

Nonetheless, Chamberlain proceeded during the months following Munich on the basis that a general settlement with Germany was by no means impossible. This meant accepting, until Hitler proved otherwise, that the Sudetenland did represent his last territorial aspiration in Europe. Indeed, it was probably part of his strategy to talk up the prospects of peace, at least in public. In private he tended to be more circumspect. The greatest catastrophe had been avoided, 'but we are very little nearer to the time when we can put all thoughts of war out of our minds and settle down to make the world a better place'.[85] Even

so, he believed that the contacts which had been established with
the dictator powers opened up the possibility of a future wide-
ranging agreement which would enable a stop to be put to the
arms race. Much of his thinking remained founded upon that
assumption of reason and reasonableness in Germany which
represented his most important blindspot:

> when the world had passed through a crisis like that of last
> September without catastrophe, it is almost impossible to
> reproduce the circumstances until at any rate sufficient
> time has elapsed for the memory of it to have become
> blurred. At the present time, the memory of September is
> still vivid in the minds of the common people throughout
> Europe, as well as in this country, and they are on the alert
> and anxious to make sure that they are not a second time
> being led unawares to the edge of a precipice.[86]

By February, however, in other words before the German
entry into Prague, it is clear that something had changed,
perhaps as a result of intelligence reports, and that the
Government was ready to adopt a tougher line. Chamberlain's
statement to the Commons on 6 February that any threat 'to the
vital interests of France from whatever quarter it came must
evoke the immediate co-operation of Great Britain' represented
the firmest declaration of a continental commitment for many
years. By the end of the month the first round of Anglo–French
staff talks had got under way. Patrick Donner remembered
returning from a lecture tour of Germany and Poland on behalf
of the British Council and reporting to the Prime Minister his
clear impression that Hitler intended war, probably in August:

> Chamberlain replied that my information 'reinforced his
> own', which was that Germany intended war in September
> and that he had already 'ordered the largest possible re-
> armament programme commensurate with the maximum
> capacity of existing machine tools'. I record the sentence,
> a note of which I made immediately after leaving No.10.[87]

Prague itself was clearly a significant development, though it
did not prompt a complete reversal of Chamberlain's policy. The
incorporation into the Reich of the non-Germanic peoples of
Bohemia and Moravia was not compatible with the racial theories which Hitler had hitherto purported to espouse. In his
Birmingham speech on 17 March Chamberlain took up again

the question with which he had toyed in his broadcast the previous September, whether Hitler's latest actions were the prelude
'to an attempt to dominate the world by force', implying a
different answer to that given six months before. His statement
to the cabinet the following day was entirely consistent with the
interpretation of his views put forward in these pages:

> Up till a week ago we had proceeded on the assumption
> that we should be able to continue with our policy of
> getting on to better terms with the Dictator Powers, and
> that although those Powers had aims, those aims were
> limited. We had all along had at the back of our minds the
> reservation that this might not prove to be the case but we
> had felt that it was right to try out the possibilities of this
> course ... He had now come definitely to the conclusion
> that Herr Hitler's attitude made it impossible to continue
> to negotiate on the old basis with the Nazi regime.[88]

By the end of March the guarantee of Polish independence was
in place. Poland was not guaranteed on its intrinsic merits – in
most respects it offered a less attractive subject for British
concern than Czechoslovakia – but because it now stood as a
test case of Hitler's intentions. Chamberlain had never believed
that appeasement meant making limitless concessions to the
dictator powers. In this light the guarantee was a statement that,
if Hitler transgressed the limits now defined, Britain would be
prepared to resist him, if necessary by war.

But if the Polish guarantee indicated that in given circumstances Britain would take military action, it should also be
understood as a deterrent designed to prevent the conditions of
war from arising in the first place. To this extent it would be
wrong to suggest that appeasement – in the sense that
Chamberlain had always conceived it as a dual policy of deterrence and the quest for a settlement – had now been abandoned.
The door to further negotiation remained open and the fact that
it was Poland's independence rather than her territorial integrity
which was guaranteed may indicate that the Prime Minister was
prepared to contemplate concessions over the Polish corridor
where, if it were possible to view the issue in dispassionate isolation, Hitler did of course have a reasonable case. Samuel Hoare,
closer to Chamberlain than any other senior cabinet minister,
described the change occasioned by Prague in the Prime
Minister's thinking:

If I described his mind in a sentence, I would say that at the time of Munich he was hopeful but by no means sure that Hitler would keep his word, but that after Prague he came to the conclusion that only a show of great determination would prevent him from breaking it.[89]

That even now, despite all the evidence to the contrary and in defiance of the increasing sentiment of his political colleagues and, as far as we can judge it, of public opinion, Chamberlain still believed in the possibility of a peaceful resolution of Anglo–German relations leaves his long-term reputation at its most vulnerable. His most vehement defenders would find it difficult to deny that obstinacy was a prominent feature in his make-up. He recognized that conflict was becoming ever more likely but refused to renounce the last hope of avoiding it until the actual declaration of war had taken place. In mid-July he doubted whether 'any solution, short of war, is practicable at present', yet could still assert that 'if dictators would have a modicum of patience, I can imagine that a way could be found of meeting German claims while safeguarding Poland's independence and economic security'.[90] Even a week later he referred to that moment when Britain's defensive capability would be sufficiently strong to enable further talks with Germany to take place. Such remarks smack of near-wilful blindness to the reality of the international situation in the summer of 1939 and perhaps make sense only if we remind ourselves again of the total catastrophe which Chamberlain believed would be unleashed by modern warfare. 'When I think of those four terrible years', he had once said of the First World War,

> and I think of the 7,000,000 of young men who were cut off in their prime, the 13,000,000 who were maimed and mutilated, the misery and the suffering of the mothers and fathers, the sons and daughters, and the relatives and friends of those who were killed and wounded, then I am bound to say again what I have said before, and what I say now . . . to all the world – in war, whichever side may call itself victor, there are no winners, but all are losers.[91]

That Chamberlain, unlike his successor, was not born under the sign of Mars was very apparent once war had broken out. His first inclination was to stand down in the belief that he did not have 'any particular part to play until it came to discussing peace terms'.[92] He could not 'bear to think of those gallant fellows who lost their lives last night in the RAF attack, and of their families who have first been called upon to pay the price'.[93] Only perhaps the fact that the war turned out 'so different from what I had expected' enabled him to carry on.[94] Britain was in no position to take the military initiative at this time, but in any case the nature of the Phoney War chimed in well with Chamberlain's vision of how it could be won. His hope was not for military victory, but for a collapse of the German home front. This would come about when the German people, realizing that they could not win the war and having to endure gradually increasing restrictions in their normal lives, forced their government to abandon the ways of aggression. 'My policy continues to be the same', he noted in October. 'Hold on tight. Keep up the economic pressure, push on with munitions production and military preparations with the utmost energy. Take no offensive unless Hitler begins it.'[95] Such thinking was of course totally misplaced, the product of erroneous intelligence about the state of the German economy combined with Chamberlain's continuing faith in the reasonableness of the German people, even if Hitler himself now stood condemned as a dangerous lunatic.

The circumstances of Chamberlain's fall from power were dramatic in the extreme. Robert Boothby, who had developed into one of his severest critics, recorded the scene in the House of Commons as the vote was announced at the end of the debate on the Norwegian campaign:

> For a moment he blanched, but quickly recovered himself, and smiled at some of his supporters. Then he rose abruptly, and walked out alone. I watched his solitary figure going down the dark corridor behind the Speaker's Chair until it disappeared from sight. I thought of him standing in Downing Street, barely eighteen months before, with the cheering crowds surging around him. All is vanity, saith the preacher. I felt very sorry for him in the hour of his fall. God knows he had struggled, according to the light that was in him, for peace.[96]

Some described what happened in terms of Greek tragedy. But the true classical hero must undergo a cathartic process whereby he recognizes his errors and accepts responsibility for his own downfall. Chamberlain, by contrast, went to his grave convinced that there was nothing for which he needed to reproach himself and content to leave his ultimate reputation to the verdict of history.

What then was Chamberlain's legacy? How well prepared was Britain to prosecute the war at the time of his resignation from the premiership? By June 1940 he felt able to endorse his appeasement policy with achievements which it had not been possible to proclaim while his primary goal had remained the maintenance of peace. 'If we get through this war successfully', he insisted to the Conservative Party's National Union executive, 'then it will be to Munich that we shall owe it. In the condition our armaments were at that time, if we had called Hitler's bluff and he had called ours, I do not think we could have survived a week.'[97] Though the last six months of Chamberlain's life witnessed a succession of major reverses in the allied war effort, the salient fact about 1940 was that the country survived the Battle of Britain. It did so by the sort of narrow margin which makes it difficult to accept that Chamberlain had been wrong to postpone war for as long as possible. 'When the battle arrived, the strength of Fighter Command was almost ten times that of September 1938.'[98] Patrick Donner recalled that on 20 July 1940 he had reported from Fighter Command headquarters that, for the first time, Britain had sufficient numbers of wireless electrical mechanics as well as wireless operators to enable the radar system along the coast to cope with massive and simultaneous German air attacks. Such attacks began on 8 August. '*The margin between victory and almost certain defeat was precisely nineteen days,* neither more nor less, and that narrowest of narrow margins was secured for Britain by Neville Chamberlain at Munich.'[99] Chamberlain himself believed that he merited some of the credit for 'if I am personally responsible for deficiencies of tanks and anti-aircraft guns, I must be equally personally responsible for the efficiency of the Air Force and the Navy'.[100] In the country's 'finest hour' it was of course the strength of Britain's fighter aircraft, the Hurricanes and Spitfires, backed up by radar, which proved decisive. That strength was largely determined by what had been produced or was already in the pipeline at the time of Chamberlain's fall rather than by some miraculous transformation in the intervening period. 'No one can suppose that our equipment has all been turned out in the last six weeks.'[101] Furthermore, and as has been shown, Chamberlain had been the key figure in shifting the emphasis of

British rearmament from the bomber to the fighter. Indeed, it seems reasonable to suggest that, had the National Government constructed the sort of airforce for which Churchill had clamoured in the middle years of the decade, 'then the Hurricanes and Spitfires would not only have been starved of the funds needed to produce them in any quantities, but their development might have fallen victim to economies imposed by the need to produce the bombers which Churchill wanted'.[102] Though contemporaries found it easier to equate Chamberlain with Dunkirk and Churchill with the Battle of Britain, it is the historian's duty to arrive at a more equitable distribution of praise and criticism.

It was probably inevitable that Chamberlain's reputation should suffer a catastrophic decline in the last months of his life – and one from which it has never fully recovered. 'Few men' he reflected, 'can have known such a tremendous reverse of fortune in so short a time.'[103] The very fact that Munich had elevated him to such unusual levels of public acclaim made his eventual fall from grace all the more dramatic. And 'when he fell there was no safety net of affection to catch him. He was not a loveable man.'[104] The setback in Scandinavia, Hitler's turn to the west, the fall of France, hitherto seen as Britain's indispensable wartime ally, Italy's entry into the war, the beginnings of the aerial assault on the capital and the apparent imminence of invasion combined to make 1940 one of the worst years in the nation's history. In such an atmosphere men looked for simple explanations and someone to hold responsible for all that had gone wrong. The war, commented the *Manchester Guardian*, 'marked the collapse of an experiment in diplomacy in which [Chamberlain's] own initiative and his own judgement had been the driving and governing force. It stamped with failure the policy with which his name would go down to history.'[105] By involving himself so personally in the conduct of British foreign policy since his advent to the premiership he ensured that he would receive either the applause or the condemnation for its outcome. By 1940 it was clear which this would be and the desperate circumstances of the time did not favour an impartial quest for the truth. All along Chamberlain's policy had been one of tremendous risk, not least because its ultimate outcome had not been his to determine. As one sympathetic MP had noted at the time of Munich, 'His policy is of course the right one – but its success depends upon Hitler first and foremost – and can one trust the man?'[106]

Chamberlain too fully understood the risk that he was running. He even seemed to anticipate the historiographical dangers his reputation would incur if his policies failed:

> I fully realise that if eventually things go wrong, and the aggression takes place, there will be many . . . who will say that the British Government must bear the responsibility and that if only they had had the courage to tell Hitler now that if he used force we should at once declare war, that would have stopped him. By that time it will be impossible to prove the contrary.[107]

But did Chamberlain have any realistic alternatives to the line he chose? Historians, who are never themselves confronted with the sorts of choices which politicians have to make, can too readily give the impression that, with a little more courage and imagination, politicians could easily avoid the disasters to which their decisions on occasions lead. Much of the criticism to which Chamberlain has been subjected, renewed and reinvigorated in recent post-revisionist writing, implies that viable alternative courses did exist, which were consciously overlooked or dismissed, but which could have averted war and even perhaps have led to Hitler's overthrow. Such alternative policies have the inestimable advantage over Chamberlain's that they can no longer be subjected to empirical evaluation. It was easy for his contemporary critics just as it is for later academic commentators to postulate courses of action which might in fact have been equally doomed to disaster. Indeed, it is possible that there was 'no good or "correct" policy' available in the circumstances of the 1930s.[108] The problem which faces the historians of this decade, judged Norton Medlicott nearly half a century ago, 'is to decide how far the leaders failed and how far circumstances can fairly be said to have been too much for them'.[109] Put simply, Chamberlain was confronted by the need to protect Britain's over-extended global interests with insufficient means of doing so. The same problem faced his successor, Winston Churchill, albeit in different circumstances and, as David Reynolds has suggested, 'the various policies [British leaders] advanced are not to be divided into separate camps – appeasers and the rest – but rather on different points of a single spectrum, with no one as near either extreme as is often believed'.[110]

It is reasonable to observe that Chamberlain spent much more of his time and energy trying to reduce the number of the country's enemies than he did trying to increase the number of its potential allies. He himself suggested that the concept of a Grand Alliance was a very attractive idea with almost everything to be said for it, 'until you come to examine its practicability'.[111] At the very least it must be conceded that there was something defective about each of its component parts. Had it come into being in 1938 or 1939 it might have reduced the attractions of the military option from the German point of view. Alternatively, as Chamberlain feared, it might have made Hitler more inclined to lash out against 'encirclement' on the pattern of 1914. At all events a Grand Alliance could not have been based on bluff. Only the conviction that his opponents were willing to fight a war against him and that they had the capacity to win it would have been likely to deter Hitler. Yet the British did not believe that, with or without allies, they could survive a German attack, at least in 1938, and had good reason to suppose that an Anglo–German conflict would be the occasion of a multi-theatre assault on Britain's position as a world power. Perhaps the risk was worth taking. At least until the spring of 1939 Chamberlain judged that it was not. As he put it that January, 'I am not a "peace at any price" man; but I must in any given situation be sure in my own mind that the cost of war is not greater than the price of peace'.[112]

This assessment has not attempted to disguise Chamberlain's mistakes and misjudgements. In relation to Adolf Hitler these were fundamental. Yet if appeasement failed and, with hind-sight, was bound to fail, there was nothing dishonourable in the attempt to make it work. To this extent there is much to be said for the idea that he was right to be wrong. In one key respect Chamberlain, in common with most of his British contemporaries not to mention several million Germans, lacked the insight or perhaps the foresight to make the correct judgement about the man with whom it was his misfortune to have to deal. His assessment of Hitler and the leading Nazis never progressed beyond vague notions of 'crazy people' or 'mad men' towards a true understanding of the nature of the Third Reich. Whether having that insight would have been a matter of genius, common sense or mere good fortune is a moot point. Yet if Chamberlain's most grievous error was to cling to the hope of peace longer than there was any justification for doing so, it was a mistake with which most of his fellow men will be able to sympathize. The final word may be left to a forty-eight year old private soldier serving in Hong Kong who wrote to Chamberlain shortly before the latter's death:

> It is easy to be wise after the event and you will be criticised for generations, but your sincerity has been transparent, and I in common with thousands of others who may or may not give expression to their feelings, have admired your efforts – particularly your efforts for peace, so heartrendingly unsuccessful.[113]

Notes

1. K. Middlemas and J. Barnes, *Baldwin: a Biography* (London, 1969), p.1063.
2. J.E. Powell, *Joseph Chamberlain* (London, 1977), p.151.
3. Cited in H.M. Hyde, *Neville Chamberlain* (London, 1976), p.169.
4. Chamberlain MSS, NC7/6/33, N. Chamberlain to Arthur Chamberlain 12 Oct.1940.
5. Earl of Swinton, *Sixty Years of Power: some memories of the men who wielded it* (London, 1966), p.108.
6. R.C. Mee, 'The Foreign Policy of the Chamberlain Wartime Administration, September 1939–May 1940', University of Birmingham Ph.D. thesis, 1999, p.291.
7. Lord Butler (ed.), *The Conservatives: a History from their Origins to 1965* (London, 1977), p.398; House of Commons Debates, 5th Series, vol.365, col.1617.
8. R. Sencourt, 'The Foreign Policy of Neville Chamberlain', *Quarterly Review*, no.600, April 1954, pp.153–4.
9. E.D. O'Brien in *Illustrated London News* 23 Dec. 1961.
10. S. O'Grady, 'Can she look the East End in the eye now?', *Independent on Sunday* 5 March 2000. A review of a reissue of M. Gilbert and R. Gott, *The Appeasers,* published in the *BBC History* magazine for August 2000, suggested that 'what is striking is how many of their conclusions have stood the test of time'.
11. N. Chamberlain, *Norman Chamberlain, A Memoir* (London, 1923), p.140.
12. Chamberlain MSS, NC13/18/949, N. Chamberlain to J. Simon 6 Oct. 1940.
13. House of Lords Debates, vol.117, col.661.
14. K. Feiling, *The Life of Neville Chamberlain* (London, 1946), p.127.
15. Chamberlain MSS, NC18/1/759, N. Chamberlain to H. Chamberlain 24 Oct. 1931. See also Chamberlain's speech accepting the party leadership in 1937, *The Times* 1 June 1937.
16. *Ibid.,* NC7/11/33/29, N. Chamberlain to Lord Bledisloe 17 July 1940.

17. J.D. Fair, 'The Conservative Basis for the Formation of the National Government of 1931', *Journal of British Studies*, xix,2 (1980) presents Chamberlain as the architect of the National Government. But see also S. Ball, 'The Conservative Party and the Formation of the National Government: August 1931', *Historical Journal*, 29, 1 (1986).

18. The phrase is W.H. Auden's.

19. J. Ramsden, 'A Party for Owners or a Party for Earners? How Far Did the Conservative Party Really Change after 1945?' *Transactions of the Royal Historical Society*, 5th Series, vol.37 (1987), p.56.

20. Chamberlain MSS, NC7/6/33, Chamberlain to Arthur Chamberlain 12 Oct. 1940.

21. *Ibid.*, NC7/11/24/15, Chamberlain to Sir F. Humphreys 8 Jan. 1932.

22. *Ibid.*, NC7/6/33, Chamberlain to Arthur Chamberlain 12 Oct. 1940.

23. J. Ramsden, *The Age of Balfour and Baldwin 1902–1940* (London, 1978), p.362.

24. I. Macleod, *Neville Chamberlain* (London, 1961), p.47.

25. Feiling, *Chamberlain*, p.321.

26. Chamberlain MSS, NC7/3/48, Chamberlain to George VI 30 Sept. 1940.

27. C. Petrie, *The Chamberlain Tradition* (London, 1938), p.234.

28. F. Williams, *A Pattern of Rulers* (London, 1965), p.135.

29. *Ibid.*, p.193.

30. W. McElwee, *Britain's Locust Years 1918–1940* (London, 1962), p.257.

31. A.J.P. Taylor, *English History 1914–1945* (Oxford, 1965), p.440.

32. Lord Avon, *Facing the Dictators* (London, 1962), p.445; the story was recently repeated in P.F. Clarke, *Hope and Glory: Britain 1900–1950* (Harmondsworth, 1997), p.184.

33. H. Nicolson, *Why Britain is at War* (Harmondsworth, 1939), p.106.

34. Note by Hankey 24 Oct. 1933, cited P. Bell, *Chamberlain, Germany and Japan, 1933–4* (Basingstoke, 1996), p.31.

35. P.M.H. Bell, *The Origins of the Second World War in Europe* (London, 1997), p.93.

36. S. Hodgson, *The Man who Made the Peace: The Story of Neville Chamberlain* (London, 1938), pp.93–4.

37. D. Somervell, *Reign of King George the Fifth* (London, 1935), pp.475–6.

38. Lord Londonderry, *Wings of Destiny* (London, 1943), p.160.

39. Albert Hall 12 May 1938.

40. N.J. Crowson, *Facing Fascism: The Conservative Party and the European Dictators 1935–1940* (London, 1997), p.43.

41. B. Morris, *The Roots of Appeasement: The British Weekly Press and Nazi Germany During the 1930s* (London, 1991), pp.6–7.

42. D. Keith-Shaw, *Neville Chamberlain* (London, 1940), pp.78–9.

43. Feiling, *Chamberlain*, p.324.

44. Speech at Guildhall, November 1937, cited in W. Rock, *Neville Chamberlain* (New York, 1969), p.118.
45. K. Middlemas, *Diplomacy of Illusion: The British Government and Germany 1937–39* (London, 1972), p.48.
46. House of Commons Debates, 5th Series, vol.345, col.440.
47. Chamberlain MSS, NC18/1/1116, Chamberlain to Ida Chamberlain 10 Sept. 1939.
48. *Ibid.*, NC7/3/48, Chamberlain to George VI 30 Sept. 1940.
49. Middlemas, *Illusion*, p.11.
50. R.J.Q. Adams, *British Politics and Foreign Policy in the Age of Appeasement* (Basingstoke, 1993), p.68.
51. Chamberlain MSS, NC L.Add.128, Chamberlain to P.E. Flandin 25 April 1935.
52. Lord Templewood, *Nine Troubled Years* (London, 1954), p.332.
53. Lord Strang, *Britain in World Affairs: Henry VIII to Elizabeth II* (London, 1961), pp.320–1.
54. P.F. Clarke, *A Question of Leadership: Gladstone to Thatcher* (London, 1991), p.122.
55. Feiling, *Chamberlain*, p.324.
56. Strang MSS, STRN4/1, Halifax to Strang 7 Jan. 1957.
57. Chamberlain MSS, NC7/11/30/141, Chamberlain to Lord Weir 15 Aug. 1937.
58. *Ibid.*, NC7/6/29, Chamberlain to Arthur Chamberlain 25 Oct. 1939.
59. E.L. Woodward and R. Butler (eds), *Documents on British Foreign Policy 1919–1939*, 3rd Series, vol.1, p.56.
60. Hodgson, *Man who Made the Peace*, p.61.
61. A. Bryant (ed.), *In Search of Peace: Speeches 1937–1938 by Neville Chamberlain* (London, 1939), p.276.
62. Cadogan to N. Henderson 22 April 1938, cited R. Douglas, *In the Year of Munich* (London, 1977), p.26.
63. Chamberlain MSS, NC18/1/1042, Chamberlain to Ida Chamberlain 20 March 1938.
64. V. Massey, *What's Past is Prologue* (London, 1963), p.261.
65. House of Commons Debates, 5th Series, vol. 339, cols 41–2.
66. See, for example, B. Bond, *British Military Policy between the Two World Wars* (Oxford, 1980), pp.280–1.
67. See, for example, G. Stewart, *Burying Caesar: Churchill, Chamberlain and the Battle for the Tory Party* (London, 1999), p.315.
68. Chamberlain MSS, NC11/12/1, memorandum by Sir Charles Bruce Gardner, c.1954.
69. N. Rose, *The Cliveden Set: Portrait of an Exclusive Fraternity* (London, 2000), p.203.
70. R.A.C. Parker, *Churchill and Appeasement* (London, 2000), p.184.
71. Swinton, *Sixty Years of Power*, p.120; D.R. Thorpe, *Alec Douglas–Home* (London, 1996), p.83; P. Donner, *Crusade: A Life against the Calamitous Twentieth Century* (London, 1984), p.236.

72. Chamberlain MSS, NC7/6/44, Arthur Chamberlain to K. Humphreys 2 Jan. 1973.
73. House of Commons Debates, 5th Series, vol. 339, col.551.
74. D. Dilks, ' "We must hope for the best and prepare for the Worst": The Prime Minister, the Cabinet and Hitler's Germany 1937–1939', *Proceedings of the British Academy*, LXXIII, 1987, pp.309–52.
75. Chamberlain MSS, NC18/1/1074, Chamberlain to Ida Chamberlain 22 Oct. 1938.
76. *Ibid.*, NC18/1/1108, Chamberlain to Ida Chamberlain 23 July 1939.
77. R.A.C. Parker, *Chamberlain and Appeasement* (London, 1993), p.206.
78. Chamberlain MSS, NC18/1/1158, Chamberlain to Ida Chamberlain 25 May 1940.
79. House of Commons Debates, 5th Series, vol.334, col.55.
80. Stewart, *Burying Caesar*, pp.315–6.
81. Chamberlain MSS, NC11/1/823, Annie Chamberlain to G. Shakespeare 17 Jan. 1950.
82. PRO, CAB 23/96, cabinet 31 Oct. 1938.
83. Chamberlain MSS, NC11/12/1, memorandum by Sir Charles Bruce Gardner, c.1954.
84. Templewood, *Nine Troubled Years*, p.383.
85. Chamberlain MSS, NC18/1/1077, Chamberlain to H. Chamberlain 15 Oct. 1938.
86. *Ibid.*, NC7/11/32/281, Chamberlain to Lord Tweedsmuir 7 Feb. 1939.
87. Donner, *Crusade*, p.241.
88. PRO, CAB 23/96, cabinet 18 March 1939.
89. Templewood, *Nine Troubled Years*, p.374.
90. Feiling, *Chamberlain*, p.407.
91. Keith-Shaw, *Chamberlain*, p.111.
92. Chamberlain MSS, NC18/1/1116, Chamberlain to Ida Chamberlain 10 Sept. 1939.
93. *Ibid.*, NC17/11/32/149, Chamberlain to Cosmo Lang 5 Sept. 1939.
94. Feiling, *Chamberlain*, p.445.
95. Chamberlain MSS, NC18/1/1124, Chamberlain to Ida Chamberlain 8 Oct. 1939.
96. R.R. James, *Bob Boothby* (London, 1991), p.244.
97. Ramsden, *Balfour and Baldwin*, p.374.
98. Stewart, *Burying Caesar*, p.316.
99. Donner, *Crusade*, p.243. Emphasis in original.
100. Feiling, *Chamberlain*, p.446.
101. Chamberlain MSS, NC18/1/1166, Chamberlain to Ida Chamberlain 20 July 1940.
102. J. Charmley, *Churchill: the End of Glory* (London, 1993), p.293.
103. Feiling, *Chamberlain*, p.455.
104. Clarke, *Question of Leadership*, p.123.
105. *Manchester Guardian* 11 Nov. 1940.

106. S. Ball (ed.), *Parliament and Politics in the Age of Churchill and Attlee: The Headlam Diaries 1935–1951* (Cambridge, 1999), p.137.
107. Chamberlain MSS, NC18/1/1068, Chamberlain to Ida Chamberlain 11 Sept. 1938.
108. P. Kennedy, *The Realities Behind Diplomacy* (pb. edn, London, 1981), p.301.
109. W.N. Medlicott, 'Neville Chamberlain', *History Today*, 2,5 (1952), p.346.
110. D. Reynolds, 'Churchill and the British "Decision" to Fight On in 1940' in R. Langhorne (ed.), *Diplomacy and Intelligence during the Second World War* (Cambridge, 1985), pp.165–6.
111. Chamberlain MSS, NC18/1/1042, N. Chamberlain to Ida Chamberlain 20 March 1938.
112. *Ibid.*, NC7/11/32/106, Chamberlain to H.A. Gwynne 7 Jan. 1939.
113. *Ibid.*, NC13/18/121. E.R. Childe to Chamberlain 4 Oct. 1940.

Chronology

1869
18 March   Neville Chamberlain born Edgbaston, Birmingham.

1876   Joseph Chamberlain enters Parliament.

1877   N.C. attends first school, near Southport.

1882
April   N.C. enters Rugby School.

1887   N.C. attends Mason College, Birmingham.

1888   Joseph Chamberlain marries third wife, Mary Endicott.

1891
25 May   N.C. arrives in Nassau to supervise sisal plantation on Andros.

1897   N.C. returns to England
N.C. joins Elliot's and Hoskins.

1904–5   N.C. visits India and Burma.

1906
11 July   Joseph Chamberlain suffers stroke.

1911
January   N.C. marries Anne Vere Cole.
November   N.C. elected to Birmingham City Council to represent All Saints Ward.

1914
2 July — Joseph Chamberlain dies.
November — N.C. elected Alderman.

1915 — N.C. Lord Mayor of Birmingham.

1916
December — N.C. appointed Director-General of National Service.

1917
8 August — N.C. Resigns.
December — Norman Chamberlain killed on Western Front.

1918
December — N.C. elected to Parliament as MP for Birmingham, Ladywood.

1920
March — N.C. declines Under-Secretaryship in Lloyd George Coalition.

1922
7 September — N.C. sails for Canada.
30 October — N.C. appointed Postmaster-General

1923
February — N.C. appointed Paymaster General
March — N.C. enters cabinet as Minister of Health.

August — N.C. promoted Chancellor of the Exchequer.

1924
21 January — Fall of Conservative government.
November — General Election returns Conservatives to power. N.C. survives at Ladywood with majority of 77.
Appointed Minister of Health.

1925
October — Austen Chamberlain helps conclude Treaty of Locarno.

1926 — Public Health Act.

1927 — Poor Law Act.

1929

May   Conservatives defeated at General
                             Election. N.C. returned for
                             Birmingham, Edgbaston.

1930

January–February   N.C. visits East Africa.

March   N.C. chairman of Conservative
                             Research Department

June   N.C. Party Chairman

1931

August   Formation of National Government.
                             N.C. becomes Minister of Health
                             again.

27 October   General Election, after which N.C.
                             replaces Philip Snowden as Chancellor
                             of the Exchequer.

1932

4 February   N.C. proposes general 10 per cent duty
                             in House of Commons.

August   Ottawa Agreements signed.

1933

30 January   Hitler becomes German Chancellor.

1934

March   Defence Requirements Committee
                             recognizes Germany as Britain's
                             ultimate potential enemy.

1935

4 March   Defence White Paper published.

April   Stresa Conference.

22 May   Baldwin admits that German air
                             rearmament has been underestimated.

7 June   Baldwin succeeds MacDonald as Prime
                             Minister.
                             N.C. remains at Exchequer

December   Hoare–Laval crisis. Eden becomes
                             Foreign Secretary.

1936

7 March   German troops reoccupy Rhineland.

10 June   N.C. refers to continuation of sanctions

	against Italy for aggression in Abyssinia as 'the very midsummer of madness'.
July	Outbreak of Spanish Civil War.
11 December	Abdication of Edward VIII.

1937

16 March	Death of Austen Chamberlain.
28 May	N.C. becomes Prime Minister.
5 October	Roosevelt's Quarantine Speech.
November	Halifax visits Germany as master of the Middleton hounds.
December	Inskip Review.

1938

13 January	Roosevelt launches 'peace initiative'.
20 February	Eden resigns as Foreign Secretary, to be succeeded by Halifax.
12 March	German troops enter Austria. Anschluss declared.
16 April	Anglo–Italian Agreement signed.
August	Runciman mission to Czechoslovakia.
15 September	N.C. flies to Germany for first time.
18 September	Daladier and Bonnet visit London for talks on Berchtesgaden agreement.
22 September	N.C. flies to Godesberg meeting with Hitler.
26 September	Daladier and Bonnet return to London.
27 September	Orders given to mobilize fleet. N.C. broadcasts to the nation, warning of imminence of war.
28 September	N.C. accepts invitation to third meeting with Hitler. Scenes of emotional relief in House of Commons.
29–30 September	Munich Conference.
3–6 October	House of Commons debates Munich settlement.
23 November	N.C. and Halifax visit Paris.

1939

10 January	N.C. and Halifax visit Rome.
14–15 March	Prague Coup.
17 March	N.C.'s Birmingham speech seems to indicate significant change of policy.

21 March	Germans seize Memel.
31 March	N.C. announces Polish guarantee to House of Commons.
7 April	Italian forces seize Albania.
May	Negotiations begin with Soviet Union.
23 August	Nazi–Soviet Pact.
1 September	German forces invade Poland. Churchill rejoins cabinet.
3 September	Britain declares war on Germany.

1940

January	Cabinet reshuffle. Hore-Belisha removed from War Office.
March	Finland falls to Soviet forces.
4 May	British forces evacuate Norway except for Narvik.
7–8 May	House of Commons debates Norwegian campaign. Government majority falls to 81.
10 May	N.C. resigns premiership. Accepts office as Lord President under Churchill.
July	Publication of *Guilty Men*. N.C. undergoes operation for cancer.
August	N.C. recuperates in Hampshire.
1 October	N.C. resigns from government.
9 November	N.C. dies at Highfield Park, Heckfield.

1946	Publication of *The Life of Neville Chamberlain* by Keith Feiling.
1948	Publication of the first volume of Churchill's War Memoirs, *The Gathering Storm*.
1967	Public Records Act reduces to thirty years the period after which most government papers are opened to public inspection.
1975	N.C.'s papers formally handed over to the University of Birmingham and opened to historical scrutiny.

Bibliographical essay

There is now a vast literature dealing with all aspects of Neville Chamberlain's career, especially his involvement in the foreign policy of the 1930s. The following is offered as a guide to some of the more important titles and is arranged to match the organization of chapters in this book.

Introduction

Chamberlain's life is charted in a number of biographies. The following are listed in descending order of value. David Dilks, *Neville Chamberlain* vol.1 (Cambridge, 1984); Keith Feiling, *The Life of Neville Chamberlain* (London, 1946); William R. Rock, *Neville Chamberlain* (New York, 1969); H. Montgomery Hyde, *Neville Chamberlain* (London, 1976); Iain Macleod, *Neville Chamberlain* (London, 1961). Information on the Chamberlain dynasty may be found in J.L. Garvin and Julian Amery, *The Life of Joseph Chamberlain*, 6 vols (London, 1932–69), D.H. Elletson, *The Chamberlains* (London, 1966) and David Dutton, *Austen Chamberlain: Gentleman in Politics* (Bolton, 1985).

In his own day

Interim biographies published during Chamberlain's own lifetime are valuable less for their scholarship and revelations than for their freedom from the impact of *Guilty Men* and all that flowed from it. Duncan Keith-Shaw, *Neville Chamberlain* (London, 1939) and Derek Walker-Smith, *Neville Chamberlain: Man of Peace* (London, 1939) may be read with interest. See also Charles Petrie, *The Chamberlain Tradition* (London, 1938),

Stuart Hodgson, *The Man who Made the Peace: The Story of Neville Chamberlain* (London, 1938) and Collin Brooks, *Can Chamberlain Save Britain?* (London, 1938). Valuable insights can be gathered from the letters of Austen Chamberlain, edited by Robert Self, *The Austen Chamberlain Diary Letters* (London, 1995). Contemporary perspectives on Chamberlain are most easily traced through the large number of published diaries which exist for this period. The following are among the most useful. Stuart Ball (ed.), *Parliament and Politics in the Age of Baldwin and MacDonald: The Headlam Diaries 1923–1935* (London, 1992) and *Parliament and Politics in the Age of Churchill and Attlee: The Headlam Diaries 1935–1951* (Cambridge, 1999); John Barnes and David Nicholson (eds), *The Leo Amery Diaries*, 2 vols (London, 1980–88); David Dilks (ed.), *The Diaries of Sir Alexander Cadogan* (London, 1971); John Harvey (ed.), *The Diplomatic Diaries of Oliver Harvey* (London, 1970); Robert R. James (ed.), *Chips: The Diaries of Sir Henry Channon* (London, 1967); Cecil King, *With Malice Toward None: A War Diary* (London, 1970); Nigel Nicolson (ed.), *Harold Nicolson: Diaries and Letters 1930–1939* (London, 1966); Ben Pimlott (ed.), *The Political Diary of Hugh Dalton* (1986); Nick Smart (ed.), *The Diaries and Letters of Robert Bernays, 1932–1939: An Insider's Account of the House of Commons* (Lampeter, 1996); Philip Williamson (ed.), *The Modernisation of Conservative Politics: The Diaries and Letters of William Bridgeman, 1904–1935* (London, 1988); Kenneth Young (ed.), *The Diaries of Sir Robert Bruce Lockhart* 2 vols (London, 1973–80).

Guilty man

Cato's *Guilty Men* (London, 1940) was republished in 1998 with interesting introductory essays by Michael Foot and John Stevenson. Among wartime publications written in the same vein are Simon Haxey, *Tory MP* (London, 1939), Geoffrey Mander, *We Were Not All Wrong* (London, 1941), Cassius, *The Trial of Mussolini* (London, 1943), Gracchus, *Your MP* (London, 1944), Cassius, *Brendan and Beverley: An Extravaganza* (London, 1944), Celticus, *Why Not Trust the Tories* (London, 1944) and Diplomaticus, *Can the Tories Win the Peace* (London, 1945). John Wheeler-Bennett, *Munich: Prologue to Tragedy* (London, 1948) and Lewis Namier,

Diplomatic Prelude, 1938–9 (London, 1948) and *Europe in Decay: A Study in Disintegration 1936–1940* (London, 1950) helped give academic respectability to this school of writing. A. L. Rowse, *All Souls and Appeasement* (London, 1961), Margaret George, *The Hollow Men* (London, 1965) and Elizabeth Wiskemann, *Europe of the Dictators* (London,1966) ensured that this vision was perpetuated for a second generation. C.L. Mowat, *Britain between the Wars 1918–1940* (London, 1955), Collin Brooks, *Devil's Decade: Portraits of the Nineteen-Thirties* (London, 1948), William McElwee, *Britain's Locust Years 1918–1940* (London, 1962) and Ronald Blythe, *The Age of Illusion* (London, 1963) took the message to a wider audience. Lord Vansittart, *The Mist Procession* (London, 1958), Alfred Duff Cooper, *Old Men Forget* (London, 1953), Robert Boothby, *I Fight to Live* (London, 1947) and Lord Avon, *Facing the Dictators* (London, 1962) were among those who used their memoirs to hone their own anti-appeasement credentials. Martin Gilbert and Richard Gott, *The Appeasers* (London, 1963) provided a forceful restatement of the *Guilty Men* thesis before the tide turned in favour of revisionism in the 1970s.

The Churchill factor

John Ramsden's work is indispensable for understanding Churchill's position within Conservative party history and its relationship to the Chamberlain era. See in particular his *The Age of Churchill and Eden* (London, 1995). Also important are the same author's *The Age of Balfour and Baldwin* (London, 1978); *An Appetite for Power: a History of the Conservative Party since 1830* (London, 1998); 'A Party for Owners or a Party for Earners? How far Did the Conservative Party Really Change after 1945?', *Transactions of the Royal Historical Society*, 5th Series, vol.37 (1987); 'How Winston Churchill Became "The Greatest Living Englishman" ', *Contemporary British History* 12, 3 (1998); and ' "That will depend on who writes the history": Winston Churchill as his own Historian', *University of London inaugural lecture*, 1997. Churchill's own account of the 1930s is to be found in *The Gathering Storm* (London, 1948). Martin Gilbert, *Winston S. Churchill* vol.5 (London, 1976) is exhaustive but somewhat uncritical. Richard Powers placed the first question-marks over the Great Man's role in the 1930s in 'Winston Churchill's Parliamentary

Commentary on British Foreign Policy, 1935–1938', *Journal of Modern History* 26, 2 (1954). Robert R. James, *Churchill: A Study in Failure* (London, 1970) now seems less shocking than when first published. John Charmley's *Churchill: The End of Glory* (London, 1993) is the flagship of recent revisionist writing. Graham Stewart, *Burying Caesar: Churchill, Chamberlain and the Battle for the Tory Party* (London, 1999) and R.A.C. Parker, *Churchill and Appeasement* (London, 2000) are valuable recent additions to the literature.

The growth of revisionism

W.W. Hadley, *Munich: Before and After* (London, 1944), Viscount Maugham, *The Truth about the Munich Crisis* (London, 1944) and Quintin Hogg, *The Left was Never Right* (London, 1945) were bold enough to speak up for Chamberlain while the Second World War was still in progress. Samuel Hoare's memoirs *Nine Troubled Years* (London, 1954) are the most persuasive of any written by Chamberlain's contemporaries. W. Norton Medlicott published a sympathetic essay 'Neville Chamberlain' in *History Today* 2, 5 (1952), while D.C. Watt had the temerity to question Sir Lewis Namier's scholarly credentials in 'Sir Lewis Namier and contemporary European history', *Cambridge Journal* (1954). The same author discusses the developing historiography in 'Appeasement: The Rise of a Revisionist School?', *Political Quarterly* (1965) and 'The historiography of appeasement' in Chris Cook and Alan Sked (eds), *Crisis and Controversy: Essays in Honour of A.J.P. Taylor* (London, 1976). Keith Robbins, *Munich 1938* (London, 1968) and Martin Gilbert, *The Roots of Appeasement* (London, 1966) showed the willingness of younger scholars to re-examine the conclusions of their elders even before the introduction of the Thirty Year Rule. John Stevenson and Chris Cook, *The Slump: Society and Politics during the Depression* (London, 1977) provides a useful starting point for revisionist writing on the social and economic history of the 1930s.

The importance of evidence
Chamberlain: an assessment

Constraints of space mean that reference can only be made to a small part of the literature which was produced after the introduction of the Thirty Year Rule. Ian Colvin, _The Chamberlain Cabinet_ (London, 1971) and Keith Middlemas, _Diplomacy of Illusion_ (London, 1972) suggested that the newly opened archives might merely confirm orthodox opinion. They were, however, far from typical. Stuart Ball, _Baldwin and the Conservative Party: The Crisis of 1929–1931_ (London, 1988) and Philip Williamson, _National Crisis and National Government: British Politics, the Economy and Empire 1926–1932_ (Cambridge, 1992) are among important recent works which throw light on Chamberlain's career before he became Prime Minister. William Rock, _British Appeasement in the 1930s_ (London, 1977) offers a useful survey of the determinants of British foreign policy. Paul Kennedy, _The Realities Behind Diplomacy_ (London, 1981) is also concerned with underlying forces. Uri Bialer, _The Shadow of the Bomber_ (London, 1980) emphasizes the importance of contemporary perceptions of aerial warfare, an impression confirmed from a different perspective by Benny Morris, _The Roots of Appeasement_ (London, 1991). R.P. Shay, _British Rearmament in the Thirties_ (Princeton, 1977), Brian Bond, _British Military Policy Between the Two World Wars_ (Oxford, 1980), Michael Howard, _The Continental Commitment_ (London, 1972) and Gaines Post, _Dilemmas of Appeasement: British Deterrence and Defense, 1934–37_ (Cornell, 1993) discuss various aspects of defence policy. Frank Gannon, _The British Press and Nazi Germany, 1936–1939_ (Oxford, 1971) remains indispensable, but Richard Cockett, _Twilight of Truth: Chamberlain, Appeasement and the Manipulation of the Press_ (London, 1989) offers a post-revisionist corrective. George Peden, _British Rearmament and the Treasury 1932–1939_ (Edinburgh, 1979) is an excellent study of the Exchequer. Anthony Adamthwaite, _France and the Coming of the Second World War_ (London, 1977) explores the position of Britain's leading ally. C.A. MacDonald, _The United States, Britain and Appeasement_ (London, 1981) provides an American dimension as does William Rock, _Chamberlain and Roosevelt 1937–40_ (Columbus, 1988). David Reynolds, _The Creation of the Anglo-American Alliance 1937–41_ is unlikely to be bettered. Ritchie Ovendale explores the importance of the Dominions in _Appeasement and the English Speaking World_ (Cardiff, 1975). Peter Bell, _Chamberlain, Germany and Japan, 1933–34_ (Basingstoke, 1996) explains Chamberlain's attitude to the Far-Eastern situation, a story continued by P. Lowe _Great Britain_ *and the Origins of the Pacific War, 1937–41* (Oxford, 1977). Wesley Wark, *The Ultimate Enemy: British Intelligence and Nazi Germany* (London, 1985) is the best starting point for the issue of intelligence. Andrew Crozier, *Appeasement and Germany's Last Bid for Colonies* (London, 1988) explores an important dimension of the appeasement story. Simon Newman, *March 1939: The British Guarantee to Poland* (Oxford, 1976) questions whether appeasement was ever really attempted. Maurice Cowling, *The Impact of Hitler* (Cambridge, 1975) attempts to set appeasement in the context of domestic politics, while N.J. Crowson, *Facing Fascism: The Conservative Party and the European Dictators 1935–1940* (London, 1997) considers how far Chamberlain managed to keep his party on side. Christopher Hill, *Cabinet Decisions on Foreign Policy* (Cambridge, 1991) challenges the assumption that Chamberlain relied on an inner cabinet of like-minded cronies. Andrew Roberts, *The Holy Fox: A Biography of Lord Halifax* (London, 1991) and David Dutton, *Simon: A Political Biography* (London, 1992) offer revisionist interpretations of two of Chamberlain's closest supporters. David Dutton, *Anthony Eden: A Life and Reputation* (London, 1997) questions the anti-appeasement claims of one who became a committed Chamberlain critic. Though the second volume of David Dilks's biography has not been written, the author has, in a series of articles, provided the most convincing defence available of Chamberlain's behaviour. In particular see ' "We must hope for the Best and prepare for the Worst": the Prime Minister, the Cabinet and Hitler's Germany 1937–1939', *Proceedings of the British Academy* (1987); ' "The Unnecessary War"? Military Advice and Foreign Policy in Great Britain, 1931–1939' in Adrian Preston (ed.), *General Staffs and Diplomacy before the Second World War* (London, 1978); 'The Twilight War and the Fall of France: Chamberlain and Churchill in 1940' in David Dilks (ed.), *Retreat from Power: Studies in Britain's Foreign Policy of the Twentieth Century* vol.1 (London, 1981) and 'Appeasement Revisited', *University of Leeds Review* 15 (1972). R.A.C. Parker, *Chamberlain and Appeasement: British Policy and the Coming of the Second World War* (London, 1993) offers the most eloquent statement of the post-revisionist case. Frank McDonough, *Neville Chamberlain, appeasement and the British road to war* (Manchester, 1998) follows the same line. Sidney Aster, ' "Guilty Men": The Case of Neville Chamberlain' in R.

Boyce and E. Robertson (eds), *Paths to War: New Essays on the Origins of the Second World War* (London, 1989) revives the indictments of 1940. At the opposite end of the historiographical spectrum John Charmley, *Chamberlain and the Lost Peace* (London, 1989) offers a vigorous defence of its subject. To set Chamberlain's foreign policy into the wider context of the origins of the Second World War, reference should be made to two seminal studies, P.M.H. Bell, *The Origins of the Second World War in Europe* (London, 1997) and D.C. Watt, *How War Came: The Immediate Origins of the Second World War* (London, 1989). Andrew Crozier, *The Causes of the Second World War* (Oxford, 1997) is also worthy of mention, not least for its historiographical discussion.

Index